The Year My Mother Died

A Memoir

Sherry Scott

authorHOUSE®

AuthorHouse™
1663 Liberty Drive
Bloomington, IN 47403
www.authorhouse.com
Phone: 1-800-839-8640

First published by AuthorHouse   04/29/2011

ISBN: 978-1-4567-3777-1 (e)
ISBN: 978-1-4567-3778-8 (hc)
ISBN: 978-1-4567-3779-5 (sc)

Library of Congress Control Number: 2011902505

Printed in the United States of America

Contents

This book is written in honor of
my mother

Dedicated to my children
Donald Aaron
Madison Gail
Tyler Caleb
Aubry Alla Elise

Acknowledgment

The author gratefully acknowledges the kindness and support of the following people: Stephanie Lane, my editor, for her professionalism and dedication. Margo Smith, for first believing. Rebecca Richey, Bonnie and Bill Neeley, the "first" readers and cheerleaders. Cliff Scott, for his patience that surpasses understanding. My first family: Vinson Shields, Alla Fay Shields, David Shields. Connie Turner, who has always believed. My palliative care friends: Cindy Beckwidth and April Coldsmith, as well as our team at Santa Rosa Children's Hospital. Dr. Anthony Infante and Dr. Javier Kane, for giving me the chance. The staff and physicians at The Howard A. Britton Children's Cancer and Blood Disorders Center, including: Dr. Howard Britton, Dr. Anne-Marie Langevin and Dr. Paul Thomas. My professors and mentors in the Department of Pediatrics at the University of Texas Health Science Center at San Antonio. Dr. Marion Primomo, a "giant" in her field. My extended family and friends, for the treasure of memories. To all the artists mentioned in this book and otherwise who have inspired me, comforted me and drawn me into their circle of creativity. Lastly, to David and Ginger Cook for photographs appearing throughout the book.

Prologue

*I*n preparation for my new position as a palliative care pediatrician (a field whose mission it is to *alleviate* the physical, psychosocial, emotional, and spiritual suffering in children with chronic and terminal diseases), I was given two books that proved most beneficial. The first was a booklet published by the Texas Cancer Council: *Pain Management in Children with Cancer.* The other one was *Primer of Palliative Care,* by Porter Storey, M.D., approved and acknowledged by the American Academy of Hospice and Palliative Medicine. I viewed the first book as a bible to approaching and maintaining adequate pain control in my patients and carried it with me always. I also kept the other one on hand and referred to it often, because it concisely covered the basic principles of hospice care and also addressed other distresses—outside of the physical—that plague the patient. In the *Primer* section on psychological, social, and spiritual distress, the opening paragraph dealt specifically with the common denominator of fear, common in people who are approaching death. The author quoted several experts in the field dealing with this phenomenon that is often repressed into our subconscious. The paragraph ends with this sentence: "A hospice worker who has examined his or her own subconscious fears is able to be much more helpful to a dying patient."

I felt that I had been adequately prepared and positioned for this job by previous life events. I had lost a best friend to cancer, and I had seen firsthand what compassionate care directed toward managing her pain and addressing her emotional fears had done. More importantly, after coming through a dark period of my own, I had been released from a long-held fear of death and its consequences.

Out of hopelessness had come hope, and I now saw death as simply a door rather than a brutal end with pending judgment on the other side. In fact, I felt so prepared that I had no problem in understanding the passage on transcendence: "When experienced, transcendence locates the person in a far larger landscape. The sufferer is not isolated by pain, but is brought closer to a transpersonal source of meaning and to the human community that shares those meanings. Such an experience need not involve religion in any formal sense; however, in its transpersonal dimension, it is deeply spiritual."

During my pediatric residency I had stood at the foot of beds watching children die, and in the recesses of my mind I knew this place in medicine—end-of-life care—was really where I wanted to be. But it wasn't actualized until years later, until I was no longer afraid of the mystery of death. People have often asked me questions or made comments regarding "the special person it must take to work in such a field," or "How does one work in an environment with so much loss?" They fail to understand what all persons in hospice experience time and again: joy, inexpressible joy in the midst of pain and suffering, a transcendence. It's what keeps the hospice nurse, social worker, volunteer, and doctor coming back to do what they have a passion for doing. I found it a privilege and honor to be invited into the inner sanctum of a family and witness with them the completion of the circle of life, a resolution like none other.

I had been prepared to do my job, but, some years later, I was not prepared for the death of my mother. I had grieved over people before: the loss of loved ones, friends, those with whom I was loosely associated, and others far off and unknown to me. Even as a child I was familiar with death, or rather the rituals associated with it. It seemed I was always frequenting family night visitations and funerals with my family. Most were distant relatives of my parents, but, whatever the case, I attended a lot of funerals as a kid. Finding a babysitter for me didn't even appear to be a consideration. I just tagged along and didn't think anything of it. As I grew older, however, and unexpected tragedies took away people with whom I was closely or distantly associated, the stakes got a little higher. There was no more familiarity with the state of death. Instead, it became a dark and ominous intruder that clouded my mind with confusion and fear, causing me willfully to suppress feelings in dealing with my own mortality. Over time, even this proved surmountable, and so I thought I had made my peace with the aspects of life and death completely out of my control. However, I was not prepared for my own grieving over the sudden loss of someone with whom I had experienced a lifetime of relational ups and downs.

I found myself in a distant land that seemed both familiar and strange at the same time—a recollection that played out somewhat like a dream I couldn't quite recall after awakening from a deep sleep. The past seemed strangely close, yet far away, and my suffering over its loss was tightly wound up within the loss of my mom. And so my journey truly began. No guidelines, no maps, and no distractions came forth that would have allowed me to disembark from the path laid before me, for a while, that is. All I *thought* I knew about bereavement quickly vanished, and as I ventured into unchartered waters, all the words I had said to comfort others, the very ones I had written to console, seemed to come back and taunt me: "You know nothing of this."

∽

Time that seemed to drip like honey on certain days, true to its nature, did pass, though, and one September morning I sat down to look back and record my thoughts and experiences over the year that had passed. It had been a surreal year that had brought significant changes with the loss, a year that would eventually lead me to reclaim parts of myself I had left behind or forgotten. The year had been affected by Mom's death, but, more importantly, her life had affected the way I lived my life, and the recalling was interwoven with the grieving.

October

I didn't think October would be the last time I would see her. I remember watching her slowly walk back up the walk in her bare feet after retrieving the evening paper. She wore a long white, sleeveless cotton gown over her blue jeans. Her new tomboyish haircut accentuated those voluminous brown eyes, somewhat glossed over and shaded by her drooping eyelids due to the medication she was taking. After having known her for so long, I was still struck anew by how beautiful she looked. My friend Gail had fought an off-and-on battle with Hodgkin's lymphoma for the past thirteen years, and on this particular mild late September afternoon, I thought she had a lot more time. I thought *we* had a lot more time. I thought her decline would be gradual, allowing time for drawn-out goodbyes, nighttime vigils, and a wearing down of the body, mind, and soul to the point of one agonizing last breath; after all, it was what she had always feared. But in typical Gail-like fashion she decided to forego all the wasting away and bedside drama and slip quietly away one October afternoon in the same room she had slept in as a teenager.

Gail officially entered my life in the summer of 1982. While at work, I had often seen her come through the hospital lab, usually stopping to talk to her husband for one reason or the other. Barker, as everyone called him, short for Tom Barker, worked in a wing of the hospital's medical laboratory adjacent to the pathology lab where I worked. Though Barker and I became good friends during the time I worked for the hospital, I was more intrigued by Gail's story. I learned from others who had worked there longer than I that she had been diagnosed with cancer in her early twenties and, after completing several tough rounds of chemotherapy and radiation, was now cancer-free. I also learned that her family owned a respected business in an adjacent small town; she had apparently lived a more privileged life than many of us, although she and Tom never put on airs. But she looked different than the rest of us, and she brought a certain presence into a room that I couldn't help noticing. My curiosity eventually won out over my awe. Little by little, I took advantage of chance meetings and conversations to learn firsthand more about her and forge a friendship that would become mutually important and binding to us both.

That particular summer, I was recently divorced and had a one-year-old son. She was in the middle of her last separation from Barker, which would eventually relegate her to the same ranks as me, though without a child. The couple had been unable to bear children following Gail's total body radiation treatments.

Gail was like a breath of fresh air to me. I had never been acquainted personally with someone so glamorous and with such a background of stories and experiences. I was enthralled with her history, medically as well as biographically, and I questioned her relentlessly about her diagnosis, treatments and life-changing events brought on by her illness. I think she welcomed the unabashed inquiries from me. Others around her intentionally avoided the subject due to her previous history of bitter outbursts and stubborn refusals over different treatment schedules. At the time, neither she nor I knew that our days spent together were probably preparing me for a life in medicine and were responsible more than anything else for instilling in me a passion for the spiritual and emotional well-being of the patient, aside from the research-proven models of medicine. She had lived a life outside of anything I had even come close to experiencing, for example, witnessing the Beatles' first appearance in Houston among a bunch of screaming junior high girls that her mom had transported to the floor of the Sam Houston Coliseum in 1965. I had never met anybody who had ever seen the Beatles in person, much less survived cancer! I was fascinated with learning more about a life that held far more interest than anything I had to share.

For starters, she was adopted as a baby from a Catholic orphanage in the Bronx. Her adoptive parents were returning from an overseas assignment and stopped in New York, on their way back to southern Oklahoma, to "pick out a new baby." She was told that her father was smitten with her big brown eyes from the start and announced,

"That's the one!" Hearing her tell the story in her southern drawl made the place of her origin seem all that more surreal. In fact, as a child she dreamt of finding her real mother, most likely a movie star or legend, like Ingrid Bergman, and made elaborate plans with her two girl cousins to travel to New York one day to locate her; charting their course carefully on road maps spread all over the floor. Years later, when the time would come for her to make a decision to pursue bone marrow transplant as a last measure for treatment, she would refuse it, owing to the fact that she did not want to risk the possibility of rejection again, if indeed she was successful in tracking down her biological family. Though she often voiced that God had given her the mother she needed the most, the best mother she could ever have, and that there was no longer any need to look for her biological parent, her adoption was something she would never get over or fully resolve. Listening to her stories from childhood that revolved only around finding her biological mother who had given her up, I was given the impression that she believed her adoption resulted from the inability of a young, single girl to care for her properly. I learned from her adoptive mother after Gail's death, such was not the case; she had been just another mouth the family could not afford to feed, a fact that was never disclosed to Gail.

She had also lived in places I had not: Japan and even Houston! When she was eight years old, her adoptive father, who had been a fighter pilot in World War II, committed suicide during a bout with depression. He had abused alcohol for many years and spent the time just before his death living alone in an apartment where Gail would visit him on weekends. After his death and for many years afterward, she blamed her mother for the suicide, goaded by loathsome tales from her aunts on her father's side of the family. Her animosity was further fueled by the fact that her mother, Virginia, had started dating a man who had been a fellow pilot of her dad's and a family friend. The bitterness Gail harbored for years was only matched by her mother's patience in waiting for her to heal.

For some time, Gail lived with her mother in an apartment in Houston, where Virginia held a teaching position. When the beau came to town on weekends, he courted Virginia at some of the city's finest restaurants and theatres with Gail in tow, always sporting a stiff upper lip. Only once did she let down her guard when out with her mother and future stepfather. He had secured tickets for the stage production of *The Sound of Music,* and throughout the night Gail sat on the edge of her seat, gripping the rail in suspense. She was so taken by the chapel scene that she left the theatre pledging a burning desire to become a nun: within the Baptist order, of course. One weekend during the special visitor's stay, the precocious, guarded, young girl made the casual observatory remark, "Aren't you guys ever going to get married?" The couple followed her lead, frantically scurried to make wedding arrangements, and was married a week later. It had taken six years to woo Gail into giving them permission.

Life changed for the new family rather quickly. They moved back to a small town in North Texas where a family business, Carl's Tasty Sausage, was headquartered. Gail went from living in the big city with just her mom to living in a Victorian four-story home with two older stepbrothers and all the shenanigans they were capable of, e.g., driving a fast car through the showcase window of the local Ford dealership in the middle of the night and knocking out a couple of the floor models at the same time. Gail's life soon became interwoven with the small town of Whitewright, population around 1,500. She showed cows in the Future Farmers of America program, made the cheerleading squad, became a class favorite, and eventually dated the head football star. She carved their initials into the railroad overpass before heading off to college at Southern Methodist University to pursue her education and high school sweetheart.

She belonged to organizations and enjoyed perks I only imagined. While at college, she was accepted into a prominent sorority, which she represented as "most beautiful" on campus one semester. This was back in the day when girls lined up for fashion inspection before leaving the dorm to attend social night functions and parties. After football season was over, she traveled around the state and country with her boyfriend to different fraternity and sorority events. She was not totally naïve to his semi-longsuffering. After obtaining a long-awaited engagement ring, she surrendered to an intimate relationship with him. "Yeah, he used to drop me off after a date and go off and have sex with a girl just down the street from me. Used to upset me real baahd," she'd drawl, which made her tale of woe sound a little comical while at the same time maddening—until she told the rest of the story.

Gail remained at SMU, and the fiancé eventually transferred to another school in the region in order to continue to play football.

During this time of geographical separation, plans for a summer wedding in their hometown proceeded through the telephone lines between school and back home. After the wedding invitations had been mailed, Gail's sorority sisters decided it was high time to let her in on a little secret, and, in this case, "better late than never," would not have sufficed.

Her girlfriends approached her collectively to tell her that not only had her fiancé been having a relationship with another girl on campus, but that she was pregnant and *their* wedding was to take place *that evening.* Gail made a mad dash to his campus, more than an hour's drive away, and arrived just in time to confront him. She ended the face-to-face encounter with, "What are we gonna tell Whitewright?"

Needless to say, the illusion of the life of a campus queen was forever ruptured. She left school. Gail stayed in her paid-for apartment the rest of the semester, leading her parents to believe that she was still in school; her tuition money was not refunded. After living for a time as the broken-hearted-one-gone-wild, she returned home one summer to live with her parents, but not before more life-changing events occurred.

Soon after the breaking news of her fiancé's betrayal, she learned that she, too, was carrying a baby of his. She kept the news somewhat to herself and did not reveal it to him, but, upon learning the truth, he confronted her one evening. She was around four months pregnant at the time. Their argument took place on the landing outside her second-story apartment, and, sometime during the heated exchange, she slipped and went down the stairs. When she finally landed at the bottom of the steps, (in her words) "the blood gushed." Her roommate helped her into the bathtub while her ex-fiancé sat devastated on the couch. "It was all a blur. She took care of me. I don't know what she did with it, but it had a form." she told me. "It was more than just bloody tissue." It would be the only pregnancy she would carry.

Sometime after returning home, Gail was introduced to the son of a distant cousin on her mother's side of the family: Tom. He was smitten with her, and old wounds healed to the point that a fall wedding took place in a small Whitewright church. She was every bit the beautiful bride, intent on starting a new adventure with someone she would forever love. Her intentions were true, but the adventure would turn out to be more than she had bargained for and would challenge the young couple in ways they could have never foreseen.

She was diagnosed with endometriosis shortly after being married and was advised that, if she wanted to have children, sooner would be better than later. Frustrated over not getting pregnant during a set time period, she insisted that they see a fertility specialist. In the meantime of planning for their own family, Tom and Gail became foster parents to a little boy who had been removed temporarily from his dysfunctional home by a court order. During one of the boy's follow-up doctor visits about a sore throat, Gail happened to ask the doctor what he thought of a large lump on the side of her neck. She was hospitalized that same afternoon following a "curbside" consultation by an oncologist in the same clinic. The biopsy obtained the next day revealed Hodgkin's lymphoma.

One of the most bittersweet pictures in her collection is a snapshot taken the day the biopsy was done, before the pathology report had been released. She is in a hospital gown, hair pulled back in a ponytail, a piece of surgical tape visible over the biopsy site. She is leaning forward to kiss her foster child who is being held up to the bedside by her husband. They are lip-locked with big smiles on their faces— seemingly unaware of the others around them. Shortly after the bad news was delivered, the small boy was returned to the foster system, while Gail was ushered through more tests to determine just how invasive her disease was before beginning chemotherapy.

The brutal MOPP chemotherapy regimen would be her undoing. Her treatment (using a combination of the drugs Mustargen, Oncovin, Procarbazine, and Prednisone) took place years before the newer anti-emetic agents were available to patients undergoing treatments known for causing severe nausea and vomiting. Some things were within her control. Others were not. She was bitter from the get-go and routinely had angry outbursts while threatening to discontinue treatment. After dropping down to eighty-something pounds, she finally got her wish. She adamantly refused the last two treatments of the protocol and started radiation. She never regretted the decision, believing she would have died from the chemo and its devastating side effects if she had continued as scheduled.

To say she was a difficult patient would be putting it *very* mildly. She threw fits, argued with the staff, took the whole situation out on her mother and husband and ranted and raved in the emergency room at all times of the day and night for analgesics, which she managed to obtain, for a while. A standing order existed for her to receive Demerol when she would show up requesting "something for the pain," until the nursing staff began to notice her frequenting the ER before the allotted time dosing interval, demanding her shot be given and arguing with the nurses over the last scheduled administration of the drug. Alarmed, her physician put an immediate stop to her scheduled doses. She was thrown into a drug withdrawal, which, at the time, felt more destructive than the cancer she was battling. During the subsequent weeks, she would throw herself down in a fashion similar to a toddler's throwing a temper tantrum: hitting her head repeatedly on the floor and demanding *her* Demerol.

When I first met her, some of her darkest days were behind her (days that had included relapse diagnoses, more treatments, more surgeries and procedures), though there would be more to come. She was in remission at the time and so there was a break from some of the things she would never get used to that were required for living with cancer, things such as needle sticks, for starters. Another friend of mine once told me that it was common knowledge to scatter and run when Gail showed up in the hospital lab for a blood draw: "Nothing or nobody could please her." Starting IVs on her was a whole other experience. Specialists such as anesthesiologists usually had to be called in while she sternly warned them, "Don't probe." Another psychological stumbling block was losing her hair.

She had been in remission for several years when I began to get to know her and discovered that she kept a full head of hair tucked under the huge wig she had worn since her first round of chemo. Her big hair gave her some kind of false sense of security. My big mouth and I eventually started harping on the subject with remarks like, "Doesn't that thing get hot?"; "Why don't you just go get a cute style done? You've got plenty of hair"; or, better still, "What are you going to do when you start going out again and end up going to bed with somebody? Are you gonna wear your wig or take it off?" I don't know what did the trick, but one summer day she came over to my parents' home proudly sporting a new bi-level haircut.

I'll never forget it. We were sitting in the backyard watching my young son play in the water. She walked through the gate wearing a pink cotton sundress. Her smile seemed to signify something new was about to begin, even though her divorce proceedings would soon be in the works. She felt a little braver, a little freer, and it showed.

The summer that heralded the beginning our friendship felt like my first summer of love. I was excited to have someone new in my life: a new best friend. We were to each other like sisters we'd never had. Six years my senior, she passed her wisdom and experience on to me; she taught me a lot about fashion sense and makeup and was with me when I bought my first box of loose facial powder. She introduced me to potpourri by Ben Rickert and designer perfumes such as Shalimar, her favorite since age sixteen. She wore her clothes and jewelry uniquely, stating that she liked to be different. She always mixed the colors of her jewelry, dismissing the rule of only wearing gold with gold and silver with silver. What she couldn't afford she made up for in creativity and style. She kept her dishwashing soap in a beautiful, tall, glass decanter and arranged petite books of sonnets by Shakespeare on her living room shelves. The clutter she kept evidenced her interest in different cultures and lifestyles and included nostalgic artifacts of favorite stars and musicians. I was glad to get whatever she handed down to me. It was as if donning something of hers made me feel a little richer inside, even if it was something outdated, such as an old football jersey she once handed me.

I wore it to class one night at the junior college and after getting out sometime around 9 p.m., I dropped by to see Gail at her job before going home. She took one look at me and started laughing, "I can't believe you wore that out in public!" I hadn't even bothered to notice the huge double digits, "69," printed on the front and back of the shirt. I thought it was just somebody's football uniform number. "No wonder that guy kept smiling at me."

The fashions, hats, makeup, and wigs were her trademarks. Thus, some people who were familiar with her in the medical setting (in and out of the clinic or in the hospital) had trouble relating to her suffering. "If she felt so bad, how could she look so good?" She took great pains with her appearance, because that's where the good fight was fought. There were times when she didn't have the strength or will, but, when she did, putting on her makeup and hiding under that wig was her way of stalling the enemy and putting forth an effort to carry on and not give up.

As leery as some people were over her past history of tantrums and demands, I found her appeal unmatched. Her charm got us in and out of scrapes and seemed to have an equal effect on others.

One night on our way to a Dan Fogelberg concert we ran into a huge traffic snag in downtown Dallas. We were in a yellow Monte Carlo coupe with a brown rear-quarter vinyl roof, an early '70s model that had seen better days. Running late and finding ourselves in the wrong lane, we were held up at an intersection by a Dallas police officer directing traffic in all four directions. Gail stuck her head out the window, flashed those big brown eyes, and in her unmistakable southern drawl asked if we could make a left turn from the far right lane. Without a moment's hesitation, the cop—honest to God—blew his whistle, stopped all lanes of traffic, and waved us through! We made the concert just in time.

We seemed to have an unspoken thread of recognition and humor between us, particularly when we had been drinking. Gail never tried to be funny, but sometimes her observations, voiced with an even slower twang after a few drinks, were so perfectly timed to what I was thinking, she would make me howl. One particular afternoon, we accompanied a friend to the airport to drop off their significant someone and ended up with a lot of time on our hands while waiting for the flight to depart. Gail and I headed to a bar within the airport (long before 9/11 security regulations), leaving the couple time alone before having to say goodbye. It was a cold, rainy St. Patrick's Day, and the margaritas we were drinking had been colored some God-awful green to commemorate the day. We jokingly referred to them as "swamp water." After enjoying a few while engaged in conversation, we looked up around 5 o'clock to find the place beginning to fill up. Business flights were beginning to arrive, and we suddenly found ourselves in the middle of a Love Field happy hour.

Sitting somewhere in the back of the room was a businessman wearing a three-piece brown suit. As he got up to leave, he lost his balance and took the whole length of the bar trying to regain it. He came hopping toward us on one leg and crashed into our table with his leather briefcase and all. After his momentum was abruptly stopped, he straightened himself up, adjusted his glasses and satchel, and, without uttering a word, turned and headed for the door. Sitting there in a "Margaritaville haze," and a very green one at that, Gail glanced at me and asked, "Did that just happen or whaaht?"

That was a great day despite the rain and a parting goodbye at the airport. I lay down in the backseat, sleepily content all the way home, listening to music playing from the back speakers just over my head.

As difficult as she could be as a patient, Gail was just as difficult when it came to interpersonal relationships. Probably stemming from her childhood and the mystery behind an adoption she never understood, she had a way of putting up walls without purposefully willing them into place. Her fight with cancer only fueled the fire. In order to survive, she sometimes emotionally cut herself off from those she cared for and needed the most. She had learned to distance herself from others in a variety of ways. She could be stubborn and unyielding, evasive and cold; she played the role of the spoiled brat beautifully when she demanded certain needs of hers be met. Just like any other couple of friends, we had fights and makeups, sometimes punctuated by long periods of silence, but she wasn't above making the first phone call.

To end one of our mutual not-speaking terms, she called me after hearing the news of a friend's tragic death in an automobile accident. He and I had dated briefly, but Gail knew him as well. She had been out of town and called me as quickly as she could after finding out; the funeral had already taken place. After months of grief and confusion, it was Gail who brought some perspective into the web of chaos my mind had woven in order to understand the mysteries associated with death. While sitting on our favorite beach, she listened to my anxiety-filled rants, empathized, and then stated matter-of-factly, "Sherry, you're asking questions no one on this earth has the answers to." And just like that, I cleared and went on living a little more peaceably with things I had no control over, as well as sleeping better and keeping my food down.

Our lives would continue to parallel, intertwine, and move apart only to intersect again at some important junctions over the next six years. Our shopping sprees, music concerts, dinners out, and trips to the lake somewhat stalled after she met and started seriously seeing her second husband-to-be. We rekindled some of our fun times together when she started preparing for her destination wedding, which was to be held on St. Thomas Island in the Caribbean. I have some great pictures and fond memories of our day spent together in Dallas shopping for lingerie and making happy hour at the original TGI Fridays on Greenville Avenue, Gail's old stomping grounds back in her SMU days.

The lady working in the boutique where we purchased her negligee wouldn't let us take pictures in the store for some bogus privacy/legal reason. As she was wrapping up our purchase, the young sales person began to talk about her own upcoming nuptials that were scheduled to take place outside in some park or square. Gail and I left the store and while walking down the mall corridor, we looked at each other and said in unison, "I hope it rains." I ended up taking a picture of Gail provocatively holding up the black teddy in front of her while coming down the mall's escalator.

The best part was that she wore *my dress* on her wedding day: my little handmade wedding dress for which I had paid a little over $100 to replicate a bridal magazine dress I couldn't afford. It was a far cry from her first wedding gown, which was exquisitely beaded and had been modeled professionally for a designer's bridal show before Gail purchased it. Of course, she looked much better in my dress than I ever did, and though the couple had a very private ceremony in the Virgin Islands, I was there in spirit.

They had been married more than a year when Gail faced another relapse and more chemotherapy, but this time things were different. Her husband had already made it clear that he had no intention of committing to a long-term relationship unless she was committed to taking care of her health: no more bargaining over treatment protocols and schedules. They were both in their thirties, and Gail was considerably more mature and wiser than when first struck with cancer. He had remained a bachelor up until age thirty; the fact that his job took him out of town often also seemed to mesh with her recurring need for distance. The couple remained close and sloshed through the rigors of chemo and more oncology appointments; Gail went out and purchased the biggest wig she could find. They weathered the storm. She survived and life went on, for a while. During their second fall together, she relapsed for the last time; this would be her final run.

Gail always struggled between two opposing forces: the desire to remain close and find companionship, and the impulse to separate and disconnect from those who loved her best. There's no question that Gail could be a shit, but then cancer had been shitty to her. It had destroyed her first marriage, taken away her foster child and the ability to have children in one fell swoop, scarred her body, and robbed her of her youth and her future. Over time, she had gotten better about voicing her impulses rather than icily removing herself, but it had taken some work on her part.

Sometime during the winter of '88, we went to lunch at our favorite restaurant on the lake. She was undergoing chemo treatments at the time and had gone back to wearing a cute pageboy wig; she didn't have the need for all that hair this time around. We had the best time reliving old times while enjoying our meal, and we laughed even harder when our waitress brought us two shots of Grand Marnier, compliments of somebody at the bar. From the lackadaisical look in her eyes, I knew that she had just taken an analgesic, and that the liqueur would only enhance the effect. It reminded us of days past when, in the middle of a good time, I would look over to find her glassy eyed. I'd demand to know what prescribed med she had taken just so I would be forced to drive her home early.

While sitting with our drinks, she began telling me about a recent experience at her oncology clinic appointment. (At this time, I was in one of the most pressure-packed semesters of my academic tract. I was enrolled at a local liberal arts college, pushing toward my goal of entering medical school.) She had been introduced to a college student who attended the same school as me, Austin College. The student was enrolled in the pre-med program as well and was following the doctor around as part of a clinical exercise for one of her classes. The young girl wanted to be a doctor in the worst way and was excited and confident about her future in medicine. Gail related how she had sat in the exam room alone (maybe waiting for a blood draw) where she couldn't help but overhear the bubbly young girl's hallway conversation with the staff. "I can tell you this: I hated that girl at that second," she said. "Why wouldn't you feel the same towards me?" I asked. Her eyes widened and honed in on me as if the effect of her medication had suddenly worn off. Without blinking, she responded, "I have."

No, it didn't spoil our lunch or the rest of the day. In fact, I was quite proud of Gail. I felt privileged to be included and accepted as a friend to whom the truth, the naked truth, could be told. She had come a long way and had never looked more beautiful. I would have preferred her blunt honesty, a willingness to share her pain with me, over her abrupt dismissals any day. I realized in time that her impulse to separate herself from others with harsh words and withdrawal was, in part, preparation for her own death; however, it would rival my tenacity for holding onto our friendship in the face of hurt. Our last fight took place the summer before her death, and, strange as it may sound, it remains an endeared memory of one of our many times together.

Gail and I had a dear mutual friend named Kyra. Kyra was the executive director and one of the founding members of the local nonprofit hospice in our area. I had known Kyra for some time before she was appointed to this position. She was a licensed counselor and had a very successful private practice before making the hard decision to leave it and follow her passion for hospice. She had been instrumental in getting the organization funded by the United Way; I had been at her office the day she returned from submitting the paperwork. I was there to see her as a patient.

While undergoing her last round of chemo, Gail's doctor insisted she get some counseling support, and, when she mentioned this to me, I told her enthusiastically, "I know just the person." Kyra had stopped seeing individual clients due to her new duties and responsibilities, but I think she knew that Gail would eventually be a hospice patient. Whatever the reason, Kyra made an allowance and took Gail on. An immediate bond developed between the two. *Kyra* gently guided Gail into comfort care when she decided to forego further invasive therapy. Kyra insisted Gail's pain management be hospice managed on a continual oral basis rather than periodic injections. Kyra firmly but tenderly confirmed Gail's suspicion that she was deteriorating beyond a point she had ever gone before and had rocked her as she sobbed at the news. Kyra gave Gail's eulogy at her request, and it was a cross belonging to Kyra (a metal cross that could be hung from the IV pole, one Kyra had purchased for her own mom while she lay ill in an ICU) that Gail requested be pressed into her hand to be buried with. It was *Kyra* who helped me understand Gail a little better.

Every year, hospice put on a huge gala to raise money and awareness for the organization; it was a big event supported enthusiastically by the medical community as well as businesses and individuals in the surrounding area. That particular summer, the gala's theme was a luau, and it was held at a resort on our area lake, Lake Texoma, with plenty of food and drink, decorations, wild outfits, and lots of limbo to see just how low you could go. Gail was looking forward to going but became ill with an infection and had to be hospitalized for a couple of days. She wouldn't be released in time to make it and wouldn't have the strength to go anyway. Kyra extended an invitation for me to attend, knowing that I couldn't afford a ticket.

It was the summer before my last fall term. I was taking a physics class on a campus a little over an hour's drive away and preparing to take the MCAT (medical school entrance exam) in the fall, while continuing to work at a Holiday Inn private restaurant and club where I had been employed since beginning classes at Austin College. Apart from my shifts during the week, I worked every weekend, including Friday and Saturday night and Sunday buffet; my social life was pretty much nil at this point, so I was excited about the invitation. My excitement was overshadowed a little by my own intuition, to which I should have listened. In my bone of bones I knew not to go if Gail couldn't go. After all, this was her baby, and she felt very strongly about her life's purpose somehow being tied in with hospice.

Toward the end of my shift at the restaurant, one of my coworkers encouraged me to go on to the party. So I drove out to the lake and arrived pretty much at the tail end of the night, with only enough time to grab a plate of what was left on the buffet and watch the limbo contest. I stuck around and helped clean up. Just before I left, Kyra grabbed a beautiful Hawaiian floral centerpiece off one of the tables, handed it to me, and told me to take it to Gail since she had not been able to come.

I arrived at the hospital the next morning, just as Gail was being loaded into her mother's car. Understandably, she was not in a cheery mood. I handed her the flowers and told her they were from Kyra. "How did you get to go?" she asked. I casually mumbled something about Kyra mentioning I could come out after work. Immediate silence as she got in the car. I knew right then that my reluctance over going in the first place had been proven correct. When I summoned the courage to give Gail a call a couple of days later, without much preamble, I got blasted. Just as she slammed the phone down on me, she screamed, "I'm sick of this sucking disease! You get to do whatever you want. I'm sick and dying, and I don't get to do anything!"

I don't know which hurt worse, the phone receiver in my ear or her screaming accusations; after all, I had known I shouldn't go. But Kyra refused to let Gail shut her out, too, so she had a talk with her. Kyra also set me straight about the need some patients had to close off from loved ones and friends as a way of protecting themselves when they saw the inevitable approaching.

A short time afterward, I got a phone call from Gail inviting me over to watch a movie with her. She laughingly told me how Kyra had smoothed things over. "They were basically cleaning up by the time she got there," Kyra had told her. "Take pity." We had our last girls' night together watching *The Princess Bride* along with her two cats sitting close by on the sofa. We never fought again.

The last time I saw her was on a Saturday afternoon in October. I was getting ready for work when I got a call. She was staying at her parents' house, because her husband was working nights, and she had had some setbacks. They both felt better about her being with someone while he was away. She called me in tears, letting me know how down she'd gotten over not being able to get around well on her own, how she missed being in her own home with her music on, surrounded by her cats. (Gail was an avid cat lover, at one time owning as many as thirteen.) It had been a long time since she had called me in crisis; I couldn't recall ever hearing her sound so vulnerable. I told her I was coming out. I'd just call in to work to tell them I would be a little late (later than usual was more like it). I didn't have time or the money to buy her anything, so I grabbed some cassettes of our favorite artists and a magazine for her. Her parents lived about twenty minutes away from me. She was in better spirits than I had expected her to be when I arrived, and she was so thankful for the music I had brought her.

It was just like old times, discounting the fact that a toilet chair was placed next to the bed, a convenience she would not use up until the day she died. She told me to spray some cologne around after I stepped through the door into her old bedroom: Obsession, her current favorite. "It smells like a rest home in here," she said. She was sitting up, and I sat next to her on the bed, surrounded by the French provincial furniture she had grown up with. I painted her fingernails bright red while we talked and looked through the magazine I had brought. I was amazed at how long her nails had grown. She said the chemicals in her body made her nails "hard as bricks." The visit was like times spent with the *old* Gail. She pointed to this and that while flipping through the pages of the magazine, remarked how she liked a particular cut in a jacket coming out in the fall—that sense of fashion, still intact. We might as well have been sitting out by the lake talking shop, except that time was ticking, and I had to get to work, and she needed to stay in bed.

For some reason, I got a little shy when it came time to leave. Instead of hugging her goodbye, I grabbed her foot and gently shook it. "I'll come by again later this week, on my afternoon off," I promised.

Even if I had known it would be the last goodbye, I don't know if I could have acted differently. I think maybe it was because I knew how much it had cost her to call out to me for help, and I didn't want to risk a breakdown on her or my part. I didn't want things to seem desperate. She looked so good sitting there with those bright eyes and red nails that I didn't want it to seem like it was any different from any other visit. But it was, I just didn't know it at the time.

Gail died on a Wednesday afternoon, before any of us were ready, excluding her. That morning was the first time she couldn't muster the strength to make it to her adjoining bathroom. Her mother said that "her little legs just shook," so she resorted to using her bedside toilet for the first and last time. Shortly after noon, her mom sat by the bed and was in the middle of a conversation with her when Gail stopped her mid-sentence, shushing her with her finger over her own lips as if to say, "Quiet, I hear something," or maybe "I'm so sleepy. I need a nap." Whatever she fully meant we'll never know, for her mom acquiesced the request and quietly left the room as Gail drifted off to sleep. When Virginia returned a few minutes later to check on her, she was already gone. Gail had dismissed everybody and had gently passed on, just like the way she had come to us in the first place: all by herself.

She had sent her husband off on an out-of-town fishing trip with some of his closest friends, reassuring him she would be fine while staying at her mom's. Meanwhile, I was at the mall, taking the longest time trying to decide between a white cotton, long-sleeve nightgown trimmed in pink or a sleeveless, slightly sexy, peach cotton gown to bring her during my visit that afternoon. My plan was just to show up. Otherwise, I was afraid I would be turned away if I called ahead, and she wasn't up to having company. When I arrived at her parents' home, I was met at the back door by Kyra; Gail had been taken away a good two hours before. No last-minute goodbyes, no tears, no remorse. I swear, when that girl made up her mind to do something, she did it all her way.

Unless I pull out an old obituary, I can never remember the exact date. Gail died around noon on either the twelfth or the thirteenth of October. I established the precedent to forget on the first anniversary of her death. I was in my first semester of medical school and had just finished my dreaded first set of exams. A year to the day since she had died, I had planned to sit by the fountain in front of the school and mark the moment all alone. The setting was important because Gail had been one of my biggest cheerleaders when it came to urging me toward my goal of attending medical school. Even when she was sick, she would mail me cards telling me to let nothing stand in the way of pursuing my dreams: "Just strive."

The day came and went unrecognized, and the next day I sat dumbfounded on the side of the fountain wondering how I could have forgotten. This was supposed to be a big deal, for, in some respects, Gail had taught me more about medicine than any lecture or textbook ever could. I had made it to where I was in part because of her, and I was determined to carry her torch. More than anything, Gail had taught me that how a person dies is every bit as important as how a person lives, but she hadn't taught me bereavement. That was something I would have to learn on my own.

◈

My mother had been dead for several months when my grieving took a turn for the weird. I suddenly felt there was no one to talk to who could relate to me, no one to go back in time with me and remember who I was before I had become who I was now. All my friends who had defined a part of me, who had witnessed my life's milestones were unavailable, or so it seemed: relocated, removed, too busy with careers, finances, family, grandchildren. It suddenly felt like we had grown up all too soon, and the past that I had taken for granted and had impatiently wished away was now infinitely precious but irretrievable and irrevocable, just like my mother's life. My own mom's death occurred nearly nineteen years to the day of Gail's death. Out of the unexpected turmoil that resulted from the loss of my mom arose the painful reminder of my friend who was no longer. Even though I had named a daughter in honor of Gail, I had shoved her memory to the recesses of my mind in order to cope and get through day to day. Now that Mom's death had brought this *strange thing* upon me, like the fiery ordeal described in a passage of Biblical text, Gail was vividly brought back to mind, and I missed her all over again.

Through a passing car window, a face in the crowd of parents watching their children perform, I began to catch glimpses of her: the upturned nose, the cut edge of her hair against her neckline, her eyes, the curve of her jaw, all viewed from a distance and in passing, yet startling near and very real to me. I missed more than just seeing her, for I longed to talk to her. I wanted her to give me some advice. I kept thinking, *If I could just talk to Gail, she would straighten me out. She'd know what to do. If she could just sit down with me and offer me some words that would bring everything back into perspective (words that would bring me peace when nothing else could), then I'd be okay.* In my darkest times, dismissing what she had been through, she had shared such casual observances founded in understanding that she became my mentor, the sister I never had.

After my mom died, I accepted that she would no longer be there for advice. If I had any questions, I would have to draw from memory or look to how she lived her life for answers. I didn't realize that, in the months to come, it would be Gail from whom I would want answers.

For as long I can remember, I had always forgotten Mom's birthday. Without fail, the first day of October would sneak up on me, and I would remember too late to get a card off in time or call until a day or so had passed. It was always celebrated, though usually not until the next time we saw each other, and so belated birthday cards were the norm for me. Six months after mom died, Dad corrected me on the date of her death. We were in the middle of a conversation, and I said something about the fifteenth. "No, fourteenth; it was the fourteenth," he said. I should have known. After all, I was there. It had been a very long day, one I would never forget, yet I had remembered the wrong date. Maybe being a day or so off when it comes to remembering the day I lost someone significant means something, just like my tendency to be fifteen minutes late for everything. Or maybe I'm just a day off.

November

I was born November 20, 1959, in Honey Grove, Texas. Located in Fannin County, it sits in the middle of the blacklands about an hour and a half northeast of Dallas. A sign on the southwest corner of town greets motorists: "Honey Grove, the Sweetest Town in Texas." Once rich in cotton farms whose subsistence were dependent on sharecroppers, where the land bosses were known to have carried pistols while on horseback, I'm not sure everyone agrees with the salutation.

My mother had such a tough time during her pregnancy with my brother that she wasn't ready to think about having another baby for at least six years. My father took even longer. My grandparents once told me the story of my father having to carry my mother to the kitchen table for her dinner; my parents lived temporarily with my dad's parents throughout the pregnancy, because Mom was too sick to care for herself. She would immediately start engulfing the bowl of soup set before her until she paused to throw up, right there at the table in a little cup, then would resume eating the rest of her meal ravenously before being carried back to bed. This meal-time routine went on throughout her entire pregnancy. Some ten or so years later, I was conceived at a Boy Scout retreat in New Mexico. This fact was verified by both of my parents at separate times. My mother mentioned it to me one day while on our way to do some shopping; my dad told the story after Mom had died, while we sat looking at old slide pictures together.

Over the years, I have met people in various places who staked some claim to Honey Grove. They would preface their story, "There's this little bitty town located . . . ," and I would interrupt, "Yeah, I know it. I was born there." With a population of around 700 and holding, there is certainly no hospital for birthing babies, but for years a family practitioner held his clinic above the drugstore building, just off the Main Street square. One cold night my dad walked my brother, who was eleven and a half at the time, to the back gate where a neighbor was waiting to take him in for the night; my dad walked back home to take Mom into town. After coming to from a light dose of ether, my mom saw me lying on the table. A large, red-headed nurse gave my father the news. The doctor came out and asked my father the name. "Sherry," he announced proudly. The doctor came back with, "If it had been a boy, would you have called him Bourbon?" Mom stayed overnight in one of the patient rooms above the drugstore with the red-headed nurse. She took me home the next day.

Today, the drugstore and clinic are gone, and the doctor who delivered me died a little over two years ago; the building itself still stands, vacated and boarded up in a part of town where bricks were once used to pave the roads. Every once in a while I turn off the main highway and take Highway 56 through the small town, noticing the laundromat, the park, the churches that still stand, before taking a right off Main Street and around the block to see the old stone building. The faded name of the last doctor who practiced medicine there is still etched on the door.

Other than what I've been told, I have no memories of life in Honey Grove. We moved shortly after I was born to a community twenty miles east: Paris. Although I have yet to determine why, some of my most vivid memories and understandings of myself originate from Paris. Maybe it is partly due to the fact that I had a good childhood, full of all the play I could stand, though I often wanted more. Although not well-off by anybody's standards, we never lacked for food or shelter, and if there were times when paying the bills caused a stretch or some gray hairs, I never knew about it. Perhaps the reason also lies in the fact that the seven short years I lived in Paris were colored by my being so young. My little corner of the world may have been influenced by the likes of *Hollywood Palace* and *Gomer Pyle,* but I saw the corner of Southwest Nineteenth and Austin Streets as one great big adventure that brought something new every day. Being young helps explain why I saw poverty and segregation as something *everyday* as well as novel and interesting, as opposed to how I saw it when I returned thirty-eight years later.

Seeing the elderly black man drive his old mule team and wagon through our neighborhood in the mid-1960s was just part of the day. I liked the sight of the mules and the sound of their hooves against the pavement and the creaking leather of their heavy harnesses. Where the man was coming from, where he was going, never crossed my mind, nor did the idea that he probably lived in a different part of town, far removed from the three-bedroom brick stretch of homes along our block. Segregation went by another name: "colored town," though I don't remember actually hearing it called by that name in my house. I didn't pay much attention to other such labels at my young age. Whatever it was called didn't matter to me. I wouldn't have understood the connotation anyway. I just knew it was one of my favorite places to visit.

During his junior high and early high school years, my brother, David, threw a paper route for *The Paris News.* Once a month he went around with a yellow leather zipped pouch and collected payment from his customers for their subscriptions. During the summers, my brother would often go and spend time with my grandparents on their farm. He would help bale hay and ride around with my grandfather to various rodeos so they could show off Molly, Granddad's beautiful paint horse. While my brother was away on vacation, it was up to Mom and me to take care of the paper route. I liked collection day the best, because we got to knock on doors and meet people. Going up and down the streets of our neighborhood soon proved boring to me on a hot summer afternoon, but, a little farther down the road, our last stretch of collections managed to perk me up.

Lining either side of a dirt road without curbs or sidewalks stood weathered frame houses with little or no paint. My favorite one was a faded green house with a small wrought-iron fence and a little walk that led to the front door. A small-framed elderly black woman would always answer the door that contained old glass panels halfway up. Her hair was streaked with gray and fell in curls just above her shoulders; she wore high-topped black leather shoes and wired frameless glasses. Her simple country dresses reached down to her shins, and she always greeted us with a gracious smile. My brother always said that she was his best customer. He knew to look above the front door frame for money she left for him to collect; she was always punctual with her payment.

I never associated little black babies, wearing nothing but diapers, playing in the middle of the road alongside the chickens pecking in the dirt, with poverty. It instead reminded me of my grandparents' farm; it was like being in the country in the middle of town. It was different from our street; I found it rather fun and interesting. I perceived people of another color, living lives much different from ours as simply our last stop on the paper route, a great way to wind up the late afternoon, just like seeing the black man coming home from work driving his mules and old wagon. Segregation was such a part of our lives that I didn't even know it existed.

The segregation I was more interested in was the separation of boys and girls at our elementary school down the block. Rosa Pearson Elementary was a three-story, red brick fortress of a building that stood on the corner of Southwest Nineteenth and Bonham Streets, a very busy intersection. Across Bonham Street, the Texaco station stood on the northwest corner, catty-corner on the northeast side of the intersection was Hank's burger and malt shop/market and butcher shop. Mr. Hindman's Phillips 66 station was located directly across from the school on Nineteenth Street. This intersection, located two blocks from my house was my stomping grounds; I frequented Hank's or the other two convenience stores in the area, Sikes grocery and the 7-Eleven, daily for penny candy and gum.

Mr. Fletcher was principal of Rosa Pearson during the time I attended school there. Whether it was his preference or the bias of the school board or some other functioning entity, excluding the classrooms, the school's campus was partitioned off concerning the activities of girls and boys. Separate boys and girls cafeterias were located in the basement of the building and separate playgrounds, outside. The girls played in front of the school where a huge stone water fountain stood among the swing sets and wooden teeter-totters. The boys played in back of the school where the same equipment existed, only they had a tetherball and a basketball goal, but no big water fountain. I only remember once during my time there the boys and girls playing outside together. It was an *extra* recess time, but it wasn't earned.

A girl by the name of Kay sat in the next aisle over from me in one of the old wooden desks that had probably been there from the time the school first opened its doors. She was soft-spoken and wore cat-eye glasses of pale blue. She wore her soft, light brown hair with natural golden highlights curled on the ends. On picture day, it was teased up on the crown, so she resembled the girls from high school with their bouffant hair and curled-up ends. The style was known as *the flip,* and nobody wore it better than Patty Duke, the star of the *Patty Duke Show,* which I faithfully watched every afternoon upon returning from school. I remember Kay's hair so well because one day she suddenly got so violently sick that she vomited uncontrollably all over the place. I can still see her grabbing her hair with her hands and the vomit being all tangled in her teased crown. Our first grade teacher quickly escorted her to the bathroom while the gaping stares from her fellow classmates followed them out the door. The janitor arrived, and we were all ushered outside for an unscheduled recess in the front playground of the school. We quickly forgot about poor Kay, or rather unabashedly thanked her for the spontaneous playtime where we sat opposite our male classmates on the teeter-totters for the first time. We sat next to them on the swings and pumped our legs furiously trying to soar higher, past their jean-covered legs.

Kay lived in a small frame house a couple of blocks down from the school on Bonham Street, directly across from Bud's market and butcher shop. The day I was forced to leave Paris because of Dad's job transfer, I stared out the backseat window at the quickly passing neighborhood. Kay's house was one of the last houses I recognized on the road that led out of town; the road that would take me seventy miles to the west and would only bring me back now and then as everyone grew up and forgot all about me.

Many years later I returned to Paris with my family. My husband had been recruited by a pediatric group for partnership through a simple headhunter letter signed by a health care system "located in Paris, Texas." Reentering the small town from the west, I noticed Kay's house was still standing on the corner of Bonham and Twenty-fifth Streets; the market across the street was basically a convenience store without a butcher in the back and no longer called Bud's. I doubted Kay's family still lived in the house that had been remodeled with new siding and paint. Even now, every time I pass it, I think to myself, *There's Kay's house; she got sick one day at school and had vomit all up in her hair, and we got to go outside and play.*

November, birthdays, and Paris just all seem to go together, in my head, at least. Several birthdays in my family happen in November. My grandmother was born November second; my sister-in-law's birthday is on the twenty-fifth; my oldest daughter was born on the twenty-seventh; but, of course, mine is the most important, occurring on the twentieth. As a child I was most proud of my birthstone, the topaz. As a teenager I was most proud of my horoscope sign, Scorpio, and, to this day, there is not a calendar I pick up that I do not immediately turn to November's page to check out what picture graces the month. I love the sound of the word November, and the way it rolls off the tongue. It has a very majestic, serene feel to it, like a still lake in the silvery mist. (I must have seen it on a calendar.) When I was younger I claimed November as my own, and it had nothing to do with Thanksgiving; in fact, I remember huge gaps of time that occurred between my birthday and Thanksgiving. Perhaps that is why I still get ruffled when someone wants to combine the two celebrations; they remain eons apart in my brain. Anyway, that's how I remembered it in Paris. My birthday trumped any other day of the year, except for maybe Christmas. They were pretty much a tie. It's not that my parties were any big deal—my mother was no *Better Homes and Gardens* hostess—rather, I think it had more to do with an age when certain traditions were impressed upon me, and that happened in Paris.

Birthday parties were modest affairs in my neck of the woods in the early '60s. There was a (usually homemade) cake with candles, decorated with those little sugar appliqués that came from the baking aisle in the grocery store, that glorious song everyone sang, party favors that consisted of a cone-shaped hat with a rubber strap to keep the thing on our heads (cutting into the skin underneath our chins), and whistle blowers that had attached curled-up, hollow pieces of thin paper on the ends, which unfurled when we blew on the whistle part. The object was to go around blowing these things in each others' faces. The only other food at the party was usually vanilla ice cream that came in little individual cardboard cups with short flat wooden sticks that passed for spoons. Pin the tail on the donkey was a popular game, although we weren't organized enough even for that. I was just excited to have friends over who came bearing wrapped gifts. Thus, from this tradition I learned a very important lesson: how to keep a secret.

Too many times I had spilled the beans about the contents of birthday gifts as well as those for Christmas, Mother's Day, and other occasions meant for surprises. I hung around with mostly older kids on the block, and it didn't take much for them to needle the truth out of me. Even my father and brother got into the act of sitting around the dinner table and baiting me until I revealed whatever it was I was supposed to be saving for a big surprise, like the color of my new dress bought for my brother's graduation. Mom would always tell me just to ignore them, but I blew it every time. After being tricked once again into revealing a birthday present bought for a friend before the party, I was determined not to be duped again. And so, when Darren Fendley showed up to my sixth birthday with a present wrapped in tissue paper so thin I could see the miniature set of china dishes in the box, I gave him a knowing sympathetic smile as if to say, "That's okay, I've made the same mistake many times myself."

For my ninth birthday I talked my mom into making me a four-tier pink cake to share with all of the two girlfriends who were invited to spend the night. She spelled the number nine on the top of the cake with broken pieces of a candy cane stick. *Way to go, Mom.* On my eleventh birthday I had a skating party and got to invite my entire fifth grade class. I skated with my boyfriend on a couple's skate, and we both crashed in front of everyone halfway through the song. After that, it was pretty much slumber parties up until eighteen.

I stopped getting excited about birthdays after nineteen. I thought nineteen was cool. It sounded cool; it felt cool. I could have stayed nineteen forever. I could already vote and drink at eighteen, so turning twenty-one was no big deal. In fact that birthday was the worst to date. I was in the middle of a disastrous marriage that young love couldn't fix, and it was unraveling fast. Turning thirty was a bit of a bright spot in the road. I was in my first year of medical school, and a friend came over with a bottle of champagne, and we went to see a concert at the beautiful Majestic Theatre in downtown San Antonio. Thirty felt a little like having the slate wiped clean. All of the dumb mistakes I had made in my twenties were behind me; I was excited about my future. Once the allure of that was over, it was back to climbing up the hill, ticking off the years, thirty-one, thirty-two, thirty-three . . . . I pouted on my fortieth, because I had been receiving all these *surprise* invitations from husbands of my friends announcing big birthday bashes and such they were giving for them. My husband came in from mowing the lawn so proud of the two presents he presented to me while I sat at the kitchen table with one kid on my knee, the other one taking a nap. He announced we were going to dinner that night. *Whoop-de-doo!* I guessed that was supposed to be a big deal, considering we went out about twice a year during that time period in our lives. Anyway, I let him have it about the *no-cake* thing.

Turning forty-eight was memorable in one way, and then again it wasn't. I can't remember what I did on my birthday, though I'm sure my dad and I went to lunch or something. Maybe he came over and had dinner with the family, something, only I don't remember. I was spending a lot more time with my dad because Mom had just died a little over a month prior to the date. He would not have wanted to be alone. Anyway, Dad never missed a birthday if he could help it—no matter how painful it was.

On November 20, 2007, I was in the middle of a grieving period that I naively thought would continue manifesting itself as it were. I thought it would eventually lift, leaving me at peace with myself and the world; a little wiser, a little more grateful for the mother I had had, who wasn't coming back. Grieving at this juncture was feeling pretty much the way it was supposed to, or how I thought it was supposed to anyway. Knowledge of grieving over the loss of a loved one had been an integral part of my role as a pediatric palliative care physician and our medical team's outreach to families who had suffered the loss of a child. We prided ourselves in offering bereavement services throughout the first year after a death. Our palliative care nurse coordinator kept in touch with the families by telephone and made home visits as well. We plugged them into the Children's Bereavement Center located locally, held annual combined memorial services for our patients who had died within the year, and marked the first anniversary of their death by sending the families a beautiful card our team had designed. Our card contained a poem from Masterpiece Theatre's production of *Cora Unashamed.* At Jessie's deathbed, Cora says:

> When you love someone they're never far away, because they're always with you. That's because love has no time or space. It just continues on forever.
>
> I will see you in the cornfields. I will see you where the green grass grows.
> I will hear you when I listen as the soft wind blows.
> I will see you in the moonlight. I will see you in every star.
> I will see you wherever I wander, no matter how far.

And I will keep looking. And I will keep listening.
And I will keep remembering long after the days have
gone . . .
That our love, my dearest, will always live on.

We thought it was a beautiful way for families to celebrate the memory of their loved one, and I in my ignorance had no idea how long that first year could be. Only once did we receive an irate note from a parent with a return-to-sender note attached to our card stating we had spelled the child's name wrong. I chalked it up to a difficult bereavement and the continuing anger within the mother over losing her daughter to cystic fibrosis. I had so much to learn.

In studying death and the grieving process I had come away with the understanding that decisions, made on behalf of a family's loved one prior to their death, would greatly influence or impact the grieving process in those left behind. Thus said, decisions made in the best interest of the patient (what was the most loving thing to do?) in place of individuals' personal agendas and the selfish concerns and wishes of other family members would hopefully ensure a healthier bereavement period. I thought it all boiled down to a good bereavement versus a bad bereavement. I didn't realize at the time that there is no normalcy in grieving and how individualized and strange the process can become. Here, there are no real rules, because the psychological footprint left on a person after a death bears a direct correlation to the relationship between those mourning and those who are mourned. Losing a child is different than losing a parent, a sibling, a spouse; each relational tie has its own weight aside from the individual closeness or distance between the two people involved. I had lost friends, grandparents, other relatives, coworkers, but I didn't understand the emotional, spiritual toil of losing a mother. I couldn't have, until it happened to me.

November of 2007 felt surreal. It was like reopening a fresh surgical wound every day, like the one Mom had inherited down the length of her sternum as a result of extensive open-heart surgery. She had so many complications post-op, it's hard to say if the grotesque surgical incision was the greatest source of her pain, but it had to have been up there somewhere at the top, the way she gripped the heart-shaped pillow that had been given to her by the hospital whenever she had to move, even in the slightest. Reliving every day: the six-week ordeal that began with her surgery continuing through an extended ICU stay up to her sudden death after a hospital readmission, helped keep it all fresh in my mind, lest I forget what it was that held me in this state of fog. Apart from dissecting the mother-daughter relationship that had been a part of my every waking moment since the time of my birth (a relationship I often neglected), as a medical professional I also dissected her medical course and decisions made by the family as well. There was one particular moment when I thought I could have made a difference in the outcome if I had spoken up, but I had left things in the hands of fate, and now I ruminated over this event as part of my daily ritual of regret and farewell.

Even all this was bearable, because I had many years ago come to a peaceful conclusion that death, being such the finality that it is, meant God was ultimately in control of larger things that I couldn't comprehend, and therefore Mom's death had not been a mistake. The God we prayed to had not turned his head for a second only to look back and say, "Oops." But the reopening of the emotional wound that I took upon myself every day during my morning walk as part of my "healthy bereavement" would only play itself out for so long. The six- to eight-week period of tears I had expected, working through regrets and fond remembrances, the vow I took never to forget her and live my life in a way that would honor her, would soon take a turn for the weird. I was to experience a full year of grieving in a way I could not have possibly conceived before. I would slowly begin to understand why the woman had sent back the bereavement card, angrily dismissing our *polite* attempt to mark the anniversary of her child's death. In some small ways, the ridiculous had already started.

It's sometimes difficult to know for sure if God has a sense of humor in a situation, if He's just, say, messing with you to see how much you can stand, or if this crazy world just turns the way it does. The morning before my mother's death, (a little less than twenty-four hours away) I opened our car door to discover the kids' portable DVD players had been stolen. The night before, I had come home late from the hospital to regroup, repack, and return to the hospital to spend the remainder of the weekend with my dad. While unloading the car from the previous stay, I had neglected to lock the doors before going inside and, so there you go, my fault. Two weeks after mother's death, non-sufficient fund charges from the bank began soaring in through our mailbox. It appeared that during one of my disjointed stays at home, traveling to and from the hospital, I had attempted to pay bills and remain financially accountable. I had failed miserably. I had apparently forgotten to record a large payment and therefore we were off by about $1,500. So, for instance, the bottle of shoe polish I had purchased to touch up my daughter's dress shoes before Mom's visitation at the funeral home ended up costing me approximately $65 instead of $5.

A week or so after the banking foul-up was discovered, at Dad's request, I went over to help clean out Mother's clothes from the closet and dresser drawers in their bedroom. After spending hours going through her things, sorting them into piles to be given away to family, to charity, to be stored and saved, I left to return to my home an hour's drive away. Upon leaving the city limits, red lights began flashing in my rearview mirror. I was staring ahead at a sign that read seventy miles-per-hour, some two hundred yards away, but had failed to realize I had just come through a fifty-five-mile-per-hour zone. Stepping up to the window of my vehicle, the officer inquired if I was in a hurry for any particular reason and if everything was okay, while next to me, a stack of my deceased mother's belongings rose nearly to the ceiling of the car. "No, sir, nothing's wrong. Everything's fine." As I handed him my driver's license and proof of insurance, the wind snatched the insurance information out of his hand and took off with it down the highway. I sat there in stunned silence with my elbow resting on the edge of the car window watching this police officer run down the shoulder of the road in pursuit of my insurance card while cars whizzed past him, probably doing seventy. I thought to myself, *He's just doing his job and looking pretty silly while doing it at that—give him a break.* So without any objection or a plea for mercy, I took the ticket with a smile and went on my way, wondering what was coming next.

November would be the last time I would openly cry over Mom. Toward the end of the month, I was excited about meeting a dear friend in Dallas for lunch and shopping, which usually meant following Emiko around to her favorite stores and "feeling the fabric," as my father used to call it.

Our family had moved to Paris, Texas, in the summer of 2005. We bought a three-story clapboard house that was custom built by the original owner to resemble the Georgian Colonial she grew up in as a child. It was painted a light yellow, my favorite childhood color, with black shutters and white trim. It was located in a quiet cul-de-sac with every house on the block sporting a different architectural style—no neighborhood association meddling going on there. As much as I was struck by the look of our house, if the one next to us would have been up for sale, I would have gone after that one.

It was a beautiful reddish-orange brick Classical Revival style home with the most elegant glass front door whose overhead and side panels allowed you to see all the way through to the set of French doors that extended along the back of the house. The builder of the house had special-ordered the door from England. It was an antique, and its many little square panes were embellished with a decorative ribbon pattern in the middle that contained four tulip-shaped pieces of red glass. In the evenings, a lamp located in the center hall of the house shone beautifully through the ruby red glass. But as beautiful as the house was on the outside, it held no comparison to the beauty within its walls—I met my neighbor, Emiko, that summer.

She was a petite Japanese woman who refused to take no for an answer one evening, after having asked me to join her Bunco game the next week. I learned she was born and raised in Japan. She met Antonio, a native of Mexico City, while commuting on the train with her daughter, Aya; he was in Japan at the time furthering his medical studies. They had been married for more than twenty-six years when I first met her. They spoke each other's languages and embraced one another's cultures. Emiko could write in Spanish as well as speak it fluently; she knew Classical Spanish music and could gourmet cook in any language. She played the piano and could knit beautifully; in fact, she would buy sweaters at second-hand stores just so she could dismantle them and use the yarn for her own designs.

The first time I walked into her home, the most wonderful aroma greeted me. In the middle of this tiny town located in the northeast corner of Texas, there was this crazy, eclectic group of ladies assembled in her kitchen with drinks in hand preparing to eat and play their monthly Bunco game. Their ages ranged anywhere from mid-thirties to early eighties. This woman drinking bourbon on the rocks, belonging to the older group before mentioned, came up to me and introduced herself as Bernice. She was dressed all in red, sporting jewels everywhere. I was overwhelmed by the many new faces and names I encountered that first night, but I would never forget Bernice. I had never played Bunco, but after eating Emiko's chicken with some kind of sauce and tasting the best French apple pie I had ever put in my mouth, I signed up as an alternate player and vowed never to miss another chance to eat, I mean *play*, at her house again. Those ladies were so loud that night that my husband said he could hear us through the walls. "What were you guys doing over there?"

Emiko helped me to rediscover Dallas after being away from the area for over sixteen years. She took me into stores where I would never have shopped before—places like Neiman Marcus and Chanel—and bought things I would never buy, like vintage dish towels from France that cost $200. But she also took me into second-hand stores that were her little secret and introduced me to designers' names I had never heard of. At most of our stops, even at the perfume and makeup counters in Neiman Marcus, people knew her and called her by name though we lived nearly two hours away. She was not only a good cook but also knew where to find good food, and so we enjoyed many great meals together.

The first time I saw her house from a distance, I envisioned some little lady living next door who would invite me over for English tea. Instead, I found Emiko who invited me over in the afternoons for Japanese green tea and wine while cutting my hair in her magnificent bathroom. I enjoyed her as a next-door neighbor for a little less than two years until she moved with her husband to South Texas. I lost a neighbor, but I kept a friend.

I met Emiko at her favorite shopping mall in Dallas, North Park. We proceeded up the escalators of Nordstrom's to have lunch and were joined by Emiko's friend, Carol. Carol had lived in Paris at one time and so she "reunioned" with us whenever she could. Carol was from Wales, and so, among the three of us at the table, I sounded the least sophisticated and the most regional. Both knew of my mother's unexpected death. In fact, Emiko's father had died earlier that same year in Japan. Our lunch ended up lasting more than two hours. The poor waitress probably wondered what was going on, for every time she came by to take our order, refill our glasses, or to ask if we needed anything, we remained in deep conversation, oblivious to our surroundings, with my occasional tears dropping into my salad.

While we ate, I sat going over the hospital course, her death, and sorting through my regrets: namely, not taking advantage of the fact that we lived only a short distance from my parents after being away for sixteen years. We had moved back to be closer to Mom and Dad, and yet we had depended on them to come over and visit with us instead of taking the time to drive one hour west and visit at their house. I had blamed it on the kids' schedules and our busy lives; but, the truth be known, I had left my hometown many years ago, and I had no desire to visit there frequently. Had I only known her time was so short I would have made an effort to get together more. Carol spoke up, "But she wouldn't have wanted you to feel this way. That's why, as a parent, I don't want my kids feeling they have to be responsible for me and take care of me when I am no longer able to do for myself. I don't wish for that burden on my children, while I'm alive or after I'm gone."

I don't know if it was that beautiful Welsh accent, her compassionate and sincere tone, or the conviction of her words, but I only knew I felt a sense of relief in knowing she was right. Mother would have not wanted me to be paralyzed with regret. She was never about dredging up the past or going back over things that couldn't be helped or reversed. Never.

After lunch, Emiko and I said goodbye to Carol and went about our favorite stores together until Emiko departed to go back to her hotel. I went on to shop for some much-needed seasonal clothes for my youngest daughter and left the mall sometime after dark. I went across the street to the Barnes and Noble that Dad and I would often frequent in the afternoons between visitation hours in the cardiac ICU. I immediately recognized behind the counter the same young man who had helped me find Mom some classical music to help ease her distress and distract her while she remained on the ventilator. He was just as friendly and helpful as I had remembered him. I started to launch into the whole story about Mom and how much it had meant in those days to have someone to connect to and be nice to us even though we were having a bad time away from our home. Then I thought, *Naw, too much unloading for one day.*

I drove along the back roads and through the neighborhoods that Dad and I had driven through regularly on our way to eat dinner out and then back to the hospital for the last shift of evening visitation hours. I ate dinner alone in a little restaurant on the corner of Preston Road and Royal Lane, and, after eating, left to take one last detour before driving home.

As my dad and I had done so many times before, I drove through North Dallas neighborhoods, until I came to Forest Lane and I took a right. Just up the road a little, I turned left at the corner light that led me alongside Medical City Hospital's complex of different specialty hospital buildings and clinics and turned right on Merit Drive, the street that ran behind the medical complex. I turned right and went past the parking booth after grabbing my ticket, into the parking lot in front of Building D, which housed the cardiac ICU. I parked the car and rang security for entrance into the building, because the doors were locked after 9 p.m. I walked through the large multi-storied glass foyer and took the elevator up to the next level to use the bathroom located just down the corridor from the CVICU (cardiovascular intensive care unit) waiting room, like I had done dozens of times before. I left the building and drove out of the parking lot after the attendant looked at the minutes on my ticket and waved me through; I recognized her immediately, though she did not seem to remember me. I took a right on Merit Drive and drove slowly past the building, staring at the first window on the third floor; just like I had done so many mornings as Dad and I approached the hospital after walking the distance from our motel just down the street.

On those mornings I always looked for movement behind the half-open blinds to try to get a feel for how her night had gone and if there were any signs of staff rushing in and out of her room for any particular reason that might signal a problem. I took one last long look and drove down Merit, past the motel on the left that had been our home away from home for about six weeks. I had watched many a late-night rerun or movie there with the volume nearly on mute, trying my best to read lips, while sitting on the floor in front of the TV at the foot of the bed while Dad slept. At the end of the street, I took another right onto the frontage road and went down the hill to Forest Lane. At the red light I turned left, went under the underpass, turned back left onto the frontage road and entered Highway 75 in the far right northbound lane. I looked across the freeway at the many buildings of Medical City all lit up with their logo displayed across the top of one of the main hospitals located in the center of the facilities. It had been a long day, but I felt good about my detour. I knew I needed to go by and mark the spot, remember, relive it, even if it was only for a drive through and an excuse to use their facilities. I had been in the flow of traffic leaving Dallas for about ten or so miles down the road when the last tear fell.

The month of my birthday was on its way out and the coming holiday season was already in full swing. I felt everything was going as well as could be expected, though I knew Dad was having a very difficult time still. I had quit going over to his house as often as before and was calling to check on him once a day now instead of morning and night. Every time we got ready to hang up he would always say, "Thanks for calling," and I knew he genuinely meant it.

I now seemed ready to put some regrets behind me and remember Mom in peace. I felt I was coming to terms (within my head as well as within my heart) with the truth that life really does go on, and the pace slows down only for a little while for you to mourn and reflect. Funny what a year will bring your way. Mine was just beginning.

December

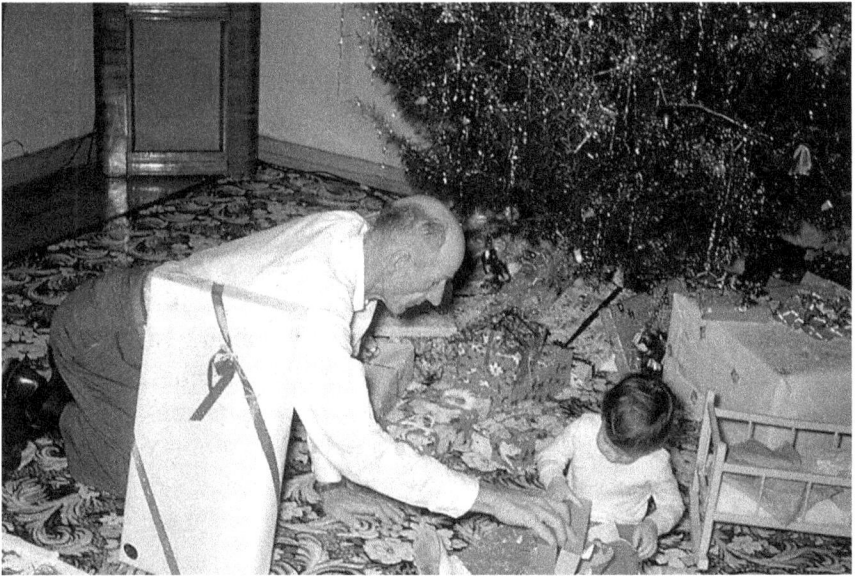

Our first Christmas without Mom. Ironically, we had already decided that this Christmas would be different from others, due to a change in venue. Mom and Dad had finally conceded to the fact that the family get-together on Christmas Eve was getting to be a little too much for Mom, and with the growth of our family due to great-grandchildren coming along, their little house was becoming too cozy for the entire family to gather. We had all agreed to celebrate this Christmas Eve at my house, then rotate every year between my brother's house and mine.

A changing of the guard, so to speak, was taking place, just as it had in Christmases past.

When I was very young, Christmas was synonymous with time spent at my granddaddy's farm in Tom Bean, Texas, population 500. The ritual was this: we had Christmas Eve at my paternal grandparents' house celebrated with their two sons' families, Christmas morning Santa Claus came and left *unwrapped presents* under the tree (so as to make the distinction they did not come from a store, but that the big guy himself had delivered them), and Christmas dinner was with whichever grandmother's turn it was. Christmas afternoon was spent at my maternal grandmother's house. The day after, everything promptly came down as my dad couldn't wait to get the tree out of the house.

My granddad loved children and being the character he was I can't think about early Christmases without his coming to mind. He had a small, wiry frame, a protuberant nose and had never had hair on the top of his head for as long as I had known him; in fact, he had lost it while yet a young man. He was impulsive, impatient, and continuously jumping into his pickup, just looking for an excuse to run some errand. He would always feign irritation if my granny asked him to pick up bread or milk from the store while he was out, rubbing his hand over his bald head and murmuring, "I knew she'd want something," as he headed for the door in a hurry. But the truth was, he couldn't wait to get behind the wheel of that old truck and kick up white-rock dust all the way down their road on the way into town. He was even happier if he had a granddaughter or two in tow, particularly when we rode in the open bed of the truck with our hair blowing freely in the wind, eating M&M's and sloshing grape or orange soda all over ourselves. It would have been unheard of for us to come back from the store empty-handed; he would have never allowed it. The first thing he did upon proudly entering the general store with us was to point to the candy aisle as a sign for us to take care of our business while he took care of his.

One Christmas morning, he came into my room mumbling something about how Santa had to parachute into the pasture due to bad weather, but that he got here just the same. I was still half asleep and couldn't figure what he was going on about. The truth was he couldn't stand it any longer and just wanted me to get up and see what was waiting for me under the tree. Santa had left me a Phonola record player with a fuzzy orange turntable. It was just like the blue and white one my friend Karen Hampton had—the one we played our favorite Beatles songs on. It had also come with two 45 records. One of the records was bright yellow and had three Christmas songs on it; the other was a regular 45 with a couple of Christmas tunes demarcated by a stripe that ran around the middle of the record. I played them both over and over the entire day. I got a lot of mileage out of that record player. I played my brother's *Golden Hits of the Everly Brothers* album on it while he was away at school; I knew every word to "Cathy's Clown," my favorite song off the album.

Another Christmas at my grandparents', I woke up to handlebars over my head. It was my first bike, royal blue with a white seat, a lot bigger than the small red bike of Janet Westbrook's on which I had taught myself to ride one glorious Saturday afternoon. I had fallen and picked myself up repeatedly trying to keep up with the other big kids on the block until I finally mastered it. That was to be the last Christmas morning I would spend with my brother: he was joining the Air Force and would go on to grow up, marry, and start his own family without ever coming back to sleep in with me on Christmas morning. I would believe in Santa for one more year, until I confronted my mom after opening *By the Shores of Silver Lake* by Laura Ingalls Wilder, the book left for me under the tree that Christmas. I was in the second grade.

My early belief in Santa Claus had been firmly secured by the testimony of a trusted neighborhood friend. One day in a heated debate on our street, the older kids began to spew their knowledge on the subject. The most damaging piece of news was told by someone who had woken up in the middle of the night and had caught their parents in the act of placing their gifts under the tree. They said it in a most matter-of-fact fashion, case closed. But Tracy, who was two years older than I, who lived across the street and did the best flips in the neighborhood on her backyard trampoline, firmly stood by her own story. *She* had awakened in the middle of night and had seen the sleigh with its reindeer parked in her frontyard. Well, that was good enough for me. Whenever that twinge of doubt would enter my head I would refer to the resolute and trustworthy look I saw in Tracy's eyes as she gave me her own eyewitness report.

Anticipation of the big day and harnessing the impatience that mounted during the waiting was also something I had in common with my granddad. I knew Christmas was on its way when we received our annual paper Santa Claus within our TP&L newsletter. My dad worked for and retired from Texas Power and Light Company, and to this day that paper Santa hangs on the tree, just like it did in the winter of 1965. Little by little, the stores would start to put out decorations and toys. Even our neighborhood food market put baby doll strollers above the produce section. The downtown square was decorated in silver and blue (mirroring the colors of the home football team) even before most people had their trees up, because unless you were allergic and had to have an aluminum tree with single-colored Christmas balls with a revolving lamp on the floor to reflect off the silver, most people had real trees; you couldn't put them out too early because they would dry out. The first year my granddad could no longer go out and chop down a tree (my father always remarked that, by the looks of their tree, "he probably just chopped down the first one he came upon in the pasture"), my grandmother picked up a used aluminum tree from somewhere and strung lights on the thing, much to my father's dismay. After all he did work for the power company.

Struggling to learn the words to "Away In a Manger" for the children's part in the Christmas pageant, the second verse to "Jingle Bells," picking toys out of the JCPenney catalog all led up to the excitement of finally heading *out of town* to spend the holidays with my grandparents and cousins, a whole hour's drive away. There, the lure of wrapped gifts under the tree, coupled with cold weather that kept us inside, tempted us into mischief.

The three granddaughters tried to stay out of Granny's way in the kitchen, where all the glorious aromas of baking wafted throughout, but we found plenty of other ways to get in trouble. Diana, affectionately called Dini, was four months behind me, her sister Karen was four years behind us, perfect for picking on and leaving out. Dini and I began to notice as we grew, our gifts were shrinking in size as compared to our younger cousins' whose continued to grow. We had become the age where our grandparents decided we would be happy with corduroy pants and shirt sets, while Karen received life-sized dolls. One particular Christmas, we got into trouble for peeling back a corner of Karen's three-foot-tall package to reveal a large yellow-haired doll standing in a box with a clear cellophane front. The adults all acted outraged by our behavior. What was the big deal? Couldn't they clearly see that the presents weren't being doled out fairly? My anticipation over Christmas was becoming matched by my increasing jealousy.

Christmases with my cousins throughout the years were hit and miss affairs. Not only was my uncle in the Air Force, but after a bad divorce, my cousins moved far away with their mother. Contact with them became sporadic until their teenage years, when they finally returned to Texas in order to live with their father. Those early Christmases spent with them were some of my most memorable holidays, hopefully as it is with all young children who experience Christmas, or at least how it should be.

As the years went by my excitement over the holiday was eclipsed by the excitement of my brother's first-born son, Chad. I was a freshman in high school the year he was born. When I started making my own money through my school co-op part-time job, he became the focus of my buying at Christmas, because never had I witnessed such a clothes horse in the body of a three year old. One year I decked him out from head to toe, cowboy hat to cowboy boots, in a western outfit that even included a cowhide belt with his name on the back. I knew there was something different about this kid when he became overjoyed while unwrapping his new down-filled jacket. I harkened back to the days of my cousin and me rolling our eyes at one another after tearing open Christmas wrap only to find brown corduroy pants awaiting us.

By the time Chad had come along, our grandparents had moved in from the country to a small frame house in town, and my other grandmother had passed away some five years earlier. Not since I was much younger had we spent the night with my grandparents on Christmas Eve due to our family moving closer to them during my first year in school. After family presents, we would drive home to our house fifteen miles away, followed by my brother and his new family to celebrate Santa with my nephew the next morning. My brother and dad would stay up half the night putting some special toy together, such as his first rocking horse, a pedal car, or a train set. One Christmas Eve, while the wine and conversation flowed during one of these construction events, I went for a ride on my ten-speed bicycle.

White Christmases are not typical or even anticipated in Texas, but that night the snow was coming down, and I wasn't going to miss it. It felt like in the poem: "The children were nestled all snug in their beds" while I was the only one out on the snow-covered streets. Save for the fresh tracks my bike made, the yards and streets were covered in snow as it continued to come down. It was so magical. I rode bravely up and down the street in front of a guy's house on whom I had an unrelenting crush. It was Christmas; it was white; and I was in love and undiscovered.

If I thought Christmas had changed when my grandparents moved off the farm, when my cousins were no longer there to tear open packages with, when everybody began to grow up and move off, I was in for real change when my grandfather died and my dad became Granddad, the official patriarch of Christmas Eve. Along with a new head to the family came a change in the venue. My dad counted twenty-two Christmases spent in my parents' modest three-bedroom home where we would experience our family grow and change over the years and eventually see our children's children straining to remain patient while the adults finished their evening meal before *finally* heading to the living room for presents. Granny would only spend a few of those times with us before dementia would force a move into an assisted living facility that would prove a necessity for her and my family's well-being. Just as all the preparations had become overwhelming for my grandmother, the same held true for my mother after a time.

Two Christmases before Mother died, I remember sitting in a chair in the living room, one leg draped over the arm, absentmindedly watching Mom through the open door that led into the den/kitchen. It was in the afternoon before everyone was scheduled to arrive around nightfall. Mom was setting things out on the stove top, getting her sandwich platters all in order, just doing her thing. I remember thinking to myself, *Embed this image in your mind—it might just go away someday,* just like the fading picture on a movie screen where the character gently fades away to convey the passing of time. That day came all right, but it wasn't expected, particularly by my father.

On the whole, I think Dad coped pretty well. The first Christmas spent away from my parents' home was different for all of us. My brother and his family had only visited my house a couple of times, being that just two years prior to my mom's death we had moved back from South Texas to be closer to the family. My house was all lit up like the one in the movie *Home Alone*—wreaths on the windows and the whole bit. We sat about eating as in times past while the kids begged us to "hurry up." Only once did Dad have to excuse himself for a walk outside, alone. My brother and I exchanged glances, acknowledging that we both knew he was having a difficult time and was putting on a brave face for the kids. I, on the other hand, was doing great; by this time I had put Mom on the back burner. I was caught up in grieving over someone else.

One morning in mid-December I picked up the morning newspaper to read that singer-songwriter Dan Fogelberg had died on December 16 after a hard-fought battle with prostate cancer. I hadn't even known he had been sick. Funny thing was that I had been listening to one of his earlier CDs, *Fallen Angel,* almost exclusively at that time. During the months of September and October, while my mom remained in the hospital recovering from surgery a good hour and a half away from my home, I stayed with my father in an extended-stay motel near the hospital. Periodically I would leave to come home to do laundry and check on things, make sure the kids were where they needed to be, after farming them out with different friends so I could remain with my father. I traveled before and after peak traffic times since the hospital was located in a highly congested area in Dallas. I would either leave after the last ICU visitation at 10 p.m. or before sunrise around 4 a.m. After leaving the interstate I traveled primarily on lonely back roads and two-lane highways to get home, always in the dark. Being in the habit of listening to music in the car and playing a CD over and over, a disc of Dan Fogelberg's had been left in the CD player. So on those lonely treks home with a lot on my mind, his music serenaded me. It was unbeknownst to me at the time that he himself was nearing the end of his own journey.

I remember the first time I was introduced to his music. I was around fifteen years old and over at a friend's house; her father was a fundamentalist preacher, and I attended their church. We sat talking in her room while admiring the cover art on an album lent to her by a mutual friend of ours at school. The album was *Fallen Angel.* As we were engrossed in some high school girl talk while she was getting ready, her father strode forcefully in the room, lifted up the album, and stated that he never wanted to see her bring this kind of stuff into their home again! I sat there dumbstruck as he walked out, firmly closing the door behind him. She half smiled, not in the least bit shaken, and said, "Never mind that—look at this poetry," and we proceeded to read the words of his songs printed on the inside of the album sleeve.

What had rattled her father was the same thing that had rattled us: the picture of Dan on the back cover, sitting in open nature with that glorious long dark hair and beard blowing in the wind, gorgeous eyes, and a beaded necklace hung around his neck. I was too young to realize the humor in the moment. The truth was, back in 1975, if there ever was anyone who was *safe* to listen to it was Dan Fogelberg, with his beautiful melodies and ballads of love, despite his long feathered locks. I didn't realize it then, but my introduction to his music, memorable for whatever reason, was just the beginning of my love for his art and even dependence at times on his music for inspiration and comfort.

In 1981, he released his double album, *The Innocent Age,* acclaimed by many as his crowning achievement, "a masterpiece." In the latter part of 1981, I was twenty-one years old, nearing the ripe old age of twenty-two while going through a divorce as a single parent. Having neglected a good part of me while being so caught up in a challenging relationship with my first husband, it was difficult to think about future goals for myself. Words from that album like, "the snow turned into rain," or "you face the future with a weary past—those dreams you banked on are fading fast" gave me some artistic expression to identify with, and by feeling my crossroads were identified in song, I began to experience hope. I listened to his music through the years, enjoyed seeing him in concert from time to time, and collected several of his CDs. I remained a fan, but as time ticked on, and I became busier and busier while pursuing career and personal goals, I stopped keeping up with the music he continued to produce.

After learning of his death, I decided to go online to learn more of his illness and recent recording history. His official website opened up to a great picture of him with his dates prominently displayed underneath; the background song playing was one of his I hadn't heard in years. The sight of him took my breath away just as it had years earlier, except this time I wept at the sight of him. I soon became obsessed with learning more about him, looking at his photograph gallery and reading all the condolences. I would stay up all hours of the night reading each message of sympathy and personal grievance, scrolling page after page. The messages represented stories of how people had come to love his music and the role it had played in their lives. I even sent one myself, which was something I had never done before. As thoughts of him began to take over my mind, as I became more and more preoccupied with grieving over the thought of never getting to meet him, I began to wonder what was going on; this so-called grieving process had taken a turn somewhere.

After my mom had died in October, after helping my father clean out her drawers and closet space, after attempting to regain some normalcy around my own home, I wanted time alone to process the journey I had been on for the past two months and to grieve in my own way: isolated. While walking my dog, I would pray for a *holy grieving,* a time to honor my mother and in so doing I would honor God as well. I wanted to live out the rest of my life in a way that would honor the memory of her, something that would be pleasing to her. It was not to be; my mother was never like that anyway. She never pushed her agenda on me, never expected or even alluded to the fact she ever wanted me to do anything with my life that would reflect well on her. She probably understood me better than I gave her credit for, or at least she accepted me for who I was even though she didn't always "get me." Whatever the case, I believe Mom's desire for me was for me to be, to do, whatever I was meant for, not something to pursue on her account. Looking back, I wonder if she was trying to tell me something then, a release of guilt for all that I felt I had fallen short of as a daughter, for all the things I didn't say, or did say. But, at this juncture of my life, it was the things I didn't say that were troubling me the most.

Prior to Mom's surgery I had toyed with the idea of asking her if she was scared, if she had any doubts. Knowing my mom, I figured she would process all this in her own way: she would smile and nod as the doctors explained the procedure, recovery process, and anticipated outcome, but would never voice any fears or concerns. I was too scared to mention my own reservation; I didn't want to cause her any discomfort once she'd made her decision. She called me one day, a month or so before her scheduled surgery. She said that, before she had this "big heart operation," she needed to see about some other medical problems she was having. She had been studying something she'd found in her local newspaper: a list of symptoms associated with ovarian cancer. She told me she had every one of the symptoms listed. I talked to her at length about speaking with her primary care physician about a gynecological exam, particularly because she hadn't had one in some time, and, if he didn't perform them, to get a referral for a gynecologist, because her previous one had retired. I told her that if she had any problem, she could call me, and I would talk to her doctor, but I agreed with her that this needed to be addressed—the sooner the better. We never discussed it again. On the morning of her open-heart surgery, it was pointless. I figured she had talked to her doctor, but, knowing Mom, she probably hadn't. She had prepared herself and was wheeled through the operating doors with a peaceful, calm reserve about her.

While going through her things after she died, I found a scribbled note in her handwriting listing the signs and symptoms of ovarian cancer and the blood tests recommended for diagnosis. We didn't talk much about her fears and concerns. Mom had always handled these in her own private way, but I still wished I had spoken up and let her burden me with some of those if she had needed to. She was very stoic in some ways—not in a haughty, confident way, but rather in a calm, trusting kind of manner. "No use to worry," she would always say. "There's nothing you can do about it anyway." And so in dealing with my pain, I had come to a juncture where guilt and remorse were replaced with something, someone else. I think she understood. I think she would have wanted it that way.

It was time to discuss this pattern of thinking with someone, and I knew just the person, April. While working as a palliative care pediatrician in San Antonio, I was privileged to be part of a palliative care team, a division under the pediatric oncology department of a children's hospital. Our team consisted of our medical director and founder, a pediatric oncologist; a program coordinator; a patient care coordinator; a chaplain; and me. Our excellent team was dedicated to the total comprehensive care of managing our patients with many challenging medical and emotional problems. As a consulting physician dealing with chronically and terminally ill children and their families, I worked closely with our patient care coordinator, an RN by the name of Cindy, and the chaplain, April—one of the most liberal, loving persons I have ever met.

One of my favorite duties was to make house calls to check on the status of a patient, usually accompanied with one or more of the team members. We made bereavement visitations as well. One of my favorite memories was visiting with a family in the final days before their baby girl expired. The infant had a terminal condition and was left with very minimal brain function, only that which allowed her temporarily to sustain her breathing, a heartbeat, and blood pressure. In medical terms, she was subsisting on "brainstem function" only, not enough to sustain her life beyond the very near future. We made a hospice visit to check on the baby and offer our support to the young parents. They were coping well, taking plenty of pictures and marking the time they had left with her. I'll never forget April picking up the baby and gently rocking and swaying with her as she sang a song from the movie *Babe*: "If I had words to make a day for you, I'd sing you a morning golden and new. I would make this day last for all time, Give you night deep with moonshine." It was the most beautiful moment, and the dad, so touched, asked to take a picture of April holding the baby.

April was like that: she brought something unique to the team. She delivered some of the most moving messages at our patients' funerals that I sometimes had to smile, even laugh, in spite of the tears. Either way, I came away knowing a little more about the child than I did before. She was open-minded about some things; she was opinionated about certain things; she was also a paradox in many ways. Never questioning God or laying any blame on him, she would still rant and rave about how things weren't fair: children shouldn't die before their parents; her own daughter should not have had to go through a leukemia relapse; her dad was too young to die at seventy-five years of a progressive neurological disease. She hated conformity, loved learning about other peoples' faith and beliefs, and called herself "a pimp for God."

After I moved away I kept in regular contact with both Cindy and April. Our first reunion after my move took place that same summer at the wedding of Cindy's son. April's father had recently lost his two-year, downhill battle with a debilitating neurological disorder, never given a name, which irritated her as much as the disease process itself. I was anxious to talk with her and see how she was doing. We found some time at the reception to catch up with each other. She began in great detail to relay the story of the recent tragic loss of her cat, Yu-mi-san. *Huh?*

Apparently, this adopted kitten, owned by her for a short six months, was a comfort to her after her father had died. She snuggled with the thing every morning and had become very attached to it. After all, she explained, her kids had gotten too big for all that cuddle stuff. Three weeks after April's father's death, the cat had come down with some kind of illness and had become septic. She had taken it to the vet and, after investing quite a bit of money already, was told they could either put the cat into the "kitty-kat ICU" to try some more therapy to salvage it, or they could put it to sleep instead. When she asked the estimated cost of an ICU stay, the vet handed her a finance plan pamphlet that could help out, up to the amount of $10,000. April had reasoned there were starving children in third world countries without adequate health care, nutrition, or fresh water who would probably be better served from that amount of money than her cat. She just couldn't justify spending that much on further treatment that wasn't guaranteed, and, besides, she didn't really think she could afford it at the time. So she did the reasonable, recommended thing: she had the cat put down. *Good decision,* I thought. Except the case was not closed. While at the reception, she droned on and on about missing the cat, maybe she did the wrong thing, even though it would have meant no summer trip for the kids if she'd spent that kind of money on the cat, and the only silver lining was that, since she was so lonely, her husband had promised her she could get a pug dog, something she'd always wanted.

At one point in the conversation, I looked at Cindy, who was rolling her eyes at me, and I said, "April, do Cindy and I need to sit down and go through a palliative care consultation with you? You did the right thing. You did the most loving thing for this kitten, and, furthermore, you'd be crazy to spend that kind of money." The point is, we talked little about her father. She was coping on that front, but she was grieving openly about the loss of a cat she'd only had in her possession for a little while. The timing of events proved catastrophic for her, or at least distorted her perception.

"So, April, tell me, two years ago when you grieved so over the loss of your cat in the face of your father's death, were you transferring? Is that what I'm doing?" She was the first person I confided in about this confusion over missing someone I had never met versus the memory of my own mother. *Was I crazy or what?*

"Dan Fogelberg, didn't he sing . . . ?"

"Yeah, that's him." I was walking around a car garage with my cell phone stuck to my ear revealing what I thought were ridiculous schoolgirl-like longings. We were back in town to celebrate the holidays with my husband's family at the time. Christmas was approaching, and I wasn't emotionally ready to be the hostess after returning to our home in North Texas. No, she didn't think I was crazy, and, yes, she did think she had transferred the sadness over losing her father onto the cat, although she still insisted how much the cat had meant to her. It had been a solace to her after her father's death. In fact, for a minute I thought we were headed back to a discussion regarding the decision to have the cat put down versus taking out a major loan in order to save it. Instead, after a long conversation about our families' dealing with their first loss and individual coping during special times, I hung up feeling somehow not too strange. I was comforted for a short while. I really did love my mother, but the bizarreness was just beginning.

Transference is just one of many tools we use to get through difficult times that confront us all from time to time. In my mind, denial runs right up there at the top of the list as a way people cope, whether employed consciously or subconsciously. I witnessed this often in my work with terminally ill children and their families, particularly on the part of one or both of the parents. I ran into this in Dallas within the cardiac ICU where my mom was a patient for over a month.

When you regularly visit with someone in the ICU, when you strictly adhere to the scheduled visitation times, when you push that big blue button on the wall that allows entrance into the secured ward time and again, you begin to notice the other patients and the coming and going of their families, particularly when others have moved on, and you're still stuck there. Such was the case of a poor man next door to my mother.

He had come in about the same time as Mom and had remained on a ventilator for some time. Off and on, the number of family members present would swell, probably in response to the patient's increasingly critical condition. One day, outside the hospital, I spoke with the wife and her grown granddaughter, who regularly accompanied her. They were from Oklahoma, but her husband had been under the regular care of a cardiologist in Dallas. Her husband had some predisposed medical condition that finally resulted in complete cardiac failure. He had no other risk factors, according to the wife. He had never smoked, was not overweight, kept himself in good shape working on the farm; it was just that his ticker was in bad shape. He had been on the transplant list for a new heart, but his condition had deteriorated rapidly. They had been told to come to the hospital for medical support while awaiting a new heart.

Something had gone wrong during his hospital stay; he had gotten into trouble during a procedure, then pneumonia had set in, compromising his respiratory status. Thus, he remained on the vent. He subsequently had been taken off the transplant list, because he could not withstand the surgery and would have to recover fully (become strong enough to come off the ventilator), before he could even be considered a heart recipient again. I listened to the gravity of the situation, nodding my head in sympathy at this poor man's plight. I thought to myself, *What this family needs is a palliative-hospice consultation to help them make some difficult decisions.* Even so, in such a situation, I listened as a fellow ICU visitor and kept my mouth shut. She talked of her faith and how she just knew he was going to get better and whip this, because he was strong and determined, and, after all, his own mother had a direct prayer line to God. She told me that she couldn't understand how she could bring a "perfectly healthy man" in here and have everything turn out like it had. *Excuse me?* The man had entered the hospital on the transplant list! How in the world could she have perceived him as healthy? He apparently had been living on borrowed time. I guess we all deal similarly with the inevitable loss of a loved one. We become used to seeing them in a compromised state and take it for granted they will continue on as such.

I had seen families use denial as a coping mechanism. I had employed it myself. After Mom died, I was looking at family pictures made during special events that occurred just prior to Mom's surgery: my son's wedding and my parents' sixtieth wedding anniversary celebration. Mom was gray. Her coloring was awful. *How could I have missed that?* After all, I was a doctor. We had all missed it. We knew she was slowing down, couldn't walk as far, rested more, had left most of the household chores to Dad, but we had "grown accustomed to her face." I had chalked it up to Mom's not being much of an exercise enthusiast. Poor thing, she had struggled silently with probable poor cardiac output, and we had just assumed that she would continue in that state. Denial had carried us for a while, but that had all changed; it was still changing. I was in for a long, cold winter.

January

*M*y husband used to say his two least-favorite months of the year were August and January. If you've ever lived in San Antonio, you could understand—about the August part, anyway. By the end of the summer we were usually under water restrictions due to lack of rain and unrelenting heat. The combination of suffocating humidity and high temperatures, water drying up all around, brown lawns, and trying to find relief somewhere besides the air conditioning in your car (which had set in the sun all day) and in your home (for which you paid a pretty penny), could explain his dislike for the last month of summer. I think most people can relate to the dreariness of January, especially after the rush of the holidays. Time to pay the piper, time to go back to school, back to the ol' grind—the whole bit.

January. I remember the challenge of learning how to spell it, that and February. If it weren't for celebrating the New Year and getting to show off what you got for Christmas, the month would be easy to dismiss from memory. I remember Januarys being a lot colder when I was a kid. Maybe it was because I was so skinny, maybe because the houses weren't insulated as well, maybe because we didn't have central heat, maybe because up until the end of the fourth grade we had to wear dresses to school. The earliest memory I have of bucking the system, crossing the line, was the day I came to school wearing pants.

The buzz had gotten around at our elementary school that some girls were showing up at the high school in pants, not jeans. There was never any official statement on the matter, but we knew "the code." So, a friend and I decided to join the movement. I showed up in my homeroom class the next day wearing one of the only two pant outfits I owned. I was greeted with widened eyes and muffled giggles by my classmates and a sly, sideways smile by my teacher. (To this day I recall her look as a silent nod of approval.) Nothing was ever said about it—no announcement made over the PA system—but the next day we were joined by the rest of the fourth grade girls with their britches on. Suddenly, we were warmer and more confident, armed with the knowledge that the dress code had been modified by the silent minority. I rotated wearing my aqua blue and rusty brown pant sets throughout the remainder of the year. Colored jeans were allowed the following year. Over the next couple of years, pants would prove a dilemma for me due to anatomical changes.

When your six-foot father marries your five-foot mother, who is extremely short-waisted to boot, someone ends up paying for this dichotomy. My brother has always lamented his short stature. He got all of Mom and her side of the family. Standing at maybe five-foot-seven, he married a girl who's a good five-nine; his two boys start out at around six feet and keep going upward. Poor guy. I, on the other hand, am a combination of my parents. I have always described my build as "dysmorphic," though there is no such word found in the dictionary, so "disproportioned" will have to do. I am all extremities, particularly my long legs, inherited from my father, with my mom's short torso stuck on top. I swear my rib bone is connected to my hip bone. The first time my grandmother on my dad's side saw me, she exclaimed, "Look at those legs! Oh, my God, she'll be as tall as Jean!" referring to her tall sister-in-law.

For years I have employed the technique of camouflaging with long tops and no belts, anything to lengthen the body. But as a growing youngster, neither I nor my mother had the skills to camouflage or fix the fit of a pair of pants on me. If my mom could find them long enough in the legs, they were huge in the waist; if they fit in the waist, they were up to my shins. I was not only skinny, I was *bony skinny,* and my legs, which went on for miles, were only appreciated by my ballet teacher, it seemed. Apparently my parents never read any child psychology journals while I was growing up, because they always employed these dinner table techniques, wild tales that I believed to be true. "If you don't eat, a strong wind will come along and blow you away." "If you don't eat, a big bird will come along and carry you off." Is it any wonder I would search the skies for a big, black predator bird that would surely swoop down at any time? It just went with the territory of being raised by parents who remembered the Great Depression, even if they were just kids at the time. "Cleaning your plate" was not only advised, it was your duty, a mission I found tiring, night after night. Nothing was to be wasted: not food, not the cold air in the refrigerator (I got in trouble once for standing with the door wide open admiring our new fridge; I literally couldn't take my eyes off the new inside part), not water, not the air conditioning, or the heat from the stove. Though conditions had drastically improved over the years, I got a little taste of another place back in time whenever I visited my grandparents and, ultimately, as a result of those relationships, understood my parents a little bit better.

Both of my grandmothers lived on the opposite sides of Tom Bean, a small farming community located approximately a hour's drive northeast of Dallas. Both their houses were old, two-story, white framed farming types, probably built about the same time, although neither set of grandparents was the original owner. My paternal grandparents' roof was blue; my maternal grandmother's roof was green. It made all the difference to me as a kid, because the front of their houses were identical. They each had long wooden porches that ran along the entire front of the house where two front doors opened onto them. The two upper-story front windows had pointed roof peaks above them that gave the houses a castle-like appearance to my small imaginative eyes. There was no air conditioning, only open windows and rotating fans that were usually heard whirring somewhere in the kitchen atop a cabinet. The heat came out of propane gas space heaters placed strategically around the house. When they were freshly refilled by the propane man, one had to be careful lighting the stove. (My Grandma Taylor was known to have scorched her eyebrows more than a time or two while trying to ignite the stove with a lit match, a little too close.) There was always a heater in the front room to keep us warm while we watched TV, one in the bathroom to bathe by, and one in the kitchen. We depended on the bedcovers to keep us warm at night. To conserve the heat, we closed off certain rooms.

In my maternal grandmother's house, a small, dark entry hall off the back porch housed her sewing machine and the staircase. Next to that was the dining room, which contained an old table with six chairs and the deep freeze, which stood up against the wall. We had to pass through both these rooms in order to get from the front living room to the kitchen at the back of the house. On cold winter nights, the two middle rooms were terribly dark and freezing cold. So, I would run from the warmth of the front room toward the light I could see spilling out from underneath the kitchen door—and as fast as I could to avoid the monsters of the dark and such.

Grandma was afraid of nothing. I mean nothing. (She was a petite woman with long, gray-streaked hair, which she liked to keep up in a bun; she incessantly fussed aloud at her hair for not cooperating.) One night, in the pitch black I hid behind the door frame in the small entry room. As she came striding out of the front room, purposely headed for the kitchen, I jumped out of the dark from behind the door frame and yelled, "Boo!" She never broke stride or even looked my way. She just patted me on the head, said, "Boo, yourself!" and kept right on walking through the pitch black toward the kitchen.

Such would have never been the case with my other grandmother, the one affectionately called Granny. I would have caused a stroke if I had done such a thing to her. Granny was loud, boisterous, laughed, and made us laugh a lot. She was quite large and anxious about everything. If there wasn't anything to worry about, she found something to wring her hands over. If the sky darkened outside, threatening a thunderstorm, or if the wind picked up, my dad would always jokingly say, "Well, I guess Granny is headed towards the storm cellar."

January at my granny's was especially depressing, because I knew the cousins wouldn't be there; they would have returned to their home after the holidays, and I would have to pretend in our playhouse all by myself. We actually had two. Now, these weren't custom-built doll houses for us. They were buildings already on site that we took over. Our "winter house" was a two-room shed located in the side yard, close to the big hen house—and when I say "big," I mean big. I don't ever recall chickens in the yard at Granny's; they were always contained in this large building with different levels of roosts for the hens. (Planks stretched from one end to the other so the chickens could perch at night.) My other grandmother also had chickens. In fact, they seemed almost more like her pets. I helped her feed them all twice a day. She would sometimes sell the eggs and always send some home in a brown paper bag with my mom when we came to visit. Granny used her chickens' eggs as well, but the primary reason she raised chickens was to eat them.

Every spring she would get about fifty little chicks to "renew her supply." My dad remembers, as a child back in the 1930s, that the mail carrier would deliver them. Our two-room playhouse was the brooder house. The chicks would arrive in early spring when it was still cold, and the floor of our playhouse would be covered with them. Devices on the floor contained a naked, lit lightbulb that the chicks would gather around in order to keep warm. How long they remained in the brooder house before they were moved to the hen house, I have no idea, but I knew what fate awaited them. I never saw it myself, but my father used to tell how, back in her day, my granny could take a chicken from the yard, have its neck wrung, body steamed, feathers plucked, cut, floured, fried, and on the table within one hour. She loved fried chicken and once told me she could eat it three times a day.

The noon meal, known as dinner, always had a piece of fried meat on the table, whether it be chicken or beef, along with vegetables from the garden, thawed that morning from the deep freeze. Yes, Granny had a deep freeze, too, but it stood against the wall in her kitchen, not in the dining room as in my other grandmother's house, for she didn't have a designated dining room, but the deep freeze did serve as a piece of furniture from time to time. It was a trunk style, as was my other grandmother's. The cousins and I were relegated to eat at either end of the deep freeze when we had big family dinners. We knelt on a chair or vanity stool in order to reach the top of the freezer that served as a tabletop. Dini and I sat at one end, and we made Karen sit by herself, way far at the other end. It was like sitting at opposite ends of a long, formal dining table, except it was just a deep freeze against the kitchen wall.

After dinner and dessert, which was usually butterscotch pudding that Granny had poured into reusable butter dishes and kept chilled in the 'frig, my grandparents sat down to watch *As The World Turns*, Monday through Friday, without fail. After the episode's conclusion my granddad returned to work out on the farm, in the fields, with the cattle or whatever he was working on. Granny would then go on about her day after cleaning the kitchen and putting the table scraps outside for the dog or dogs. I always smile to myself when I hear precautions against feeding dogs chicken bones. My grandparents always had a dog on the place, and they never bought a bag of dog food, ever. The chicken bones went out into the yard everyday along with the gravy and other trimmings. When they moved into town, Granny set out the table scraps every day in the yard even when they no longer had a dog. Didn't matter: the town's dogs knew where to find fresh meat. That skillet was licked clean every time, chicken bones and all.

I enjoyed lots of stories, good meals, and good times at my grandmothers'. Over the years, particularly during tough times, I would draw comfort from their memory.

It wasn't just the remembering, I believe it was their strength that flowed through my veins, their no-nonsense approach to life and work: the way they filled their day with endless chores and duties that seemed to suit them well as they hummed, sang, and scurried about. Their downtime, or time set apart for them, was still something that ultimately benefited others but allowed them to create or work at their own art of gardening, sewing, baking, mending, etc. Strong, independent women, never afraid of an honest day's worth of work yet willing to let me tag along and make memories that would serve me well when I needed to believe I was forged from something that would see me through.

That was not to be the case this particular January. I didn't want to remember my grandmothers, my origin, my background, my own, or the fires I'd been forged from, and certainly not my mother. I wanted desperately to be somebody else, to be originated from someone else, not as quaint, not as simple, not as unknown.

January couldn't get cold enough for me. As the temperature dropped, bringing warnings of freezing rain or ice, my resounding sentiment became, *Bring it on*. I wanted to hole up and be left alone. My kitchen became my cave. I would shut off the two sets of French doors that led into the kitchen, turn on my music, and work while my mind wandered. I would prepare dinner, clean up afterward, and somehow stretch out the time spent so that I was in that little room up to three hours every night. It was my space, and anybody who entered got the message: "Back off. Get out of here. Can't you see I'm busy?" I really wanted to be left alone with my wandering thoughts and dreams that took me far away—dreams of being somebody better, more important. After all, life was futile, and I had better hurry up and make my mark, because time was running out.

What served me well during this darkness was what had always carried me, my imagination. I had years' experience of being who I wanted to be, being with who I wanted to be with: I always got the guy; I always had the look, made the song a hit, or got the top award. When I was young, I would shut off the two sets of doors to our living room and dance and sing on top of the marble-top coffee table to my brother's old Motown album collection. I sang along with Marvin Gaye and Tammi Terrell, and I *was* the voice of Tammi.

I couldn't actually sing along to *this* music playing in my kitchen, and I sure didn't want to get caught by my kids. I've always had an affinity for Christmas music and usually play it well after the holidays are over, usually until the kids go back to school, but the year my mother died I played it right up until spring. It wasn't choral music or any of the traditional pieces; instead, it was instrumental selections off some *Winter Solstice* CDs by Windham Hill artists. Some have a lonely, melancholy sound, beautiful but sad. I liked it that way. One of the pieces, *Asleep the Snow Came Flying* by Tim Story, has one of the loneliest melodies with beautiful oboe and cello solos that almost sound as if they are mourning, especially the weeping cello. Prior to Christmas, while driving across the pasture lands back and forth from checking on my father, the song would bring memories of Mom, particularly haunting memories of our days spent in the hospital. Now it was just a lonely tune.

My family never said a word. Aside from the kitchen, I basically let the rest of the house go and prided myself on at least getting dinner on the table and laundry done. I kept the calendar as free as I could from any unnecessary activity, a "no, thank you" to invites of any kind. I managed to get the kids to where they had to be and coped with their schedules as long as they didn't try to ask me questions along the way while I had the music cranked up. I vacillated between wanting to escape and wanting to cocoon myself in for the duration of winter. So, when I said I needed to go to Colorado, my husband said, "Go."

It's funny how distance sometimes brings people closer together. Jill and I had been friends for many years, dating back to our days of working in different parts of the lab at the hospital in the town where we both lived. When she moved to South Texas we still kept in touch, but when she moved to Colorado, northeast of Denver, we really became better friends. I would visit from time to time, and after I remarried and started another family, we would take family vacations there together. We had a lot in common: our older children were the same age, my husband loved the camping and fishing to which they were accustomed, and Jill's husband and I loved to give each other a hard time. Jill called one day and was having some difficulty in a new position at work, and I was, well, whatever I was, so we were both excited about *a visit* to Colorado that we thought we both needed.

The day I was scheduled to fly out of Love Field airport in Dallas, my dad came over about mid-morning to go over some final instructions. He would be staying at my house while I was away to help out with the kids, dog, cats, meals, etc. Prone to anxiety anyway, he came over with not "twenty-one questions," but at least fifty. He followed me around the house as I was hurriedly getting my luggage and stuff together, going over everything from what I had written down pertaining to the kids' activities to what days the garbage truck ran. He asked me questions I not only didn't know the answer to, but also questions I had no idea how to go about even attempting to answer; "Wonder if you'll have any delays due to bad weather that could occur?" After I closed the front door behind me, I sprinted down the front walk, threw my bags in the back of the van, and drove off. This was my first time to fly off somewhere since Mom had died and even though I knew Dad was having a bad time and was just going through his "be careful" spiel, I had to get away.

The airport is a good two hours' drive from my house, so in order to check in on time, I had to stay on schedule. It's always nerve racking when I start out because I know I'm under the gun to get there on time, and there's a lot of road between me and my flight. I therefore nearly panicked when I looked down at my gas gauge to see it sitting on empty and I was a good twenty minutes from the next town. *God, after struggling to get out of the house, now I was going to be stranded in the middle of nowhere.* Luckily, I cruised into a shopping center gas station on fumes, gassed up while battling the wind that was determined to slam the car door on me, and made my flight, after running through the parking lot and down the concourse. Thankfully, there was a guy running behind me, running for the same flight, so I wasn't the only one they were waiting on. Oh, yeah, there was a delay in Las Vegas waiting on a connecting flight—bad weather somewhere, I think.

Jill had made arrangements for us to stay up in the mountains with a friend who had rented a condo up in Winter Park for the winter. "Don't worry," she said, "I'll take care of all the ski wear. I've got everything we need." I'd heard that one before—I should have learned. The first time I ever skied was with Jill and her extended family who were all staying at a ski-in lodge at Winter Park resort. She said I could wear one of her aunt's old ski outfits. From the look of things, her aunt wouldn't have been able to get a leg in, not so much because she had gained some weight, but because the thing had to have been an antique. It was a powder blue two-piece set that was reminiscent of the ones worn back in those early Andy Williams Christmas specials. (I must be thinking of his ex-wife Claudine Longet photographed in her ski attire.) Anyway, I looked far and wide over those mountains and never saw another soul wearing anything like what I had on. By the end of the day, I was so excited about making gains on the bunny hill and surviving after they'd talked me into going up on top of the mountain, that I'd forgotten about my attire (or at least until I saw the pictures).

While preparing for our stay in the mountains, we went into the guest room closet. Jill began pulling out odds and ends from what looked like her kids' snow gear from years past. She decided on these two pairs of snow bibs made out of nylon with polyester insulation, good and bulky, tight through the butt (probably because they used to belong to her kids), and festively colored in shocking pink and neon blue. After layering, we looked like female prototypes of the Michelin Man. Guess who got to wear the pink! Again, I looked high and low over those mountains and saw no one wearing anything that resembled what I had on except some eight-year-old-looking girl who did have on the same shade of pink. Good thing my bulky pink silhouette could be seen from all the surrounding mountain peaks: otherwise everybody would have missed how I came off the lift (after I was forced manually to go up to the top of the mountain, after having not skied in fourteen years). I slid feet-first underneath the operator's shed, causing the lift to stop temporarily while this really cute guy sprinted out from his station to help me disentangle my skis from all the shovels and rakes falling around me. Or, how I crashed and came out of my skis and miserably thought, after many failed attempts of trying to get them back on, I was just going to have to slide down the mountain on my padded pink butt.

After returning from two days in the powder, even Jill's husband who is an avid fisherman and hunter, who lives in nothing but flannel shirts, couldn't believe we went skiing "looking like that!" "This is what I wear," he said, pulling up a pant leg to reveal sporty black Under Armour thermal leggings. *Yeah, you and everybody else we ran into cross-country skiing the day before in their L.L. Bean gear,* I thought.

Jill did try, though. We embarked on beautiful drives into the mountains, where snow was falling in record amounts; in some places the powder was so thick and deep there was a danger of being buried alive if we'd wiped out. We stopped and had coffee at little quaint cafes along the way. We ate out frequently and always made it a point to take Bailey's with our coffee in the mornings while deciding what to do with the rest of the day. She took me shopping for a pair of new jeans and sunglasses; we had our nails done; and then we headed to her favorite restaurant for martinis and fish while dodging the Super Bowl game that was on back at her home. On my last full day there, she took me to Boulder, the one place I had really wanted to go back to, because it had been nearly fourteen years since I had last visited there; I wanted to see if I recognized anything along the Pearl Street Mall.

It couldn't have been any better; we ate and talked over lunch a good two hours while the snow came down outside the window beside us. The snowflakes were so big I could see individual patterns of the flakes on my blue sweater. Still, I knew Colorado wasn't the answer. It was almost time to leave. I had managed to get away for a little while, but I was returning home with as much restlessness in my soul as the day I had left. There was one moment of consolation, though.

The first time I visited Jill after her move to Colorado, I was in my first year of medical school. We discovered the store Peppercorn while strolling along the Pearl Street Mall, downtown Boulder. I thought it was the most fabulous place, specializing in household items, cooking wares, and accessories. There was so much to see, and I remember thinking, *This is how I want to live someday, if I could just get past all these tests so I could afford some of this stuff.* Peppercorn was still there, and there was still a lot to see, but, after fourteen years and a lot of water under the bridge, I wasn't as drop-jawed as the first time I visited the store. There are times, however, that I believe small things happen because a *Higher Power*, God, lets you know your idiosyncrasies, desires, longings—however childish—are understood, maybe even valued.

While in the store, I remained alone, tucked in a corner of discounted Christmas items. I was looking at a rack of cards when the song "Dancing Shoes" came wafting from the store's overhead speakers. After moving to Colorado, during his first winter spent songwriting in his mountain house somewhere outside of Boulder, "where it would get so silent he could hear the snow fall," Dan Fogelberg wrote the songs for his *Nether Lands* album, released in 1977; "Dancing Shoes" is the third selection on that album. Tears in my eyes made the cards I was reading seem a little out of focus as it continued to snow softly outside on Pearl Street Mall. Time to go home.

It's always been hard for me to leave the snow, because we seldom get it in Texas, and I never saw any while living in San Antonio, but this time it was just hard returning home, period. I hadn't missed the family or my house and certainly wasn't looking forward to getting back into the routine of provincial small town life. So, it was back to my kitchen and crosstown escapes in my van. I ran kids, made extra trips to the grocery store, and looked for any excuse to run an errand, just so I could envelop myself in music and be alone. I didn't realize it then, but a remnant of Mom was developing in my everyday routine that I didn't associate with her memory until months later. What first started out as a source of comfort and pampering became a survival tool. I was developing a love for coffee.

I used to think my mom was the ultimate coffee drinker. My brother once told me she would be sitting at the kitchen table drinking coffee when he left for school and upon his return at the end of the day, she would be sitting at the same place drinking her afternoon coffee. For years she took it with cream, and then one day just started taking it black. Although she said Maryland Club was the best, she always drank Folgers. (Mrs. Olsen represented our brand. In fact, she was still Mrs. Olsen to me when she played Katharine Hepburn's nosy neighbor in *Guess Who's Coming to Dinner*. I recognized her at once, being a great connoisseur of commercials.) My Grandma Taylor always used Maxwell House, and Granny drank Sanka (I guess because of the "nerves factor"), but neither grandmother drank coffee the way my mother did. In fact, the only person who may have surpassed Mom in coffee consumption was our neighbor from across the street, Ruth Aylor.

Some of my fondest memories of our little house on Nineteenth Street are of the days when Ruth would come over with her two dogs, Joe and Lady, and two packs of cigarettes: one was a package of L&M's and the other, some kind of menthol. She would alternate smoking cigarettes out of the two packs. The dogs, the former being a large Rottweiler blend with a black coat and brown eyebrows and the latter, a small black cocker spaniel, would dutifully park themselves on the back steps by the kitchen door. Mom would make a pot of coffee, and the visiting at the kitchen table would commence, with Ruth smoking cigarette after cigarette while both consumed cup after cup of black coffee.

I just assumed when I grew up I would drink coffee and smoke cigarettes, because that's what all the adults around me did. In fact, cigarette smoking was such a part of the culture, I don't remember the scent of cigarette smoke on our clothes or in our hair, although it had to have been ever present. It's a wonder our school teachers weren't sick all the time from bronchitis or asthma attacks. However, they were probably acclimated to it, for I recall (more than once) walking past the teachers' lounge as someone was leaving, billows of cigarette smoke trailing behind them.

Cigarette commercials on television and in magazine ads were everywhere, and I could readily identify the brand smoked by most of the adults around me, because the ads were so catchy and attached an image to the cigarette and its owner. Mrs. Hampton from down the street would rather "Fight Than Switch": she smoked Tareytons. One of my aunts smoked Salems, which my dad disdained because of the menthol, and the other aunt preferred Benson and Hedges without a filter. My dad was a Luckie at one time, because he smoked Lucky Strike, with that great big red circle in the middle of the package. Then there was Marlboro—a very Western brand that my granddad smoked, although he preferred a cigar and finally switched altogether from cigarettes to Swisher Sweets. Cigars were a whole other kind of thing. As kids, we all knew about those as well, because every year at the beginning of the school year we went down to the corner convenience store and asked for an empty cigar box to hold our pencils and crayons; everybody had one in their school desk. In fact, cigar boxes were probably on the school supply list, or at least implied as essential.

Some of us actually emulated our parents' habit by pretending to smoke while playing house and such. Candy cigarettes were a big hit: nothing but chalky white sticks of sugar with fuchsia food-colored tips that represented the lit end. Then there was always the real thing. Once I kept a cigarette butt stashed on the side of the yard for pretend. I never lit it, but the effect was great, especially when I had to hide it from Dad, who seemed to suspect something was going on around there. Don't even get me started about watching adults with their lit cigarettes, during *adult* conversations, to see how long they would allow the tip of ashes to grow before they decided to flick them, or (oops!) just miss the tray. Ashtrays were actually decorative items in the home, placed strategically about the house, particularly on coffee tables and end tables. They were viewed as much as a part of the decor as a necessity. They made great Christmas gifts and vacation souvenirs too. I always knew when Dad was trying to quit by the absence of our two ashtrays in the den. My favorite was a comma-shaped tray, made out of bright yellow Bakelite; the other one was clear glass in the shape of a flower. Mom would store the ashtrays in a cupboard over the kitchen stove until it was time to bring them out again.

Once in the second grade we made match holders for our dads for Christmas. We took two plastic blue tiles and sandwiched four little (filled!) matchboxes between them with little brads stuck through the fronts of the boxes for handles, so they could be pulled out like little drawers. I argued with Mrs. Looney that, because my dad had just quit smoking, this would not be an appropriate gift for him. She promptly told me that matches could be used for other things besides lighting cigarettes, and that this would be a perfectly good gift for my father. *That's okay,* I thought, *I'll just give it to Granddad for Christmas. He still smokes.* My mom finally got rid of the ashtrays after Dad's last and successful attempt in the late '70s. Mom never smoked.

I never smoked either, unless you count those occasions when, after having too much to drink, it would just seem the thing to do—light up a cigarette. Then the next morning I'd remember what I'd done by the taste in my mouth. I never drank coffee either. People often used to ask me how I managed to get through medical school without it. I usually drank cup after cup of hot tea and rewarded myself with a piece of Pepperidge Farm triple-layer chocolate cake after having read through so many pages. During test weeks, while enduring fatigue and increased anxiety, out of sheer desperation I would read while walking through the aisles of the library or outside on the campus in order just to stay awake. A couple of times during continuing education medical conferences and seminars, I would suffer through a cup of coffee as long as I had a doughnut or something to eat along with it, just because I didn't want to sleep through a lecture I had paid for. Then, after I moved to Paris, I started not only drinking coffee but enjoying it—always a cappuccino at one of the local coffee shops, still taken with food, either a cinnamon roll or a dessert.

After Mom died, I started drinking regular coffee. For the first time in my life, I started brewing coffee for myself, purchasing coffee beans and whipping up milk to put on top. I started in the morning and added the afternoon as a pick-me-up, and suddenly I was making frequent runs through Starbuck's drive-through for a bag of beans, because our supply was dwindling faster now that I was drinking more coffee than my husband. I don't know where it came from, but it was something to look forward to, the one thing that was a part of my reality that seemed to spark me while the rest of me continued spiraling deeper into a place of isolation and aloofness. I didn't do it intentionally, but I believe it also began to serve another purpose: I began making a pot of coffee for just me and my dad to drink together.

My parents had always enjoyed coffee together in the morning. For years, they drank from their favorite designated coffee mugs. Both were a sturdy ceramic style: my dad's, tan colored with a thick rim on it; Mother's, a smaller version in white with a much thinner brim. He took sugar, she took cream, until one day they both went black. Since Dad's retirement in the mid-'80s, coffee in the afternoon had become their ritual. It was that time of day to start settling in for the evening, the beginning of the "news hour." They would begin watching one of three news shows while enjoying their coffee. They would start with the world and national news then end with the local news broadcast before beginning dinner. My father was now spending that time alone. I had often wondered since Mom's death about those lonely evening hours, particularly when people would ask how he was doing. I had once witnessed how deep his grief ran.

The morning after the day my mother died, I was awakened in the early morning hours to the sound of my father weeping in the den, the place where they had gathered every morning. The day before had been the longest of days. After returning to his home from the hospital, he and I had stayed up talking until around 2 a.m. while my two daughters slept in my old bedroom. I had cried silently, listening to him speaking candidly of his losses over the years: grandparents, parents, aunts and uncles, cousins on both sides of the family, "but I've never lost anything like this," he said. Tears streamed down my face as he began to outline plans of how he would take care of himself. "I'm going to buy myself some fresh green beans and carrots and keep stuff I can fix ahead and store in the freezer so I can continue to try and eat healthy."

And so it had gone on, talking and sharing to the point of exhaustion, so sleep would come easy once he decided to go to bed. But no more than three hours later, his internal alarm had gone off. Upon entering the den before the light of dawn, no one greeted him, save the grim, stark reality that Mom was not coming home from the hospital. I lay in bed listening to him, too emotionally and physically spent to get up to try to help him. I knew this scenario was probably relived from time to time, particularly in the early morning and evening hours in the home where they had spent forty years together.

By January, my dad's fragile and grieving state was apparent, even though he was trying so hard. I had been calling twice a day and visiting him two times a week immediately following Mom's death. Now my visits were less frequent, and I tried to remember to call at least once a day. He struggled with wanting to be alone with his grief but was so desperately lonely he would show up to spend the night from time to time: sometimes after calling; sometimes, unannounced. We would take long walks with the dog out at the lake and talk about old times while living in Paris, but he would grow anxious and begin crying by the next day, saying he couldn't keep himself from it and felt like he needed to go back home even though I would encourage him to stay.

Even so, he still looked forward to our times at the coffee shop before either heading out to the lake with the dog or after dropping the kids off at school. I would have my usual cappuccino with skim milk; he would drink the regular brew black; and we would each eat huge heated cinnamon rolls with the best icing ever. Before the kids came home from school in the afternoon he would always ask if I had anything sweet to eat with the coffee I made for the two of us. It wasn't the same, of course, but he at least liked my coffee. We at least still had that.

> The depression drips down
> and glazes the ground
> > "The Last Ride" by Todd Rundgren

February

*I*t's a Todd thing. It came on one day and was hard to explain away, but it seemed to serve a purpose, for a while anyway. One Saturday I gave in to repeated requests by my son to accompany him to the local bookstore so he could use me to rent a game for his *new system.* Whoever came up with the idea of combining a bookstore with music, movie and game rentals, tons of magazines to peruse for those who don't read seriously, and access to the internet while partaking of the new drug of choice—coffee—was a genius. Never is this fact more evidently witnessed than while living in a small town. Our local bookstore is a Mecca of activity for all age groups, and never is it more fun than on special nights celebrating the arrival of an anticipated book, particularly one within the *Harry Potter* series. I never thought I would have teenagers who would ask to be dropped off at the bookstore on a Friday night to meet friends, just to hang out and have fun, or, stranger still, who would ask me to deliver them there so they could use their own money to purchase a book!

At any rate, I found myself reluctantly hanging out in the store one afternoon while my son searched the Wii games in the locked-down rental section. Meanwhile, I sauntered over to the music section to look for artists' names I recognized and to stare at the pictures of those I didn't recognize. This alone was enough to make me feel old. I missed digging through the record bins.

While growing up in another small town, the 1970s brought about many changes locally, but one stands out in particular: we got a mall. The downtown square was soon evacuated and left to resemble a ghost town that the railroad had bypassed—suddenly we had a new hangout to frequent every Saturday. Just off the central atrium stood the music store, Musicland, which catered to the young and their choice of rock and roll. The young and lean guys who worked there had long hair and wore dress pants and dress shirts with wide psychedelic ties. The store was a standard stop every time we were at the mall, regardless if we could or couldn't afford a new album or an eight-track. Part of the thrill was just thumbing through all the albums, divided and labeled under the different musical artists, and checking out all the wild covers.

Along with the explosion of new music, there was a plethora of pop art and a psychedelic movement in graphic design as well. Our spiral journals and three-ring binders featured such artists as Peter Max, my personal favorite, as did the album covers of different bands and individual singers. If we weren't caught up in trying to interpret the graphic art designs, we were mesmerized by the otherwise graphic displays of peace, love, sex, and drugs on the covers. The twelve-by-twelve vinyl record jackets, otherwise known as LP covers, were great visual advertisements for the artists too; they were like mini posters. I was once visiting with a girlfriend who kept an album cover of Neil Diamond propped up on her bedroom dresser. His eyes stared out at her so intensely from that cover that she demonstrated how she had to turn him to the wall when she was getting undressed. That's a powerful visual.

On this particular Saturday, the only recognizable hint of my old music store were some of the names I remembered from the days of having enough spare change to spend on music just for me. So, I picked out a CD, *The Very Best of Todd Rundgren,* and headed to the checkout with my son after the man with the keys had obtained his game from the case. Little did I know at the time what havoc that purchase would bring upon me, those around me, and my repressed inner sanctum of grief and buried dreams.

Todd Rundgren was somebody whose music played in the background of my preteen and teen years when my ears were beginning to perk up and become more attuned to the surrounding times and trends. He was somebody on the radio and was probably only heard by me on an AM radio band, for that matter. It was the mid-1970s, before some of the more popular FM stations from Dallas began to invade the airwaves of my small town and replace the AM station we all listened to for popular music. (It eventually went country.) The last time I could recall a *new* Todd Rundgren song announced over the radio was in regard to "A Hammer in My Heart," a song that came out in 1982.

He was someone whose music I knew I liked, but he didn't command any more of my attention than casual listening. I didn't keep up with him; never bought any of his stuff; never thought of him as more than just someone on the radar of popular rock music at the time. My one memory of him was a picture of this gaunt face with large eyes framed by long hair in a feathered style with light-blond streaks. I remember trying to weld the image of this guy with some of his hit songs, but the two didn't seem to go together. The selections I loved of his were these sensitive love songs, beautifully sung, and here was this guy in some zany outfit with this strikingly different, charismatic face. I remember thinking, *What's up with this guy?* That was the extent of my curiosity, until thirty-something years later I purchased his CD just for the heck of it.

I was listening to my new CD, taking my daughter to a friend's house, when everything changed after the third song on the disc began to play. It was "I Saw the Light." "I remember this song!" I exclaimed. "I can't even begin to remember the last time I heard it." But I did remember the way I used to *feel* when I heard it. For me, if any song written in that era was targeted to get into the mind and heart of a young girl, it was that one. Mr. Rundgren skillfully tapped into this whole idea of getting to a girl, or at least understanding where she's coming from, by just looking her in the eye. *If a way into a man's heart is through his stomach*, then the way into a girl's heart, her world, her pants, is through her eyes, I always say.

It brought back memories of me as a young girl pining over someone like the singer in that song to make such a connection with; to be able to relate silently through my eyes into another's my desires so they would understand without words and would, of course, gratefully commit the same back to me from then on. Wow, such a picture of me at fifteen while riding around in someone's backseat to who-knows-where, with the wind and radio competing with each other for my ear space: too young to drive, too young to love or be loved.

I dropped my thirteen-year-old daughter off at her best friend's house for an afternoon of doing whatever young girls do these days. In my day, it was sharing our secrets about boys and dreams while listening to our favorite songs over and over. I turned up my music louder as I drove off, envying them for having more time than I had left, time to make dumb mistakes along the way to living out the rest of their lives. I was supposed to be past all that, but the music had got in my head, and I was beginning to experience the cover over the well of my "young girl's soul" being lifted off. The restlessness it unleashed was just beginning.

The music scene in my van drastically changed from that point on, blitzing all reason. It wasn't just returning to my rock-and-roll roots from glory days gone by, it was all Todd. In fact, at one point, all six slots in my car CD holder were reserved for him and him alone. You could forget about the Disney radio station, the collection of Disney and children's CDs, or requests for "our music" coming from the kids in the backseat. This was my van, my music, and I needed this escape; if I couldn't go back to nineteen, I could still listen to what nineteen sounded like while shuffling a carload of kids here and there. Hearing the same music over and over began seeping into my kids' heads as well; they began to sing to the lyrics and request repeated play of their favorite tunes. The fourteen-year-old downloaded Todd's rendition of "Lord Chancellor's Nightmare" on her iPod. My ten-year-old son had to hear "Bang the Drum All Day" to and from ball practice, good and loud. Yet the most persistent requests came from my five-year-old daughter, who wanted to listen to "We Gotta Get You a Woman" over and over. On the way to her school, she would let down the window in the back and lean her head outside, singing and swaying to her favorite song.

Meanwhile, my husband watched all this in a state of dismay; he called our van the "Todd Van" and would have no part of it. I knew I had to be somewhat respectful of this and found I needed to mute some of the words when I realized my five year old was catching on pretty quickly; she started to sing the words to "Piss Aaron" one day, and I knew that wouldn't fly around the dinner table.

Although I was trying to be discreet, appearing to be the minivan/ cab service for three active kids, smiling and waving to other moms during drop-off and pick-up, I was in another world with my music blaring to the point that the kids would exclaim, "Mom, turn it down!" No errand was too small or any distance too great. In fact, I looked forward to any excuse to get out of the house and turn up Todd. Instead of the obsession showing any sign of abating, it became all the more consuming when one day I decided to Google him online, just to *see what he was up to these days,* or, better yet, to see if he was even still alive! I guiltily typed in Todd Run . . . one night, and page after page of websites popped up. I was shocked. The guy was not only still around, he was flourishing and had an impressive entourage of fans that, to say the least, *were faithful,* if not obsessed to the point that I had become. So, I read on.

Outside of his biographical history (place of birth, where he grew up, etc.), I learned that he had gotten an early start in music and, as early as 1967, a year out of high school, had fronted the rock group Nazz before moving on to form the band Runt, which showcased his songwriting, vocals, instrumentation, and production work. ("We Gotta Get You a Woman" was a hit in 1970 on Runt's first album. My youngest daughter was obviously adept at recognizing emerging talent.) Apparently at this stage in his career he was becoming recognized as much for his technical skills in music production as his musical giftedness exhibited as a solo performer. With the release of his self-produced double album *Something/Anything* in 1972, at the ripe age of twenty-four, everything seemed to change. He was propelled into stardom with probably his most famous hit, "Hello It's Me," assuring him a place in the hearts and minds of many fans from that time to the present. Declared by some critics as his "masterpiece," the double album features him as the solo performer on three of the four LPs: lead and backup vocals, all instrumentation, which included lead guitar, bass guitar, keyboards, percussion, and saxophone. He wrote all but two of the twenty-five recorded songs as well, establishing him as an accomplished musical artist.

The '70s were chockfull of recorded works featuring him on solo albums and with the band Utopia. He formed the band in 1973, and they collaborated over a decade in the studio and on concert tours. The massive amount of creative musical artistry that Todd Rundgren wrote, performed, and self-produced was only matched by his prolific production of albums for other individual artists and bands throughout the same time period. By the 1980s, he went on to further his interest in combining music and video technologies by becoming a pioneer in the field. He produced some of the first videos aired on MTV when the concept of airing musical videos was in the beginning stages. His love for technology as well as music kept him busy right up through the mid-1990s when massive internet access allowed yet another medium of exposure for his work. He rose to the challenge with innovative works on two albums that were made and marketed for interactive listening. Features on them actually allowed listeners to remix the way they wanted to hear the music while on their PC, as well as a CD that followed with a featured interactive video content—way before anybody conceived the *Guitar Hero* phenomenon. Collaborating with others, he developed an internet project, Patronet, that offered his fans access to his new music for a subscription fee, cutting out major record labels as the only vehicle for showcasing his work: again, way before many self-made internet artists chose this as a way of exhibiting their own musical creations and recordings. He continued to release and tour with his own solo works into 2005 as well as touring with other groups and ensembles. His self-named radio show and a list of credits ranging from stage musical and TV scores to self-written songs featured in movies and commercials were also listed. *Where the hell had I been?*

I grew dizzy after a while from trying to wrap my brain around the idea that one person could be so talented and accomplish so much at an early age and then continue to proliferate musically in so many diverse ways while approaching innovative technology as a natural means of advancing his own creative visions. Computer-challenged myself, I found it amazing that under the umbrella that housed the art of Todd Rundgren existed this spectrum of a charismatic, idiosyncratic musician/performer (who seemed to march only to the beat of his own drummer), as well as the persona of a techno-computer whiz who seemed to thrive on the gadgetry as much as he did on the music.

The dizziness soon turned into a knot in my stomach as I pondered my own life's accomplishments, then eventually vaporized into a cloud of envy that began to settle over my head and follow me everywhere I went. The thought of meeting my newfound obsession was not only ludicrous but tainted by the fact I would have nothing to bring to the table. Seemingly caught in midstream, floundering in career transition or rather paucity, feeling as if the current were carrying me closer to the drop-off point as age continued to remind me, "Time is running out," I felt miserably small and without purpose.

I had recently come across a poem by Patrick Larkin while thumbing through a children's book in the public library:

Days

What are days for?
Days are where we live.
They come, they wake us
Time and time over.
They are to be happy in:
Where can we live but days?

Ah, solving that question
Brings the priest and the doctor
In their long coats
Running over the fields.

I asked myself what I was doing with a day; what was Todd Rundgren doing with a day?

Caught up in learning more and more about the artist was causing another cloud to form as well; whereas envy fed into my ongoing depression and kept me shut down, restlessness caused a stirring within that would not go gently away. Personal characteristics of the singer were sprinkled throughout articles written about him, whether in musical reviews, interviews, or just biographical stuff. Descriptions such as "notorious," "arrogant," "eccentric," "control-freak," "cult-star," references to his "libertine lifestyle," and quotes like, "Todd got around," not only dispelled any preconceived ideas about some quiet guy sitting at the piano writing love songs, but intrigued me all the more. The wild side of being a rock star in the '70s was a persona we all bought in to, thought it was just part of the gig, and while growing up in that era, the idea of *that kind of guy* appealed to me as well as to lots of girls around me. Fate prohibited me from exploring this for myself up until the end of high school, and so when I did finally tap into the wild side, I got more than I bargained for, let's just say. In fact, it became a hard habit to break, and so like most addictions, after having been rehabilitated for many years, falling back into a growing fascination with the *bad boy* felt natural.

And so the flame of obsession was fanned by a growing knowledge as was my discontent with the status quo and everything around me. I was even more discontented with myself and my situation, even though I had worked hard to put myself in the very place I was: financially secure within a stable family. My world seemed all the more uneventful and small, shrinking to the point of suffocation as I began to play the poisonous game of comparison. Feeling as if I had missed out, I began backtracking over the years and comparing the relatively unknown life and times of me to the years of some of my favorite Todd albums' releases. He seemed to be right in the thick of the rock-glam years. I had been too young.

As already noted, with the release of his self-produced album in 1972, Todd Rundgren would become a household name; destiny had called, and his place in pop music history had been secured. I was in for a world of change as well, though not as dramatic or known. In the fall of 1972 I entered my first year of junior high/middle school. It was the first year that our small town decided to make the transition from three years of junior high—grades seventh through ninth—to middle school—grades sixth through the eighth; thus, I stayed in elementary school up through the sixth grade, and our classmates in the grade behind followed us to middle school instead of staying where they were. This was good for possibly two reasons, one for sure: this assured us that our class would not be the youngest class to be picked on, and we would only spend two years at middle school before moving on to our freshman year at high school. The last point was debatable; we would miss out being at the top of the heap as freshmen in the junior high system. Somehow it didn't feel so big being an eighth grader when it came our turn to be the graduating class.

A lot of changes seemed to be going on around me, and I seemed to be the only one standing still, especially when it came to changes noted in the girls' gym locker room. It was bad enough we had to suit up for gym class—I missed outside recess time at our old school—but feeling we were being compared by more than just our physical skills out on the court was unnerving. Certain *things* had changed over the summer for some of the girls, and, of course, some of the girls had been on that track for some time, but not me. Getting dressed and undressed in the locker room was initially unnerving for another reason as well; my friends and I dressed on the back row with only the stacked rows of wire baskets with combination locks separating us from a whole row of black girls who dressed on the third row.

At the time, our school system was set up so that there were two competing intermediate schools in town, and the football rivalry was renowned and fierce. The designated elementary schools fed into each middle school as defined by boundary lines drawn up by the school district. This meant that all the kids from most of the elementary schools went to the same middle school because of the district lines, but such was not the case of my elementary school. Our school was split down the middle: half of us went to Piner Middle School, located downtown in the old high school building; and half of us went to Dillingham Middle School, located farther out, on the northwest side of town. During that two-year split, many of my good friends I grew up with in Wakefield Elementary were like strangers to me when we came back together for our high school years. One of the schools that fed into Dillingham was Fred Douglass, an all-black school that was located just off downtown, close to the Martin Luther King Park. Considering this was 1972, segregation in the public schools had not been in effect all that long, but we were unaware of that piece of landmark legislation; we just knew that having as many black classmates as white was something new for us.

I knew one of the girls on the third row already. Terrence was a neighborhood friend of mine. Her family was one of the first black families to move into our modest all-white neighborhood; she lived on the street behind ours. Her brother Robert was one year behind us, so they both caught the bus with the rest of the neighborhood kids at the end of my street. Terrence was athletically built like her brother; in fact, she towered over him and most other kids her age, but she was likeable and fun. She always seemed ready to laugh about something, all her big white teeth showing, but she could be no-nonsense as well. I was glad she was my friend, so I thought I had an "in" over on the third row, where some of those girls looked like they had been growing for a lot longer time than I, in every way. Little by little I got used to seeing the girls styling their afros with Vaseline and adorning them with "cake cutters." Otherwise known as picks, they were conveniently placed in the back of the girls' hair for repeat usage.

What I never got used to were the sometimes "mixed fights" that happened in the school halls between classes. Just like a traffic jam caused by rubber-neckers, the hall would become blocked by all the students circled around trying to get a view of whomever was in a fight, until one of the coaches would come down the hall to break it up; sometimes it would take more than one coach. Fights, as intriguing as they were, carried a different weight when they were between a white and black. It seemed to me to represent more than just two kids with different ways of seeing things. The threat of what I was feeling was probably attributed to the fact that these fights represented generations of *different ways of seeing things* passed down to families who sent their kids to school with the same old generalizations and stereotypes discussed around the dinner table. They *were* more threatening; they threatened to unravel our rights to go to school with other kids different than ourselves, to meet somebody new who lived on a different side of town and experience living in a world that was bigger than the one handed down to us.

Still, it was unnerving, and everyone had a moment of truth, or so I had been told. The message was, "Do not look or act scared," or else I would be tagged as a potential target to be picked on from then on. Whether this truth held up or not, I'm still not sure, but I decided to buy into it one day when I was shoved in the hallway for no reason other than to be shoved, by Valerie Howell, one of the girls on the third row, and Terrence was not anywhere around. So, I shoved back. Valerie must have understood "the code," because she cut me this smile while continuing to walk beside me. It seemed to say, "I'm proud of you, girl. I didn't know you had it in you." From that day on, the third row didn't seem like such a scary and distant place, and I went on to enjoy having some of those girls in my classes up through high school. I was better for knowing them: Kim, Paula, Sonya, Barbara, Valerie, Carol, and Terrence, to name a few.

If I thought getting used to new friends from other schools I had never heard of, navigating the halls of a school that was bigger than anything I had ever been in, while still managing to get to class on time, was a challenge (not to mention the cafeteria food), all that was cake compared to getting used to having a new house guest, no matter the reason.

Sometime in October of that year, my mother brought my grandmother home with her one day after going out to her house to see about her. She lived in a small town about twenty minutes from where we lived. She had been recently diagnosed with gastric cancer, although unbeknownst to her. My mother's oldest brother was adamant about my grandmother's not knowing of her diagnosis. It was in such an advanced stage that nothing could be done to prevent its deadly spread; she was eighty years old. My grandmother couldn't understand why she wasn't getting any better, and, on top of that, my bachelor uncle who had lived with my grandmother all his life began staying away more and more, sometimes not returning at night. Whether this was due to her bad news or not, I will never know. My mother, alarmed by how quickly things were going downhill, packed her up, brought her home, and moved her into my parents' bedroom where she would remain over the next two excruciating months.

Living with the dying in the days before hospice (in our neck of the woods, anyway) was to be an experience I would never forget. The family doctor instructed my mother to keep my grandmother with terminal stomach cancer home and as *comfortable* as she could. When Mother asked the doctor about any medicine that could help with her pain, the doctor stated it wouldn't do any good to give her anything, because she would just have to be re-dosed over and over again and eventually would top out at the dose she could be given.

The audible sighs and groans coming out of that room eventually turned into cries. The desperate sounds reinforced my parents' insistence that I be quiet while in the house: no phone calls, no loud TV or music playing, no friends over to visit. Thankfully, my mom had given me a new Carpenters album for my birthday; my dad owned a pair of headphones, the standard model at the time, made up of huge, foam-padded earpieces that resembled something that might go on the head of *Atom Ant*. They were as comfortable as they were big and, good thing, because I would wear them for hours while standing in front of our stereo cabinet with the inside sleeve from my album propped up so I could *silently* sing along with Karen Carpenter to "Bless the Beasts and the Children," over and over. As my grandmother's disease progressed, so did the requirements of her care, which was primarily carried out by my mom.

Sometime in November, my aunt and uncle from Dallas came to stay and help out as well, and we all got into playing chess. The set was another birthday present I had received that same year, as well as a telephone in my room, though outside calls coming in were discouraged at this time. My aunt and my mom took turns changing, turning, and feeding my grandmother, but when she began to extrude bloody tissue into her diapers, my aunt had to bow out and leave the rest of her care to my mom. Her cries had now turned into howling, and nothing could soothe her, not even the goat's milk they'd found at some private farm outside of town. I should have realized something was up when it was decided I should spend some of my Christmas holidays with my other set of grandparents.

I wasn't there the day my grandmother passed away in my mother's bed. Her incessant crying and delusions had been warning enough to my parents that her time was drawing near. Still, her final day on earth, the minutes before she lapsed into a coma before dying hours later, would stay with my mother throughout the rest of her life. She hadn't been able to keep her comfortable, though she had tried.

In 1974, another double album simply titled *TODD* was released with the cover bearing the aforementioned's picture, the light cosmically playing off his red and green highlights. Cosmic is also used to describe the mix of music that the singer-songwriter was churning out during the early to mid-1970s that was further illustrated by his elaborate stage sets. Moving further away from his celebrated pop success, he took his fans on a psychedelic journey as his music took on more of a progressive rock sound that was diversified as ever with instrumental tracks as well as his noted ballads and love songs. That same year, his progressive rock band *Utopia* debuted with its first album, and his much-publicized supermodel girlfriend, Bebe Buell, was *Playboy's* playmate of the month in the November issue.

In the fall of 1974, I was a freshman at Sherman High School, home of the "fighting Bearcats." Our mascot was a hybrid of a bear and some kind of wildcat, a ferocious cat with the body of a bear that could rear up and pounce at the same time. Glad to be a part of the whole high school thing, I lived vicariously through my good friend Lauren who was in the band. I held my breath for her every week as the chair placements for saxophone were announced. The competition was stiff, and, with a surplus of saxophone players, only so many were allowed to play with the marching band during the Friday night game's halftime program. It was even more important to make the cut for out-of-town games, because all kinds of good stuff happened on the buses. Lauren filled me in. The notorious drummers and the all-girl flag corps and twirlers rode together on the fourth bus. *Go figure.*

While the fashion, music, and freedom lifestyles of the 1970s were in full swing at my high school, at the time I was attending a fundamentalist church that adhered to a different code and stressed modesty over self-exposure, humbleness over self-glorification, and sacrifice over self-fulfillment or indulgence. While girls all around me were experimenting with tight skirts and tops (that they could get by with), bell-bottomed hip-huggers worn with platform sandals, heavy makeup, and first-time drug and sexual encounters, I was wearing blue-jean skirts down to my knees, avoiding makeup, and not letting the scissors touch my long, straight hair. Though heavily involved with my youth group, I still found myself spending long hours in my room listening to the music of the day and pining over the *wrong kind of guy*. Far from being anything glamorous or someone in the mix, keeping under the radar most likely kept me somewhat protected from getting in too far over my head too soon. But it didn't keep me from dreaming or looking for ways to get close to my subjects of longing. Feeling out of depth didn't stop me from looking forward to passing a certain someone in the halls twice a week when our schedules converged, to see if our eyes would lock as they once had. In order to make the most of the opportunity I only bought flat shoes, because it was apparent my legs were still growing, and his had stopped. Therefore, when Lauren asked me to accompany her on the piano for a regional band competition that would put me in close proximity with some of the *drummers*, I jumped at the chance.

Lauren had recently switched to the bassoon at the suggestion of the band director. He thought she had talent; there were just too many saxophone players to assure her consistent playing time. She pushed herself to try out for a spot in the solo and ensemble performances for a regional competition in which her performance of a selected piece would be rated by a judge. First, however, she had to qualify by playing for the two head band instructors. Though I hadn't taken piano in years, the accompanying piano part was easy enough, so I agreed to stay after school one day so we could audition in front of Mr. Parnell and Mr. Howeth.

The audition took place in a small, dark auditorium, located across the hall from the school's main auditorium, which was used for smaller stage performances such as chorales and poetry readings. My friend Lauren was a lovely girl with Scandinavian features: very light blonde hair, blue eyes, and fair skin that indicated when she was upset, nervous, embarrassed, or humored by turning a brilliant red. You couldn't miss it, because she was so fair-haired that she would blush right up through her roots. On this particular day she was so nervous she could barely hold onto her bassoon, so I encouraged her a little as we took our places on stage. The glaring spotlight focused on her sitting in a chair in the middle of the stage. I sat behind an upright piano, and, thank God for that, because the only person who could see me was Lauren, poor thing. As we began to play, her nervousness increased to the point that she could barely hold the bassoon in place much less play it because she was shaking so violently, not to mention the beet-red hue her complexion had turned, clear up through her scalp. I was laughing so hard behind that upright that I could barely see to play the keys. All she could do was look hopelessly at me and continue. It was so bad that the band instructors felt sorry for her and passed her on to perform at the competition, noting that it "took a lot of guts to want to compete," because she had been playing the bassoon for such a short time.

We earned a three at competition. She didn't shake quite as much or turn quite as red, and I didn't laugh while sitting at a piano in full view of the judge. After we played, the judge encouraged Lauren to keep up the good work and praised her for attempting to learn a new instrument after playing the sax for three years. The best part of the competition for me was getting to watch the drummers practice their ensemble piece. We were all at the same competition, though, unfortunately, the drummers rode a different bus. They had adopted their motto, "SHS Drummers say 'Stick It,'" from the cover of a Buddy Rich album and proudly shouted it in unison after learning they had received a one rating. *What a turn on!*

In 1978, Todd Rundgren's *Hermit of Mink Hollow* album was met with positive reviews and critical acclaim for his musical genius—he once again single-handedly produced, arranged, and performed all the vocals and instruments. His return to beautiful ballads and pop melodies put him on the charts once again, namely with "Can We Still Be Friends," supposedly written after the dissolution of a long-standing relationship with his girlfriend.

My senior class of 1978 observed such events as the airplane crash of Lynyrd Skynyrd (denying friends of mine the use of their pre-paid concert tickets for the band's scheduled New Year's Eve show in Dallas), the return of Jackson Browne with his successful album, *Running On Empty,* and the summer movie release of *Grease.* I had left my church shortly before graduation and, during that summer of freedom, was experiencing my own first encounters with sexuality, love, and alcohol, though not always in that order. The church had consumed so much of my time and personal commitment that I hadn't given much thought to life after high school, until life after high school happened.

I continued my pathology lab job at the regional hospital. I had begun working there as a student in the health careers job co-op program my junior year. The most logical next step was to take some classes at our local junior college to at least appear I was interested in continuing my education. By the time enrollment came around in the fall, I had fallen in love over the summer, and the night classes couldn't compete with where my heart and mind usually hung out, with the exception of my English literature class with Mr. Carnathan.

Mr. Carnathan, rather short in physical stature, frequently referred to himself as a "sawed-off son-of-a-bitch," and for a good reason. He liked to get his ideas across or gain other peoples' attention by shocking them. He knew it, and he liked it that way. Sitting in a cinder-blocked room with primarily adults (it was night school) from all different walks of life, I was still trying to get used to the idea of actually being in college, when in walks Mr. Carnathan who introduces himself and with a twinkle in his eye asks the question, "What is English?" "English, well, it's what those brown *spics* speak, it's the language of those black *niggers*, or white *honkeys*," etc. This hush instantly fell over the class as some of us began to squirm nervously in our seats, and he breaks out into this laugh and says, "Oh, how I love to skate on thin ice. Someday, somebody's going to come up here and pick up this little sawed-off son-of-a-bitch and throw me clear out the window." Well, he had my attention, right then and from then on.

His style of teaching allowed a freedom that encouraged open discussion on topics ranging from sexuality to politics and further lent itself to expressing ourselves more freely in our writing. As for me, I no longer viewed school as a place where the absolute truth was presented. It was up to me to decide what I accepted as truth or not. During that semester, I was introduced to Emily Dickinson as one of the great writers of American literature. The various poems of hers selected by Mr. Carnathan for our class to discuss not only led me to question what was regarded as fact, but to disagree vehemently (albeit secretly) with it as well. The selected readings I recall must have centered around love, because he kept returning to make the point that there had never been any evidence of Emily's ever having been in a relationship with anyone intimately, and that her writings were more of an imaginary sort rather than autobiographical descriptions of personal experience when it came to matters of the heart. There was no way I could ever believe that, not with lines like:

> At least – 'tis Mutual – Risk –
> Some – found it – Mutual Gain –
> Sweet Debt of Life – Each Night to owe –
> Insolvent – every Noon –

(From the poem, "I gave myself to Him")

She was writing about what I was experiencing for the first time, and she pegged that yearning, that obsessive trail of thought in a young girl's heart and mind where the only thing that matters or holds any significance is the next place, the next time, you will come together for what has started to consume you. I knew she had to have had a lover somewhere along the line; she was writing my soul, putting into words perfectly what I had only just begun to know. That had to have come from experience, not imagination.

> Wild Nights – Wild Nights!
> Were I with thee
> Wild Nights should be
> Our luxury!
>
> Futile – the Winds –
> To a Heart in port –
> Done with the Compass –
> Done with the Chart!
>
> Rowing in Eden –
> Ah, the Sea!
> Might I but moor – Tonight –
> In Thee!

Why all this paralleling, returning to the past, one in which paled in comparison to the high points in *another's* lifetime of experiences. Remembering a time when I couldn't get enough, wanting something I could never have, wanting to meet someone I would never cross paths with, past or present. Regressing to a time when my mother was still alive, and I was safe within the walls of my own room where my dreams were as limitless as the sky.

Grieving takes on many shapes and forms. Some are accepted as protective, allowing us to get on with what it is we need to do; others are more subtle and seem to accomplish little more than fuel the distance between ourselves and the rest who regard curiously the "change" that has occurred in us. In my own case, dissociation was working well; Mom was officially held at bay, and, therefore, I was getting on with my life. I prided myself in getting the kids where they were required to be, laundry done, grocery shopping, dinner on the table, the list checked off—all except for housekeeping, which quickly went by the wayside. Regression, on the other hand, was killing me.

This intense desire—to go back in time somehow, to take back with me all I had learned and experienced in order to be able to withstand all that life would throw at a young girl's heart and still look good at the same time—became my escape and, at the same time, my trap. Somehow replacing the finality of death and loss with an illusion built around a life of fame and glory did more to fan the flames of panic over the inability to allude time and its swift passage than to pacify me. Bound up within the irreversibility of losing my mother was the stark reality of loss of youth and the inability to go back and retrieve any treasure found or remembered. Even more painful was the inability to return and live out another path, one that was definitely closed to me now, something I was painfully reminded of every time I looked in the mirror.

Even staying up late watching old videos of Todd on YouTube verified the same sense of loss. All the imagination of *what if,* conjured up over watching him perform thirty-four years earlier, seemed to dissipate into thin air when more recent video footage revealed the passage of time on his frame and face. Although his talent remained intact, that tall thin, charismatic heartthrob had been replaced by a seasonally matured man sporting dark glasses instead of baring his baby blues. Viewing him as through the eyes of a physician, I noticed the weight gain as well as the hyperemia (redness) in his face when wailing away on his guitar. I found myself wondering what his blood pressure reading was and hoping to God that he didn't stroke out anytime soon; I didn't need to lose another one.

In a letter to a dear friend, I confessed that I used to find comfort in age. "Well, at least I'm not as old as so-and-so, I used to say." I wrote on, "Now, I hate seeing people age behind me, and I hate seeing people age in front of me. There is no longer any consolation in age."

Irreversible, final, and forbidden as death was, it still had a work to accomplish in me by whatever vehicle or voice was available and recognizable. A musical artist from my past had ensnared me, laid full claim to my attention through his words and had me longing for more than just a good time while back down memory lane; I wanted to create something, live more fully, leave something significant that would outlive me. I was working my way out of a tunnel that would require months of self-exploration, but the agitation and restlessness I felt helped to propel me forward, determined to return to a truer self. The part of me that had been put aside for years in order to pay the bills, make it through school while single-parenting, succeed in career and live responsibly, was begging to be rediscovered. Instead of regretting past mistakes, as I had done for so many years, I began to recover a sense of me and even wished I had done more, if only to be able to say I had at least expressed myself to the fullest before the constraints of adulthood and having to "behave" had laid claim on my time and energy. I wanted to uncover what Mom had seen in me while trying to afford me the opportunities to develop what it was I longed to express. Whether in word, dance, or music, it would take some time, but I was beginning to reclaim myself, no matter how weird and dissociated I felt.

Later in the summer of that same year, I attended my first Todd Rundgren concert at the House of Blues in Dallas. Unknown to me at the time of all this obsessing and pining over a '70s rock star, the artist himself was at work on his twentieth solo album, *Arena.* He chose his sixtieth birthday party that June to introduce the new CD and kick off his tour, which arrived in Dallas on July 20, during a heat wave and soaring gas prices. Struck by the timing of all this, I ended up purchasing four tickets just to secure the best seats I could in order to get a good look at this icon. I hadn't kept up with my emails to notice a prompt by a ticketing agency that my "favorite entertainer" was coming to town, so I missed out on first dibs, but when box seats opened up I jumped on them, brandishing my credit card again and ended up eating two extra tickets—a point I neglected to mention to my husband.

I invited a cousin of mine to go with me, being a 1972 high school graduate, I thought she would have a greater appreciation for the music and would more likely remember him. Linda had recently returned to Texas after spending most of her adult life in Vermont raising a family.

Though she had divorced while her girls were in their early teens, she stayed put in the far Northeast until they both graduated and then returned to Texas just in time to help her mother care for her father who was dying of cancer. (My uncle was my mom's oldest brother and her last living sibling. He died in February before my mom passed away the following October.)

Todd had slimmed down and was dressed all in black. He delivered everything the initial reviews had raved about. It was loud and full of guitar-laden songs perfect for the acoustics of the intimate auditorium that included standing room only in front of the stage and box and balcony seating above the floor. Prepared to hear only his new music, I was pleasantly surprised, along with the crowd around me, to hear him start the show with some of the old favorites, including "I Saw the Light," the song that had sparked the whole obsessive return-to-my-youth thing. As entertaining as Todd was, it was almost just as much fun to take in the audience around us. He is widely recognized for having a faithful fan base. It was out in full force that night, every bit as diverse as the entertainer's historic repertoire: everything from guys with braided ponytails down to their waist to groomed, terminally gray-haired professional-looking types, generations of families sitting together, and older guys in groupings of two's and three's who had probably been unable to talk their wives into accompanying them. The crowd of die-hard fans that stood just below the stage intrigued me the most, though, none of whom looked younger than forty-five, including more than a few who looked old enough to be carrying AARP cards. They began gathering excitedly before the show and stood there throughout the two hours, never waning in zeal, all the while demanding more, which turned out to be a good thing for "our hero" in more than one way.

Reading about all the stunts the performer had pulled in his early years of entertaining, I wondered if I had waited too late and missed out on the glory days, since I was enjoying a concert that was on the tail end of forty years' worth of shows. That doubt was soon dispelled. During one of the beginning numbers, he stepped forward to do a guitar solo, and while whirling about he missed his footing and fell off the stage into the outstretched arms of his adoring fans. *Fell off the stage!* Now, I've been to a lot of stage performances in my time: music, dance, theatre, but I had never witnessed anybody *unintentionally* forget where they were and fall off the stage. He went one way, his guitar went another way, and both were swallowed whole by the crowd. After a couple of seconds, these two long arms emerged from the sea of people, followed by his head as if gasping for air while coming up to the surface. "He's probably being groped," my cousin remarked. His guitar was hoisted back onto the stage as the same was done to him, and "the show went on."

Surprisingly, I considered the best part of the night to be spending time with Linda, getting reacquainted and reconnected. Three very tall guys sat next to us. They'd traveled from Little Rock, Arkansas, to see the show. One of them traded seats with me, because I had trouble seeing around him and sat next to Linda. The guys were extremely nice and offered to buy us beer throughout the concert, to which we both declined—me, for fear of having to get up to relieve myself and miss something. *No telling what else Todd might do!* After the concert she turned to me and said, "My face hurts from smiling so much." That about summed up the whole experience for me as well. Todd had played my favorite song, fallen off the stage, and had made my cousin happy. I got my money's worth.

> If I thought I knew what was good for you
> I would have done it for myself

"Sons of 1984"—Todd Rundgren

March

The beginning of March brought a pleasant surprise: it snowed. Though it came overnight and was gone by the next afternoon, it snowed. It had been so many years since I had actually witnessed it snowing where I lived.

Once, while living in San Antonio, some snow flurries were reported in the Hill Country, a topographical area outside of San Antonio that stretches northwest to the city of Austin and a little beyond. While walking through a shopping mall parking lot I noticed several cars with snow piled up against their windshields, probably owned by people from that region who had driven into San Antonio for the day. I watched a mother excitedly grab a handful of the snow and pelt her son with it gleefully as they laughed over his probable first sighting of the stuff: that's how rare snow is in South Texas.

There was book club meeting at my house the night it started coming down. Book club usually breaks up around 10:30 or 11 p.m. After we've discussed the book for about the first thirty minutes, we move on to other topics; how long that lasts usually depends on what we're drinking, how much we're drinking, and the subject matter, of course. So that night after our meeting, we all ran out into the street, lay down and made snow angels in the middle of Abbott Lane; we were so excited.

Snow and particularly ice tend to scare the school districts in Texas, and so, to the dismay of people who relocate here from colder regions, sometimes schools, roads, and businesses will close or at least delay openings due to the cold weather conditions. Such was not the case this time, however. The roads were fine the next morning, but the effect of the drooping, snow-laden tree branches that came together like a canvas over the streets was breathtaking. After dropping off the two older ones, I took my five year old for a drive instead of taking her to school. People stood in their yards taking pictures with their little ones, and even the poorest of streets, with laundry still left on the line, slanted houses with failing porches, looked magical. There was such a lightness and feeling of excitement in the air, even though the snow was beginning to drip from the trees as the morning sun beat down. We hurried home to build a backyard snowman and take our own pictures. It was almost like a gift, for I was craving winter and wanted it to stay longer, despite evidence of the coming spring all around me. It was a bright spot in a very gloomy time; after all, we were in the season of Lent.

Over the years, the word Lent has evoked different memories. When I was a kid, it was just a word that would show up periodically in the church bulletin of the Presbyterian church we were attending. It disappeared when I quit going to church with my family and began attending a fundamentalist church with friends. (There were no church bulletins or markings of the traditional church calendar year.) It took on a whole different meaning the year I sank into a major depression some nine months after the birth of my third child.

In the middle of that Lent I wrestled with thoughts over the goodness and sovereignty of God versus the origin of evil and judgment unfairly dealt. *If God were so good, how could he look upon all this evil, and if he was omniscient, could he be the source of evil as well as good?* Battling through spiritual oppression redefined grace for me. So for some years afterward I operated in a zealous manner, gladly participating in all of the established church calendar events because I was back worshipping in a traditional Protestant church.

I had read that the English word "Lent" is derived from the Germanic root for "long," because Lent occurs in spring, when the days lengthen. It felt long all right. Lent was unwelcome and unwanted this year.

Though the monthly calendar on my kitchen counter was penciled with kids' activities and events to attend, my distancing and self-envelopment was increasing and ever more noticeable, particularly to those closest to me. Except to the smallest child in our family, whom I still prided myself on getting ready and delivering to preschool three days each week, there was an ever-present (although invisible) wall that separated me from the rest of my immediate family. I no longer participated in the morning regimen of my two older children living at home (probably to their delight). They set their own alarms, got up and dressed, watched their favorite shows, had breakfast, and rode to school with their father as I slept until it was time to get the youngest one up. Though I delivered kids to and from the soccer practice field, violin and theatre lessons, Boy Scouts, and ballet, I was more concerned with listening to my favorite CDs that played over and over instead of listening to them. Conversation had grown sparse between my husband and me as well. And to the one who knew me best, to God, I held my hand outstretched in front of me as if to say, *Back off! I need some space. I need to breathe.*

It's interesting to note that sometimes we find permission and support from the most unexpected places or people, even when we're not looking for it. At another book club, the discussion of age came up, and I voiced the need "not to panic" as this oncoming wave of middle-age woe and inner rebellion kept surging toward me. I also shared my need to back away from God. Though I wasn't mad at him, I just wasn't into the whole self-denial thing that consisted of the same old rhetoric, intent on restraining my mind from wandering to places of self-indulgences. The girl sitting next to me, whom I probably knew least among our group of "snow angels," looked me straight in the eye and said emphatically, "You don't have to do the Lent thing! Let it go." To which another friend across the table added, "Sherry, it's a different kind of year for you," with a knowing smile. She had lost her mother unexpectedly the year before. Maybe it was the wine that had helped me express myself so freely and honestly, or maybe it was the desperation that was stealing over me.

Whatever it was, I'm sure my husband would have appreciated some of the same honest talk, but I was far away. When I was a young child, pretend had always been a coping tool. I look back on it now and wonder what purpose it served me as a child, other than helping to develop emotional and adaptive skills. (My need to pretend to be someone else was so strong that I continued practicing it even into my middle school years.)

Comparisons—whether to people, their belongings, homes, talents, accomplishments—has been a part of my psyche for as long as I can remember. Karen Hampton's kitchen down the street was small and U-shaped with a little kitchen window over the sink that always seemed to contain a sweet potato vine growing out of a glass jar perched on the windowsill. Their kitchen was darker, had yellow and copper accents and just seemed cooler than our kitchen somehow. Karen was two years older than I. She had two sisters; her dad wore a college ring on his right hand; she was tall and blond, always with a tan; her grandfather had a boat she got to drive; she had a Chatty Cathy Doll, a blue and white record player in her front bedroom that had a large window that looked out on our street, a bricked-in patio and, *golly gee whiz*, her family finally traded in their car for a station wagon! Our kitchen, well, it was just a regular kitchen with a large window by the table that let in a lot of light as did the window over the kitchen sink. Our windowsill featured a Dixie cup dispenser instead of a plant. I had a brother nearly twelve years older than I who was never around; neither of my parents had attended college; I had plain brown hair and, though I would tan after the summer's first sunburn, I had freckles across my nose instead of smooth brown skin. I had ridden in a boat once; my first talking doll was a Baby Secret, cute but not as cool as Chatty Cathy; my record player was orange and white; my bedroom was sandwiched between my parents' and my brother's rooms with a window that looked out on Mrs. Wilson's carport. Our steps out the back door went straight into the yard, and my parents traded in the

Falcon for a Chevrolet Malibu, a four-door model, of course. We would never own a station wagon.

When I got older I considered other things than where someone lived or what their parents drove. Popularity traits in school were some kids' God-given rights: good hair, straight white teeth, big boobs, long eyelashes, dark tan, cool clothes, etc. Then as perspective entered the picture at some point, pertaining to what things really mattered, it was a matter of comparing intellect, professional degrees and success, big weddings reported in the local newspaper with exotic honeymoon destinations, time management, the perfect house, the perfect "look," the perfect life. Of course, everyone gets caught up in the comparison trap from time to time, but I dealt with my feelings of inferiority in a different way, even as an adult.

When I was a child, my little room with its homemade table and chairs and kitchen cupboard could be transformed into anything, anywhere. For years, my tricycle had made trips to the grocery store, bank, dropping off husband and kids while circling my driveway over and over (because there was no sidewalk, and we lived on a very busy street). My parking space was between the Nandina bushes by the front porch. As I became older my imagination continued to take me to places of grandeur, success, and personal happiness. Sometimes I even found that reality could not live up to the images cooked up in my own head; it was not conformed to my idea of how things should be.

Once, when I was thirteen, a dear neighborhood and school chum gave me a poster for my birthday. It was a black-and-white print of a young lion cub sitting in a wicker high back chair with one leg casually draped over one of the arms of the chair. The caption read, "It is my opinion and it is very true." My brother and father laughed over that for years, though I couldn't see what the big deal was until much later, after life had graced me with enough skids and recoveries to see myself maybe in a little truer light. My friend was quite astute for thirteen.

Imagination and pretend had never hurt anybody. Many times, imagination had given me something to strive toward, and even though the goal was sometimes unobtainable, it had kept me reaching. So my alter ego became the focus of my day, the thing I placed the most energy into while going about the mundane tasks and business of everyday life that seemed to be closing in on me. If I couldn't turn back time, I could at least go to a place where time was on my terms:

My name is Joee (pronounced Joey), short for Jo Antoinette Marsh. Yes, my parents are a little *out there* because they named me after the fictional character Jo March in the book *Little Women.* My mother lets my father name me Jo with the understanding that I shall be called Joee, hence the additional e, and, yes, it leads to many interesting conversations and mispronunciations by my teachers over the years. I may even resemble a young Joey Heatherton, who had that cute blond asymmetric haircut long before anyone had ever heard of Victoria Beckham. And of course my Joee has a knockout figure like the real Joey's with skin that stays beautifully tanned. I am not only young and beautiful, but I'm smart and talented in many ways, fiercely independent as I have been shaped by a previous tragedy. At the age of fifteen, my parents are tragically killed in an automobile crash, forcing me to leave my home in North Texas and join my only brother in Manhattan where he is employed. I am an emancipated minor by age sixteen and decide to stay in New York City after my brother is transferred with his job to another major city in the Midwest. I find a roommate, of course, graduate early due to my higher IQ and abilities, and continue to thrive independently while carving out a living off my writing and art. I play the cello well (which is not the case in my own life, as I struggle to keep the bow on one string at a time and make a nice sound on the D string, especially that damn G note on the D string). Far from just being cerebral, I am also charismatic, sexy, and fun, and did I mention a great dancer? I have been sexually active since fifteen but have managed to continue with my education and artistic goals in spite of my rebellious years and romantic detours. I am a survivor, admired for my looks and daring behavior as well as for my spunk and God-given talents. Don't forget, I'm young.

So even though the mirrors in the bathroom, the dining room, and the car said one thing about me, my second self said another. Once my counselor asked me, "What burden does Joee carry for you that you can't carry for yourself?" At first I thought I knew the answer readily, "Growing older, of course." True, coming to terms with *becoming my parents*, as my forty-eighth birthday was some months already behind me, was difficult (is still a difficult pill to swallow), but I knew there was more; my alter ego carried a much heavier weight than middle age. It would take me months to figure her out.

I had lost my mother just as Joee had lost her parents, but she was well past that, or rather she was able to express herself artistically and thrive in spite of the hard knocks. I felt as though I were flailing about with no shoreline in sight. Joee had talent and a future ahead of her. I felt like everything I had strived for was in the past, and in some ways such a distant memory that I couldn't even lay claim to the accomplishments. Acknowledging the "M.D." behind by name was a painful reminder that I wasn't currently practicing. Maybe it had all been for naught anyway.

Relationships. I was fuzzy on that one. Joee had been in relationships, most likely was not seriously involved currently. She would catch the eye of someone, probably famous, be pursued and would have a hot fling, knowing all the time it was temporary no matter what the ramifications, possibly even an unsuspected pregnancy. All the while, she would keep her distance emotionally, never allowing her own personal goals to be derailed, never allowing herself to lose *herself* in another person. After all, sudden and unexpected tragedy at a young age had taught her that life was precious. She had learned life's lessons far beyond the reach of her own years.

I was struggling within the stranglehold of a marriage to a good man, the "right one," my counselor wisely named after I'd stated my plight of feeling trapped and wanting to revert to my primal instinct of finding excitement with the "wrong kind of guy." Losing myself in others had been a hard habit to break.

"Would you do it?" she asked me point-blank during a session. "Huh?" "If you could get away with it; no one would ever know; there would be no consequences. Would you give up all that you are, to lose yourself in a consuming relationship that rocked you to the core? Would you do it?" This question stumped me for a moment, and then, much to my surprise, I said, "No." It was like hearing the sound of my voice coming from the end of a long dark corridor. No, I had come too far, learned too many lessons the hard way and didn't want to give up ground I had gained, but I was restless and wanted to move in some direction, any direction to keep from suffocating.

For years I had felt some guilt, some unease regarding my tendency to put up my guard in a good, trusting relationship, guilt over not being able to connect the way my husband seemed to do so naturally. Why couldn't the two come together? Why couldn't Mr. Right, Prince Charming, or whatever you want to call him, come riding up with long hair atop a hot dangerous ride instead of the white steed, or, in my case, the economical black Honda Civic. Why couldn't the naughty, the charismatic, the bad . . . be good?

Joee was the embodiment of lessons learned over the past thirty years. Experiences and knowledge she gained over a four-year period were compressed into her petite, tight frame. What she had learned was that not all the answers were found in a relationship, be it with Mr. Right or in a fling with Mr. Wrong, whatever the combination. The "lack of" was found within her. She answered that with creativity and drive, and though she was eventually a single parent (like I had been for eleven years), she did not look ultimately to having a future partner as being "all that." She stayed secure in her ability to thrive by tapping into the energy around her and holding herself accountable. Tough lessons, but she looked so good pulling it off. In not so dramatic a fashion, my mother had been a role model of a woman in love but not lost to another.

My parents were married for sixty years. They had met while my mom was still in high school. My father was nearly four years older. Their dating period had been interrupted by his time served in the U.S. Navy during World War II. They had continued to correspond by mail while he was overseas in the Pacific. My father returned in the summer of 1946; my mother began her senior year that fall. She was assigned the position of Tom Bean High School's first band majorette. It forced her to give up her cheerleader position, which she would have preferred, but her teacher had urged her to take on this new leadership role.

That winter she was involved in a car accident while on a picnic outing with friends. She suffered a closed-head injury, which was further complicated by a course of meningitis while still in the hospital. This being in the late 1940s, she wasn't expected to live. Her oldest brother was called from his duties in the Army, and my dad lent him his car so that Uncle John could deliver the family back and forth from the hospital. My mother recovered, got the mumps, and still managed to complete her senior year, graduating as the class valedictorian in the spring of 1947.

My parents were married that summer in the front room of my grandmother's home; my dad, in his old car, flying down hot, dusty white-rock roads (so dusty he had to jump out of his car repeatedly and brush himself off), hurried to make the wedding. The preacher was pacing the floor when he finally arrived; he had a *summer revival* to preach that night in addition to marrying my parents. My dad had just started a new job and couldn't exactly ask off early, so things were running a little late. My brother was born the next summer, June 19, 1948.

My mother didn't attend college. I don't even know if she ever thought about it. Living in a rural setting and following the natural course of marriage and starting a family was a common way of life back then, even for the class valedictorian of a country school. She did suffer from some residual effects of her brain injury, but I don't think that blocked her from pursuing a college education; it just wasn't her path. She once told me, "You appear normal to people on the outside, but there is something changed on the inside that you and you alone know is different. For instance, a word is sometimes just beyond my reach." I had been completing sentences or interjecting words, usually descriptive words or names of things or persons, for Mom for years just because I would get impatient waiting for her to complete a thought. Well, I had finally learned the reason.

My mother set about making a home for the family, doing all the domestic stuff while working at different jobs to supplement the family income. She primarily worked part time, usually in secretarial positions, until I got further up in my elementary school years. She then worked full time until some years after I completed high school. She was very humble. Though her life hadn't taken a turn for the most glamorous lifestyle, she never showed any resentment or regret.

After she died, I found the most simple but elegant handwritten letter, addressed to the local newspaper in response to a job advertisement.

1808 W. Hunt
Sherman, Texas
March 6, 1968

Box B-4
C/o Sherman Democrat

Dear Sir:

In answer to your advertisement for a receptionist experienced in dealing with the public:

I am 38 years old, married and have one child in school. My husband is employed with Texas Power & Light Company. I obtained my grammer school and High School education at Tom Bean, Texas.

We have lived in Sherman one year. From September, 1967, to January, 1968, I worked as secretary at the Grand Avenue Presbyterian church. In addition to the general office work and handling of the church correspondence, a good bit of my work consisted of talking to people, both in the office and on the telephone.

Should you wish to know something of my character and ability, I refer you to the following persons:

The Reverend Edward Matson
        Grand Avenue Presbyterian Church
        901 N. Grand   Ph. 3-1921
        Sherman, Texas

Joe Pannell   Pharmacist
                  Restand Pharmacy 3-8155
                  110 S. Crockett ~~3-8155~~
                  Sherman, Texas

Mrs Dan Creamer   Teacher
                  Home Economics Depart.
                  Dillingham Jr. High School
                  1807 W. Hunt 3-5850

I hope that you will be interested in talking to me about the position. My home telephone number is 2-8908 and my address is 1808 W. Hunt, Sherman.

                Very truly yours,
                    Fay Shields
              (Mrs. Vinson Shields)

I cried after reading it. That modest letter in no way represented all that she was, all of which she was capable, but it captured the essence of her, the simple acceptance of herself. Yet she saw a world of possibilities for others, namely me.

I never lived under the threat or even hint of divorce, even though my parents fought occasionally, disagreed on many fronts, and responded differently to situations, whether trivial or emergent. My father took after his maternal side of the family, always finding something to worry over or be anxious about. He was punctual, frugal, impatient at times, overreacted at times, *lost it* at times, was true to his word, dependable, and a good man. My mother refused to worry, "No use to worry when you can't do anything about it anyway." She played solitaire when she couldn't sleep. She took her time, was very patient, kind, sympathetic to the plight of others, and when she *lost it*, it was just plain scary. She was very charitable: my father always joked when the phone rang during dinner, "That must be the Firemen's Association calling again." She was a good woman. She was our mother. Though she lived a simple life she always retained a strong sense of self. She knew who she was.

For a period after my paternal grandfather died, my father began drinking more. He was not a heavy drinker by any stretch, but rather the type in which two beers was about all it took to make a profound change in him. This continued for some time (which I now understand better, standing in the shadow of a loss), and, one day, over lunch with Mom, I expressed my frustration about Dad and his behavior. "How do you stand it?" I asked, after voicing my differing opinions in regard to his. (This was coming from someone who lived for the weekends and partied with the specific goal of getting drunk.) Mom steadily replied, "Sherry, I made up my mind a long time ago that I could not let the actions of your father affect me. I am not responsible for him. I am only responsible for myself."

Mom was like that. She saw herself accountable for her own actions and words and didn't hold onto resentful feelings over what may have been done to her through the words or acts of others. Once, Mom and I were on some outing, just the two of us, and she was driving. We were discussing some of the dynamics in our family. I don't remember exactly how it came up, but she said, "You know, I would have probably been considered abused as a child, verbally abused." Looking out the window, she added, "But my mother was old when she had me." She did not expound on the subject.

My mother was the last of six children born to my grandmother: two older sisters from Grandma's first marriage, three older brothers and my mom by her second husband, the grandfather who died the year before I was born. Come to think of it, I never heard warm fuzzy stories about my grandmother. Mom never relayed tales about family life on the farm. But Mom honored her mother, always fostered my relationship with her, making sure I had ample opportunities to stay with her, and, in the end, it was Mom who cared for her the best she could without the aid of pain medicine while she died from stomach cancer in my mother's bed. Mom never uttered a bitter word or stories of blame.

∽

March hadn't always seemed so bleak. The saying "March comes in like a lion and goes out like a lamb" usually applies well to weather in Texas, particularly the region where I grew up. The order of these events is not as important as the significance of change. There is a saying around these parts, "If you don't like the weather, give it another forty-five minutes, and it will change." That accurately sums up memories of this month, which teeters on the edge of spring but can still bring snow and freezing temps that keep us reaching for coats and sweaters, regardless of the blooms on the trees or in the yards. Unlike snow, the wind is one force of nature that can be regularly counted on, particularly in the early spring. Remembering my bare legs' bracing against its blast and trying to keep my hat on brings to mind an important time of the year: Camp Fire Girls candy sales.

While I was in school, the Camp Fire Girls' division for younger elementary years was known as Blue Birds. My cousins, who were stationed in San Antonio with their father at the Air Force base, were Brownies, but I was a Blue Bird and proud of it. My Blue Bird leader lived down the street from me, and, if memory serves, our meetings were held every Thursday after school. Her oldest daughter, Lisa, was in the same grade as I, and we were neighborhood pals as well as schoolmates. Camp Fire Girls candy sales were traditionally every year from January to March; it must have been March for our area, because

I can recall cold days walking against the wind as well as bright sunny days when we ran and laughed along the way. I can't remember how many years I was in Blue Birds before being promoted to Camp Fire Girls, but I know this: within our group, Lisa and I had top sales every year, and we meant business.

Now, some girls sent boxes of almond caramel clusters (so good I can still taste them) with their moms to the banks or to other job sites where they were employed and got a little help selling, but Lisa and I hoofed it. We would don our Blue Bird uniforms after school, meet at her house, and set out, each carrying a cardboard box with a handle in the top. We had a plan and a different route to cover every day during the allotted time of candy sales. We rehearsed a speech to say in unison: "Hi, we're Lisa and Sherry. Would you like to buy some Blue Bird candy?" Then we would stand there and charmingly smile side by side, with the cardboard boxes at our feet. We took turns with the profits: if I got a house, it counted for me; Lisa would get the next sale, no matter how many more houses it took. This way we were bona fide partners. We always came in at a tie. We were both winners, and if one was ahead near the end of the sale period, our mothers made up the difference. We clearly understood from the get-go that this was how it had to be. We lugged those boxes for miles, and I am serious about the distance covered, because, as an adult, I can go back over the streets and neighborhoods we covered and verify the distance. (Yes, there were hills but no snow, and we wore shoes.)

During our campaign of door-to-door sales, we would always pick out our top three customers and rate our disasters as well. The nice man just one block over from our street said yes to us, even though he had already purchased a box from someone else, because the candy was "so good." And two little spinster sisters insisted we come in and warm ourselves. They kept wanting to give us sweaters or shawls to put on so we wouldn't catch our "death of cold out there," and bought two boxes to boot. They were our number one sale. I remember a couple of rejects as well: one stands out due to no fault of ours; the other, due to our swift revenge that followed the decline of our product.

We rang a doorbell and stood poised to deliver the pitch, when this woman, seen through the front plate glass window, came purposely striding to the door with a look of fire in her eyes. She flung the door open and, right in the middle of our rehearsed sentence, spat "NO!" and slammed the door in our little Blue Bird faces. We were shocked.

Only now, as I will go to any length to screen solicitors over the phone, do I have some understanding of why she acted in such a fashion. One too many Blue Birds at the door. The other poor soul who rejected us, well, let's just say we had great fun in mimicking and getting back at her.

We were selling in one of the finer neighborhoods in town, hoping to rack up some points. We rang the doorbell on about the third house on the street and waited for what seemed a very long time for the sound of approaching footsteps. When the door finally opened, there stood this little white-haired woman, slightly bent over with her bun askew and still wearing a robe in the middle of the afternoon. After our little speech delivery, she said, "I don't believe so, honey," and promptly shut the door. I don't know if we had become hardened or just wanted to have some fun, but we waited for some considerable length, giving her time to get back to what she was doing, then we went back, rang the doorbell, and ran. Not exactly the Blue Bird way, but the sun was out that day, and we ran giggling with our cardboard boxes down to the creek behind her house to hide.

Only one time was I miffed over the idea of looking like a Blue Bird: class picture day. Apparently I hadn't received the memo, or I forgot about it, but on a certain Thursday, I showed up at school with my uniform on, ready for the meeting after school. (We got little birds on our chart for wearing our uniforms to school.) We were apparently exempt from that obligation on picture day, because I was the only one wearing mine.

I had always prided myself for making it up to at least the second tier of the risers for class pictures. Once I even ended up on the third row. (The back row was usually reserved for the taller boys and poor Kay Ellen, who was always head and shoulders above the rest of us, in the days when self-conscious tall girls usually slouched in order to appear shorter.) It was not to be this year. That blasted photographer not only placed me on the front row but in the dreaded position next to the teacher. *Egad!* Right up against Mrs. Blurton on the front row for everybody to see me clearly in my Blue Bird skirt and vest. In the picture, I am clearly not happy about the situation. I am slumped and visibly pouting. Mrs. Blurton is standing like a monument beside me, stoically representing her third grade class of 1969. It is the same class that held our own mock 1968 presidential campaign, hotly contested between the Wakefield Elementary Humphrey and Nixon supporters.

Mrs. Blurton evoked an image of the great Kate Smith in more ways than one. She was statuesque, wore her hair like Kate's with just the right touch of red lipstick, and she could sing. I don't remember if it was "God Bless America," but she once sang in front of a school cafeteria/auditorium capacity crowd for some assembly. Our principal, Mr. Scott, of whom I was in awe, introduced her by making it known that she had given up pursuing a professional musical career in order to do what she loved best: teach. Coming from him, it forever put Mrs. Blurton on a different plane for me. She was a powerhouse of a woman. Once I challenged her by asking why we couldn't rotate like the other third grade classes and go to the formal music class across from the cafeteria. She smiled and said, "I teach the music in my class," and she did. She had us marching around that room in song every morning right after our Pledge of Allegiance and "My Country Tis of Thee."

Relationships: putting off God, my marriage, excusing myself from my kids and memories of Mom, the beginning of healing within myself unrecognized, remembering school days and old friends. Some things I couldn't go back to even if I wanted. At the end of March I learned that my childhood friend, Winifred Bauer, had died of metastatic breast cancer in British Columbia, Canada, where she lived with her husband and two sons. She was affectionately known by many as "Wini." When we were very young I had called her "Winifer," too young to appreciate the written English language.

She had lived on Northeast Sixth Street along with her parents and three older siblings. She had a great big red tricycle I absolutely adored because we could both ride on it at the same time. One could stand on the back red metal step while the other pedaled. Their house was a dark green three-bedroom frame that had a hedgerow of trees on one side and two concrete steps with curved sides that led up to the walk in front. It had a great screened-in front porch just off the front room that was accessed through two French doors. We played there as well as around and up on top of the large upright piano in the living room. The house was a little cluttered, always full of noise with kids coming in and out, and the best place in the whole wide world to play. A block from their house stood a large, dome-shaped aluminum building resembling a Quonset hut like the ones seen in *Gomer Pyle*. It faced the one-way street my mom and I regularly traveled on returning from the grocery store, post office, and doctor's office. Always staring out the window at the passing buildings and houses, I would become ecstatic on the occasions when she would turn our car onto the street that ran beside the domed metal building. I knew she was taking me to Wini's to play, an arrangement previously made by our moms over the phone.

Our family moved from Paris in February, 1967, just when I was at the age of really understanding friendship and that spark that happened every time you got to spend time with each other. Only seventy miles away, we rarely ever came back to visit, and so I eventually lost contact with all friends from school, church, or the neighborhood, but, on the occasions when I would return, the one place I could always find was the Bauer house on Sixth Street.

The last time I saw Wini was the summer of my senior year. I had not seen her since around the second year after we had left, and Mom and I had returned for a brief visit. Although we were only two months apart in age, Wini was a grade ahead of me in school because her birthday was in September, so she just barely made the cutoff. Anyway, she was so smart and full of curiosity that her parents couldn't have held her back another year. She had finished a year at the local junior college and was getting ready to leave for University of Texas at Austin, where she had been accepted into the symphonic band. In fact, the day I stopped by, she had just returned all of her books to the local college, and she felt like celebrating.

She was particularly excited about showing off her new flute. She had gotten a good deal somewhere on a silver Gemeinhardt flute, made in Switzerland. I believe it was secondhand, but it was beautiful, just the same. It was solid silver, with intricate engravings on it, laid gently in a dark purple velvet-lined case. I knew nothing about the flute, but I was impressed. Reconnecting with her was easy. She was just as I had remembered, even though I hadn't seen her since I was a kid. She had a gorgeous head of long blonde hair, big bright eyes that probably saw beyond what most people did, and a free spirit and way about her that made her memorable.

We decided to see a movie that night before I drove back home. We finally decided on *Smokey and the Bandit,* starring Burt Reynolds and Sally Fields, who were both all the rage that summer, although Wini expressed interest in another film, *Julia,* starring Vanessa Redgrave and Jane Fonda. *Julia,* as I learned many years later after watching it, is a lovely movie based on author Lillian Hellman's memoirs detailing her involvement with an anti-Nazi movement in the 1930s. She became involved at the request of her friend, Julia, the title role played by Vanessa Redgrave, who received an Oscar for her performance. It is a film about friendship and the lengths one will go for a cause and the lengths another will go for the sake and belief in a friend. I missed a great opportunity that night. All these years later I wish I would have chosen to see that movie with Wini. Instead, I was some young foolish girl caught up in exploring my newfound sexuality, choosing to laugh at the ridiculous and vulgar. *Smokey and the Bandit* is tame by anybody's standards today, but a great literary work of art, it is certainly not. Wini, at the tender age of eighteen at least had interests rooted in good taste and in learning more about the human condition.

Wini went on to play her flute in more than one symphony; she graduated from the University of Texas, married, had children, and finally wound up in Canada, as free-spirited as ever, I am told. I never saw her again, but I still remember the friend who was a part of what made my childhood memories something to smile over and draw hope from: an inner belief that the world could be a place of sunshine and free, unspoiled fun, even if just for the day.

March had come to an end. Spring would be coming soon. I still wanted winter to stay.

April

"I've got pieces of April
I keep them in a memory bouquet"

—Three Dog Night

April usually brings Easter, although it can come at the end of March, though not as often. The weather at home can be volatile and unpredictable, but my memories of Easter, particularly those as a child, were sun-filled days pretty much exemplifying "spring," though I recall spring coats and sweaters sometimes worn. Easter seemed a long way removed from anything. It was a long way from Christmas, a long way to summer vacation—an in-between holiday when spring would declare itself officially present, but you could never tell when that final frost might still sneak up and nip everybody's flowers.

Perhaps that's why everybody who planted according to the *Farmer's Almanac* covered their newly planted gardens with the top halves of bleach and laundry detergent bottles. That surely was the case of Mrs. Windom across the side street from our house. Back in the day when vegetable gardens in backyards were not an exception, our neighbor always planted early. She always had blue, white, and turquoise plastic jug tops over her plants whether in the garden or on the windowsill.

Both my grandmothers gardened until they could no longer, due to failing health of either body or mind. My father's mother, Granny, gardened an acre plot of ground. It was an immense vegetable garden always bordered with flowers, usually petunias, bachelor buttons, lantana, zinnias, and some fluffy, light green bushes that were perfect for rolling around in. That garden was an extension of my grandmother, every bit as much a memory tied to our childhood spent on the farm or even at the little frame house in town. It was our playground. Granny spent time there day after day from early spring well into fall, planting, hoeing, picking, and tilling for the next year. While she worked, my cousins and I would start by helping with great vigor; however, we'd soon grow tired and take to playing army or hide-and-seek among the rows or take our toys under the pear tree until the bees ran us off. Granny always wore a man's work shirt over her dress to cover her arms from the sun and a homemade sunbonnet. Cardboard pieces from a shoe box, sewn into the fabric of the front of the bonnet, made it stretch straight out in front of her face. She never could understand the concept of our wanting to get a tan or why we would expose our bodies to the sun.

As a child, she had hoed and picked cotton along with her older siblings day in and day out under the hot summer sun. She told us of how she and her sisters hated the way the sun browned and freckled their hands, how they envied the white hands and arms of the other girls at church who didn't have to work in the fields. If we wore our bathing suits or shorts she would always call us "naked" or say things like, "Put some clothes on." Granny was our playmate: she made us laugh; she sprayed us with the water hose; she baked cakes for us, sewed our clothes, and learned to do the Twist right along with the three of us.

The early Easters I remember on the farm were cool and breezy; one time, my dad held me up so I could see blue robin's eggs on a nest in the cedar bush. From then on, I looked for bird eggs every time I walked by that bush in the backyard. You would have thought with all the eggs on the place our Easter egg hunts would have included real dyed eggs. I don't recall it that way. I don't recall ever believing in the Easter bunny either, though I loved to sing about Peter Cottontail hopping down the bunny trail. My dad and my uncle were the Easter bunny, and we knew it. We waited impatiently inside the house while they scattered those sugared colored eggs in little clear wrappers all over the yard. I don't know why we were so intent on finding as many as we could—I guess it was either the competition or the thrill of the hunt—because the eggs were pure sugar, and we were sick to our stomachs after eating only a few. My granddad always helped my younger cousin cheat, so that she always ended up with more eggs than Dini and me. Jealousy always reared its head when we three got together. It was always *us* against her.

We had to have dyed eggs at some point, though, because I have a very vivid memory of a turquoise blue colored egg. I brought it home from my grandparents' and buried it in our frontyard, hoping the warmth from the ground would cause it to hatch. (I apparently didn't get the whole chicken-and-egg concept.) I checked on that hard-boiled egg for weeks, waiting for something to happen, until one day I finally dug it up myself, figuring it just couldn't get warm enough.

Easter was a lighter affair when I was younger. I got into the Easter outfit and Easter basket thing, whether to go with traditional green plastic grass for my basket or another color such as pink or yellow. Easter bonnets or hats worn by both mother and me eventually went out of style, and I settled for a ribbon in my hair up until about the seventh grade. It was around that time whereupon one Easter morning, entering my Sunday school class proudly wearing my white cotton, very "Eastery-looking" dress with pink flower appliqués across the bodice, that I had to endure snickers from all the boys as my teacher complimented me on a "pretty dress." If only as young girls we could have recognized the *ridiculousness* in a large group of adolescent boys, who really had nothing more going for them than mouths that they over-exercised in spewing forth their ignorance and obvious lack of experience. I was the only girl in the class that year; my teacher was a cool, handsome college student at the liberal arts university across the street. I liked him. Too bad I let the boys run me off; I volunteered to help in the kindergarten class instead of staying with the class to finish that year, or any other year for that matter.

Easter, 2008, came six months after the death of my mother. I guess one could say I was in the "nadir" of my grief. It's a term describing the lowest point, and we use it in medicine to indicate the lowest point the white blood cell count reaches after a patient receives chemo and radiation during a bone marrow transplant, before the new stem cells from the transplant begin producing new blood cells from a healthy line. Although I didn't recognize it as grief over Mom, it was grief over something else lost, something else unobtainable. It was youth. Time.

In February, I had come across an editorial in *The Dallas Morning News* about "middle age and the reason it makes us grumpy." I was so struck by the journalist's review of a Dartmouth College study that connected peoples' feeling of psychological well-being with their age, over any other factor (money, relationships, geography, etc.), that I tore it out of the newspaper and saved it to read over and over. In her article, Meghan Daum, an essayist and novelist in Los Angeles, quoted Andrew Oswald of the University of Warwick, who cowrote the study, explaining why "middle age can feel as grim as the Middle Ages."

"One possibility is that individuals learn to adapt to their strengths and weaknesses and in midlife quell their infeasible aspirations . . ." Daum then commented, "Am I crazy or is this sciencey-speak for what we can figure out on our own? Doesn't Mr. Oswald mean that part of getting older is recognizing that you're never going to be a rock star/compete in the Olympics/marry a supermodel, and that this knowledge becomes less of a bummer as the years go by and you're just glad not to be dead?"

Boy, did she hit the nail on the head or what? I had always wanted to be some kind of a star, or maybe just be *with* a rock star. I had many times visualized the Olympic gold around my neck in several events, including individual and pairs ice skating as well as swimming, setting new records as I went, or I wanted, like any girl, at least to look like a supermodel. Of course she was talking about more than just these listed accomplishments. She was addressing the bigger hurt that comes with dealing with our own mortality. Dreams are no longer just that; they become a series of closed doors that we are not allowed to go back through, and we are left instead with the only option of turning around and facing the future staring back at us. It can be a scary thought, particularly when you don't like what's looking back at you from the other side of the mirror.

During my high school years, a beautiful song, "At Seventeen," was penned and sung by Janis Ian. For me, it captured the feeling I had watching other girls who seemed to have it all going for them, myself only dreaming of a life that seemed to be as out of reach as the famous ones I saw myself on the arm of.

> "And those of us with ravaged faces, lacking in the social graces,
> Desperately remained at home, inventing lovers on the phone
> Who called to say, 'Come dance with me,' and murmured vague obscenities . . ."

I not only regretted but was angry at not having a time I could point back to and say, "Remember when I was fab?" It was like I had never peaked. I could not think of a time when I had been the girl everyone would have given the chance to be for just one day, or at least *look like* for a day. The desperation that went along with the regret, the anger, was further triggered by the constraint of time and its relentless march, carrying me along with it whether I wanted to go or not. And what did I have to show for it? It was more than just a pretty face I wanted to look back on: what was my legacy going to be? What was I going to leave behind besides my kids? I wanted to be known for something greater than the sum of my parts, and those parts were aging without a warranty. It was a midlife crisis woven in with grief over something, someone, I couldn't get back.

I had faced the fear of aging some two years prior to this, but some pressing interruptions had sidetracked me, and I apparently did not process it thoroughly. Daum's quote about the Olympics brought it all back.

About eight months after our move to Paris, population around 26,000, from San Antonio, population around 1,000,000, I hit a wall. *What the hell were we thinking? Remind me again why we moved!* I can pinpoint the day it happened. I was secluded upstairs with a stomach virus, trying to sleep it off and avoid spreading it to the others in the household. It was during the 2006 Winter Olympic Games. Though I had not watched any of the games that day, I knew that Apolo Ohno was scheduled to skate for his last chance to win an individual gold in short-track speed skating. Still feeling ill, I tuned in just in time to watch the skaters. By the end of that race, I was up on the edge of the bed, screaming as Apolo finished the 500-meter race in first place, miraculously feeling much better in the short time that it took him to claim the gold medal.

Then slowly over the next couple of days, which turned into weeks and then months, I sank into a depression over age and over never being able to return to or even pursue a dream such as that, or even relate to or draw interest from someone as talented or as young as those I had just witnessed at that level of competition.

I could function and do what I had to do, but I felt as if I were in a small boat without oars, and I was without any means to steer or slow down as the current carried me toward the sound of a waterfall just ahead. I could either hold on and stay put, or jump out into the swift current and be swept away. There were no other options. I could not stop time; it was carrying me with it. My husband thought my dim outlook on life had something to do with some news we had just received, but I thought I had been dealing with that okay, just as I had always dealt with news from my son.

Over the years, phone calls out of the blue from my oldest son have gone something like this: "Mom, this is Aaron. I got caught with pot today at school. Mr. Short, the vice principal, wants to speak to you." *Greeaat.* "Mom, I've been talking to a recruiter, and I've decided to quit my job and join the Marines instead of going back to college." *Well, I'm so glad we're already in Baghdad. Now won't that be fun.* Then, in early 2006, "Mom, we're pregnant, and I don't need a lecture." *Oh, joy, and this is the girl you told me about two months ago—the one you were going to take it slow with?*

We were going to be grandparents and initially took the news hard. My husband reasoned that we had failed him somewhere along the line, but, by day two, I was mad. "It's not like they're fifteen and sixteen; they're twenty-five and twenty-six! Is it that hard to get a hold of some birth control in California?" On the third day, I had come to some sort of peace that held for a while, until I watched those Winter games. I realized I was old enough to be Apolo Ohno's mother and competing in any kind of event of that caliber was *unfeasible.* I would never be a world-class athlete or any other nonsense I could dream up. Though I still longed for the impossible, for youth, my depression was somewhat sidelined as we maneuvered through the year.

I met the girlfriend and liked her, said goodbye to my son as he set out for a Pacific tour aboard a Navy ship, and tried to remain optimistic about a future for the two (soon to be three) of them. I flew to California for the baby's delivery and bonded with my first grandchild over a ten-day stay, hosted the girlfriend's family for Thanksgiving, and got the news that my son and she were engaged shortly after his return from the Philippines. We planned and attended a wedding in May, got together with our whole family to celebrate Mom and Dad's sixtieth wedding anniversary aboard a chartered yacht on the lake in July, braced ourselves for Mom's open-heart surgery in September, and then all came back together again in October for her funeral. Now here I was again, picking up from where I had been interrupted, though feeling even more desperate than before due to death's final say. The world, spinning ever faster around me, always seemed to display the accomplishments of others everywhere I turned.

Friends who used to be so easy to get a hold of, so quick to respond to my calls over troubles or disappointments were now too busy with jobs, children and grandchildren, deadlines and financial burdens. My mother was gone, my best friend who would have set me straight was now dead over nineteen years, and I did not want to confide in family about the self-pity that was plaguing me day and night. I turned to my longtime mentor, Kyra. Even though we hadn't spoken in two years, and I hadn't seen her in fifteen, I needed somebody.

So, one night after everyone had gone to bed, I sat down with paper and pen and a full glass of red wine. With Christmas music still playing, I wept and wrote down my soul on page after page, front and back, totaling at least nine tear-stained notebook paper pages of handwritten scrawl. In all fairness to the compassionate soul she is, I began with, "Please don't be alarmed when you read this. I'm okay. I just need to get this down, and even if you never receive this letter, I feel better for writing it." I wanted her to know that I wasn't desperate enough to do anything harmful to myself or anyone else, but, in truth, everything was so gray that I often thought about death.

It was more like a "whatever" attitude. I thought quite frequently that death would be preferred over living the rest of my life in emotional, spiritual pain, feeling useless and without purpose, never obtaining the desires of my heart. Suicide never entered my mind, although I sometimes felt I was tempting fate by my arrogant attitude: *Go ahead, God, I don't care!* Curbing myself in front of the kids somewhat, my language and state of defiance was one in which one day I told my husband, "If God doesn't have a sense of humor in all this, if he doesn't *get* that he put us down here in the middle of all this mess in the first place, and if there is no allowance for screwing up, then I don't want anything to do with him anyway!" This attitude of rebellion, thwarting conformity, wanting to turn back time and live an even wilder past than I had was in stark contrast to another dark April, one in which I had pleaded with God for mercy and solace.

According to the *Diagnostic and Statistical Manual of Mental Disorders IV,* published by the American Psychiatric Association, "A person who suffers from major depressive disorder must either have a depressed mood or loss of interest or pleasure in daily activities consistently for at least a two week period." When compared to learning anything from a book, especially in the field of medicine, the entity takes on a whole different meaning when you experience it yourself. The most descriptive passage I have come across that masterfully attempts to explain a major depressive episode is found on the first page of Sherwin B. Nuland's book, *Lost in America:*

> The solitary torment of a depressed mind eludes any attempt to make it apprehensible to those who have not experienced it. And even for those of us who have endured those desolate months or years, no matter the generalized similarities of the depression, each of us has suffered uniquely, and alone. Neither vivid description nor the empathy of others can pierce the darkness of the long night.

I could not have said it better myself. The isolation of my pain and the loneliness of my depression caused me to think of myself as evil, for why else would I feel so abandoned, even while still in the midst of a sea of people. I remember the day I plunged into "the night." I remained there for a solid two months, grasping for sanity sometimes moment by moment.

In February of 1998, I was standing at a gas pump filling up my car, when I had the thought: *What if I could see all the evil acts, all the wrongdoings by people toward other people occurring all over the world right now, as they are happening. Well, God can. God can see everything that occurs. How can God stand to look upon such evil? I couldn't bear to see such stuff. The beatings and rape of children, murder, neglect, the selling and prostitution of human beings . . . on and on. If God can stand to look upon this stuff and not do anything about it, then how can God be good? Is God evil?* Hence, I took a plunge that would paralyze me and keep me desperately dependent on family around me for days and weeks to come.

I dangled on the edge for a couple of days, but the morning I couldn't seem to get the spoon into the baby's mouth for all the warring thoughts inside my head, I cried out for help. It went something like this, "Mom, how is everything? I just called to say hi, and tell you everything is okay here." After the third phone call that day telling my mom everything was fine and I was "okay," she and my dad decided to get in the car and drive the seven hours it took to reach my home. When my husband arrived home that evening and found out my parents were on their way, he realized this was something more serious than a "phase."

The first night of their arrival, so terrorized was I by the night and the thoughts in my head, I climbed in between my parents as they lay sleeping on our fold-out couch. The next morning as I prepared to go to work, I remained optimistic about seeing my panel of pediatric patients until I started panicking in the shower. I managed to get dressed and then, while reaching for the car keys, told my husband, "You call Dr. Johnson and tell him I can't come to work. I don't care what reason you give him. I'm going to get help." If my parents thought they were coming for a short stay in order to check things out and visit with the kids, they were mistaken. My dad ended up going home alone. My mother stayed for the next several months.

It felt like a spiritual oppression. A wiping clean of the slate was what it was, for out of hopelessness came hope, but it was not without a battle, a resolve that required holding on by just the nail of my little toe at times. I spent my days in the surrealism of sitting in a room with others while in a vacuum, behind a glass wall that could not be penetrated, while somehow recessed in some kind of tunnel. Though I could speak and be heard, touch and feel, listen to the sound of others, I was someplace else, further removed than the illusion of present space would have others to believe. There was no escape; the problem went everywhere with me, because it resided in my head. It was a part of my every waking moment, that thing that kept me separated from others. Painful anxiety was its companion. It drove me into a therapist's office one morning, whereupon arrival for my appointment I was asked to fill out a form.

It is standard in the practice of medicine to have the patient state the reason for their visit; it is the most crucial part of the examination and is referred to as part of the medical history. In psychiatric evaluations, forms with questions regarding the patient's symptoms aid the therapist, counselor, doctor in the initial interview. It is only a part of the comprehensive process that helps to determine the diagnosis, the severity of the patient's condition, decide an initial course of action, and assemble an ongoing treatment plan.

With no holds barred, I sat down and began to answer the questions with brutal honesty, admitting on paper that I was afraid of exposing myself to Satan and that I possibly might somehow be offsetting the rules of the game between him and God. I sat there and thought, *My God, these are some of the same words I remember reading on intake forms during my third year in medical school while rotating through the psychiatric ward at the veteran's hospital, and I thought those guys were messed up!* The therapist took one look at my haggard face and said, "Do you trust me? You need to be started on medication. I usually have trouble with professionals in the medical field, though it is usually with the nurses more so than the doctors." She scheduled me to see a psychiatrist.

The battle raging in my head over taking medication went something like this: *Well, if I take this, doesn't it mean I'm giving God some unfair advantage, and, if I get better, what does that prove? Is God's weakness being revealed?* Then, the other side asked: *Will I be in the wrong if I take this? Will I be further abandoned for my lack of faith? Is this evil? Am I evil?* I got to the point where I would tell myself, *Just shut up,* and I would close my eyes as well as my thoughts and swallow the pills as fast as I could, before I started thinking about it all over again. I did come across something that helped, a touchstone I could come back to when I needed to. On the eve of my first appointment with the psychiatrist, some words from the Old Testament came to me. From Psalm 139:

> Whither shall I go from thy Spirit?
> Or whither shall I flee from thy presence?
> If I ascend to heaven, thou art there!
> If I make my bed in Sheol, thou art there!

If I take the wings of the morning
and dwell in the uttermost parts of the sea,
even there thy hand shall lead me,
and thy right hand shall hold me.

If God could be in hell, then surely he could be in the medication, and I would not be cursed for taking it.

There were other touchstones, words of wisdom I would cleave to in moments of desperation, either snippets of the Psalms, words written to me in cards that started arriving at the house (to this day, I keep them sealed in a plastic bag), or words spoken by others in message form or conversation, written down in song or in books. While reading some of the Psalms, I could read and process only small excerpts at a time. Eventually, I began to feel not so all alone and found I could relate to the pain of people down through the ages, and to think those guys didn't have any Zoloft available! Words like:

I am poured out like water,
and all my bones are out of joint

Be gracious to me, O Lord, for I am in distress;
my eye is wasted from grief, my soul and my body
also

My tears have been my food day and night,
while men say to me continually,
"Where is your God?" . . .
Why are you cast down, O my soul,
and why are you disquieted within me?

I am reckoned among those who go
down to the Pit;
I am a man who has no strength,
like the one forsaken among the dead,
like the slain that lie in the grave,
like those whom thou dost remember no more,
for they are cut off from thy hand.

and one of my favorites from the book of Jonah:

> The waters closed in over me,
> the deep was round about me;
> *weeds were wrapped about my head*
> at the roots of the mountains.
> I went down to the land
> whose bars closed upon me for ever;
> yet thou didst bring up my life from
> the Pit,
> O Lord my God.

Seaweed in my head. Yep, that's a pretty good description.

Mom was there. She helped with the kids, even got up to give 3 o'clock bottles, helped around the house, and listened to my questions asked in angst, my grapplings with God, my attempts to explain him in such a way that he would be definitive, like tabulations done in nice and neat columns with a tidy answer at the bottom. Unable to work, unable to eat, I sat at the kitchen table in a distressed state, looking out the windows onto our wooded lot where no answers could be found. Mom never pretended to know what I needed. Instead, she did as she had always done. Instead of talking and trying to fix me, when I got to a state of "at wit's end," she would calmly ask, "Would you like a cup of tea?" And as we sat together and drank tea at the table, I somehow felt a little better, for a time anyway.

She only gave what she knew to give: her presence, her service, little comforts like her *tea,* and a deep abiding compassion I could see in her face. I now clung desperately to the same mom I had pushed away since childhood in pursuit of my independence. In the past I had shied away from sending her mushy cards at birthdays and holidays, yet I wrote in a card the Mother's Day following the winter of my depression: May, 1998, "What a special Mother's Day for us, for you have truly been my rock . . . . I know I've struggled with believing God knows what is best—but I have no difficulty believing that He gave you to me."

I did eventually emerge from the darkness. I still didn't have all the answers, but, as I told Mom one day over the phone, "Though the questions still circle around in my head, I'm not *submarined* by them anymore." From out of the land of confusion, I came to a place where

I believed God was wiser than me. It had taken a good twenty years to get there.

An April now ten years later, I was in pain again but not in that kind of pain. Though I had learned a lot, I never wanted to go back to that place even though it had prepared me well. The literature addressing working with hospice/palliative pediatric patients and their families states how important it is for individuals who enter this field of medicine to "consider their own beliefs and philosophical commitments, face their own mortality." Well, I had faced mine, and I had come away with the belief that death was a passageway, every bit a part of life as birth, in fact a *rebirth* after a time of labor. Death was not an end, and there was good on the other side: hope, by definition. Maybe I was so sure of that hope that it explained why I seemed to be more comfortable attacking my pain with anger and argument than with humility and contriteness. If I didn't agree with God, I flat out told him, flat out told him I didn't want to mind or behave. While I felt I was pushing the envelope of defiance and distance, I somehow did not feel abandoned.

In fact, one morning during my morning swim, working my way through the drudgery of my laps and dealing with inescapable thoughts, I heard Mom above the rabble, "It's okay." Typical Mom. No matter how bleak life could get, no matter how confused or ornery I could be, she never acted out of despair, never gave up on hope, not on our family, not on me.

April. I liked the song, I liked the name. My brother's first calf for his Future Farmers of America project was April, named after the month of her birth. She was velvety brown, with long, soft ears, and a white face. My friend's name was April. One day in conversation, she mentioned a book. Little did she know she was throwing me a lifeline.

I started reading *The Artist's Way: A Spiritual Path to Higher Creativity* in the spring, and, on April 25, at the request of the author I wrote my first "morning pages," a sort of exercise in journaling. "It's the unattainable—the huge expanse (literally) between my fantasy and reality. Oh well, that's always been about me—kid performing on back of the truck bed, high school *pinings* and here I am again. Thank you for the writing."

Though I didn't recognize it at the time, I was beginning to lift the lid and let God out of the box. I was beginning to get a look at God through my mother's eyes.

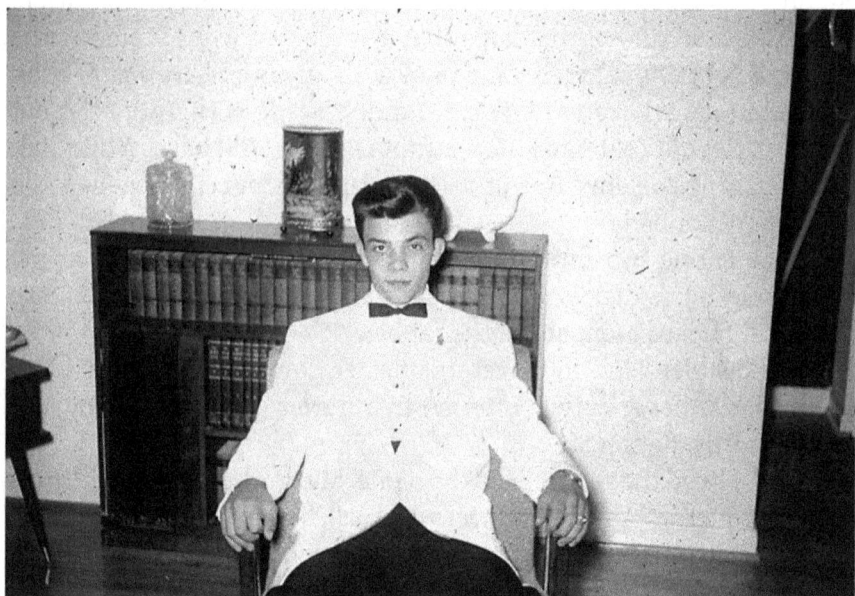

May

here is a tradition I remember, a tradition from my childhood: we would pick some fresh flowers, arrange them in a spring bouquet; then we'd lay them at the doorstep of a neighbor, friend, or anyone, ring the doorbell, and run. The owner of the home should find at their feet a pleasant surprise, anonymously given, a reminder of spring. It is called May Day. May 1 marks the end of the agriculturally dormant half of the year in the Northern Hemisphere and has been associated with raucous celebrations since the early ages. I wouldn't call it raucous, but I do recall the thrill of *legitimately* getting to run for a good cause after ringing a doorbell.

May, a month that used to sneak up on me: I was so busy complaining about having to go to school and take tests and hand in papers, that the end of the school year would suddenly steal up behind me and often find me not quite ready for the abrupt changes and closure. May is a month of transition and sometimes goodbye.

I remember the May of my first grade. My family had moved in February of that year to Sherman, a town seventy miles west of Paris. I went from Mrs. Bills, who taught on the first floor of an old three-story red brick building with old wooden desks, to Mrs. Ables, who taught in a modern one-story school called Wakefield Elementary. Even though only an hour's drive away, it seemed eons of years removed from what I was accustomed to; it still does, to an extent. Seventy miles *east* of anything in Texas makes a difference. Upon my first day in a new school, I was soon to learn there was a different way of going about things.

I was assigned to the top reading group circle on account of recommendations given by Mrs. Bills. When it came time for us to find our chairs in the reading circle, I made a beeline for a small boy with beady eyes and jet black hair Brylcreemed back from his face. I knocked chairs aside in order to sit beside Harold. He looked positively affronted, and the other kids chimed in immediately, "No cutting the butter!" I had never seen or met anyone like Harold before.

He was always immaculately dressed with every hair in place. (In our school class picture, he is wearing a suit.) Each time we went to the library he had some space or science-type book in his hand. Harold just looked smart; I wager that if I could see him today he would be a high-powered lawyer, CEO, or an ominous research director, still short, of course. Harold must have gotten over the shock of meeting me, because I was eventually invited to his birthday party that same year.

He lived in a cul-de-sac (another first for me) several blocks from my house; it was in a neighborhood where the houses took on a distinctively different look and feel from where I lived. I think it was attributed to money. I thought his home was the most beautiful one I had ever seen. We played games inside, had cake, and opened presents in our Sunday best. Harold and I became pretty good friends and often played together after school, which is why a certain occurrence near the end of the school year caught me by surprise.

Our class, as well as every other class at Wakefield Elementary, received a *Weekly Reader* to take home every Friday. It was a reader formatted like a newspaper and was written specifically for each grade level. It also featured a little cartoon bear named Buddy Bear. Buddy Bear was all about being a good citizen, so at the end of the week, Mrs. Ables selected the best citizen of the week based on our behavior. The person selected would receive a "Good Buddy" sticker (a round picture of Buddy Bear) to go on the corner of his or her desk. The whole class sang some song while she ceremoniously placed the sticker on the best citizen's desk. It was a big deal. My moment of glory finally came one Friday afternoon, and, during the singing of my song, Harold starting chanting, "Boo! Boo!" while laughing with a neighboring friend. Mrs. Ables promptly went over and snatched Harold's Good Buddy sticker off his desk to his sudden dismay. I've never seen a smile turn so quickly into a scowl as it did on Harold's face; I can see it clearly even today.

I had never experienced *Weekly Readers* or fancy kids like Harold at Rosa Pearson Elementary. Our school in Paris was so old that each individual classroom had an adjoining cloakroom and wooden desks that were probably the original ones when the school was first built. We could either enter the classroom through the front door, or we could hang our stuff in the cloakroom and enter through a door at the front of the classroom, close to Mrs. Bills' desk. Mrs. Bills had prematurely white hair; she wore cat-eye glasses, had a warm smile, and taught me how to read. She often wore a beautiful brooch of the world made of shimmering crystal beads on her dress. I have an autographed school picture of her wearing that brooch. Sometimes it's nice to know some things are what you remembered them to be.

Every morning we stood by our desks and said the Pledge of Allegiance while facing the flag, sang "My Country 'Tis of Thee," sat back down in our seats and with our hands folded and our heads bowed recited the Lord's Prayer. Mrs. Bills taught me the Lord's Prayer, and I was very proud of that fact. One morning in Sunday school class our lesson was on the Lord's Prayer and I raised my hand in order to show I knew it already. After relating the tale of my first grade's morning ritual, my Sunday school teacher looked at me dumbstruck and announced, "That's against the law." *Oh, my God, Mrs. Bills was breaking the law! Mrs. Bills was going to jail, and I had helped put her there!* Sometimes I think adults are totally clueless about the confusion they impart on the innocence of children; oh, that we could remember as much when we become the adults.

Well, I'm pretty sure Mrs. Bills didn't go to jail, and I never knew when or if she stopped teaching first graders the Lord's Prayer, but many changes occurred after I moved away from Paris. Our old school was torn down to make room for a bank and a large water tower soon after we left. A new one-story modern school was built down the road, and Mrs. Bills died a few years later from cancer. Many years later while digging through my old trunk of memorabilia my dad put together for me, I came across my first grade report card from Paris. On the back of the card in a note to my new teacher, Mrs. Bills had written down the different books we were working in and how far I had read in each, in order to help with my transition to a new school. She also wrote: "Sherry does excellent work and is a lovely little girl. I wish I could keep her." Closing in on forty, I must have been at another juncture of self-doubt, because I cried after reading those words. I had always remembered myself as some skinny, knock-kneed kid with stringy hair who never gave much thought to what she wore to school—anything but "lovely."

My first May in Sherman brought many new things my way. I discovered a new best friend named Wendy; she followed me home from school one day. I found a new place of beauty just down the block. Missing my favorite woods at the end of my old street, I discovered three green maple trees right in a row one day while riding my bike. They stood in front of a white house that housed a family with four kids; I would soon get to know them very well. Their mom would become my Blue Bird Leader. It seemed to have taken such a long time to close out my first year of school, far removed from where it all began.

We had an end-of-the-year picnic in the park just up from the school, and we were told to bring a change of play clothes to school for the party. I brought my shorts and shirt to school in an old Hallmark box instead of a sack. While standing in line outside of the girls' bathroom waiting to change, our teacher assistant stopped and asked me if I was going to change into a "box of cards." I got my feelings hurt. Our playtime at the park was cut short because of rain, but at least we got out of the classroom for a little while.

I missed the last day of the first grade due to illness. I stayed home with a fever, missing the completion of a vocabulary notebook we had been working on all semester. We were supposed to put the cover on it the last day; mine was never finished. I was very emotional as well as sick. I was missing my brother and the celebration of completing what was probably considered one of the most pivotal school years of my life. My parents repeatedly told me that my brother was "on the other side of the world." He had been deployed to Taiwan after completing his basic training in the Air Force. (My father had insisted that he sign with some branch of the military to avoid the draft and Vietnam; in his case, it worked.) I remember tearing up listening to Petula Clark's "Don't Sleep in the Subway, Darling" while it played on the radio that afternoon. He had recently sent me a book of pictures from Japan, some postcards, and a necklace with a smooth shiny heart made out of shell. At some point I lost the shell heart, but I wore that chain at my first wedding.

At the end of May I saw my first ballet in the municipal auditorium downtown and was forever charmed by dance and the stage. Miss Peggy of Miss Peggy's Dance Academy lived right next door to us. I had never paid much attention to her before I started taking lessons. At the time, she was a divorced woman who never seemed to spend much time at home. After seeing the ballet her studio put on that spring, my mother enrolled me for lessons the following summer.

I don't know where she hailed from, but she had been formally trained and brought a wealth of expertise to Sherman. She embodied everything expected in a ballet headmistress. She was a perfectionist and a stickler for details. Her end-of-year recitals were fashioned after themed ballets, such as *Cinderella* or *Babes in Toyland*. The theme was interwoven throughout the ballet by her advanced dancers on toe, but she managed to showcase the younger dancers with individual numbers interspersed throughout the program.

In a little building on South Elm Street, which now houses an appliance repair store, I was in another world for a short while among the ballet barres and classical musical strains that wafted around the tall, tile-ceilinged room. Being one of the smaller pupils in the class, I was relegated to the barre facing the wall with two other dancers; we were called the "Little Pickles." Stretching my long legs in positions I had never experienced before, I soon prided myself in displaying a perfect point. With one hand on the barre and the other held out to the side, I could look down the length of my leg and see only my big front toe as I held it in a point position out in front of me, just like Miss Peggy wanted. Working on my plies and leg extensions while facing the wall earned me the lead position in the dance of the tip toe elves in the production of *Snow White* the following spring.

On May 29, 1968, I debuted on the stage of the municipal auditorium, a remnant of the old Kidd-Key College for Women originally established in the late 1860s. It has a fantastically high ceiling to accommodate the balcony with large, nearly floor-to-ceiling windows that, thankfully, opened to the outside back then, because there was no air conditioning. I recall the flapping of programs used as improvised fans that night every bit as clearly as the colored stage lights that blinded me from the audience's faces. A beautiful teenage girl by the name of Nancy Darling, the daughter of a popular doctor in town, played the lead role as Snow White. After taking a bite of the deadly apple and dramatically falling to the stage floor, Snow White lay still while three tip toe elves one at a time came timidly out from behind the side stage curtains to touch her foot gently and scurry away. I was the lead elf. After we had surmised she wasn't going to wake up, we took our place at the front of the stage and performed our dance with me—yes, me—out in front, the proud leader of the fearful, shy elves.

Just having returned from his Air Force tour in Taiwan, my brother had to sit through more than two hours of ballet performed by the young and budding students of Miss Peggy's Dance Academy in a packed house where the whir of ceiling fans managed to do nothing more than move the warm air around. Payback time for missing my kindergarten program.

Well, it wasn't exactly *Swan Lake,* but my love for the arts was firmly implanted. A year or so after my first ballet lesson, I began taking piano as well. Being a very elemental student, I kept recalling a melody from the *Snow White* ballet that I tried to play for my teacher. It had played during the hunt in the fantasy forest scene. Some of the most experienced dancers from the studio had performed on toe, a beautiful dance as deer to this haunting music; one was shot and mortally wounded by the huntsman. Listening to me picking out the melody with one finger, my teacher immediately recognized it as Edvard Grieg's "Morning Mood," a selection from a play, *Peer Gynt.* It would be some years later before I was accomplished enough to attempt to play the piece on the piano. Though middle school got in the way of seriously pursuing ballet and piano further, I continued to perform in May ballet and piano recitals for some time up into the preteen years. Miss Peggy ended up remarrying and leaving Sherman long before I did. She danced in our last performance and graciously, as well as tearfully, accepted our long-stemmed red roses on stage as teenage girls were reduced to tears as well. May, a month of transitions and goodbyes.

School days seemed to drag on relentlessly. I would wake up and, upon attempting to gain some orientation, would proceed to complain and voice over and over how much I *hated school* while working my way through breakfast. My poor mother was subjected to this routine every morning while she ate buttered toast and drank her coffee. But I always went. Elementary years that I thought would never end at Wakefield soon dissipated as middle school and its rites of passage stretched on for two more memorable years. Then suddenly one May, high school had come and gone.

Strains of Gerry Rafferty's "Baker Street" played on the radio while I sat in the backseat of a friend's green Mach 1 Mustang, riding around making party arrangements and picking up the graduation cake. We had just come from the football stadium where we had rehearsed our processional for graduation and were instructed on etiquette and behavior expected for the night's proceedings. Nearly free at last (or so we thought in our blissful ignorance), we were all talk about the latest buzz heard throughout the stadium bleachers. A lot of parents, or I should say *most* parents, had nixed plans for lake graduation parties that night, on account of some escaped convicts on the run.

The Oklahoma State Penitentiary in McAlester, located across the Red River in Southeast Oklahoma, has a history of prison breakouts and escapes, including a notorious riot in 1975 that went on for days. On April 23, 1978, two convicts escaped from the institution and went on a month-long killing spree that took them through parts of North Texas and Oklahoma, to Alabama, and back again. On the day of our graduation, the local newspaper ran a front-page spread and a picture of their stolen get-away car (belonging to a murdered woman from Alabama), hidden and vacated in some trees under Carpenter's Bluff bridge, some twelve and a half miles downstream from the Denison Dam over Lake Texoma. In other words, *the boys* were back in our neck of the woods.

Lake Texoma is a huge man-made lake on the Red River that separates two states, hence the name *Texoma*. Constructed by the U.S. Army Corps of Engineers in the 1940s, it covers over 89,000 acres and is known for its fishing and recreation. "Texoma Land" is the name given to the surrounding communities, the two largest being Sherman and Denison, which stand adjacent to each other. The Sherman Bearcats and the Denison Yellow Jackets are long-standing football rivals, and competition between the two schools is not taken lightly. But, there is a connection. Growing up in Texoma Land means that the lake impacts your life in one way or another. If you find yourself drawn to it, it becomes more than just your backyard playground; it becomes the place where you grow and learn, where friendships are forged out of mutual experiences, the common ground for those who live near it and come to call it theirs. Many firsts occur in and around Lake Texoma, and, as a person grows up there, those firsts and their consequences take on a different weight.

The first time I viewed Lake Texoma, I was sitting in the backseat while my dad drove the family across the Denison Dam to the picnic grounds and designated swimming area on the Oklahoma side. It seemed so immense and expansive down below me that it might as well have been the ocean, stretching out to the horizon, aside from all the white-capped waves stirred up by the strong spring wind. I fell in love with it immediately. My family didn't own a boat, so I was relegated to family picnics and swim time after Dad got off work, intermittently throughout the summer or on special occasions when out-of-town family or friends would visit. But when I got into high school and could get a ride, or, better, when I got my own set of wheels, the lake became an intricate part of my life, the backdrop for a lot of life's lessons. It got even better once I found friends who owned a boat, or even friends who knew other friends who owned a boat.

I learned how to ski there, got the worst sunburn of my life, survived drinking and driving while on the water and driving back home from a day spent there. Some of my best and most memorable times were spent there watching some of the most gorgeous sunsets while sitting on the beach dreaming of the day I would own my own boat. Lots of good times with good friends. I dreamed big and lived big while on the lake. Therefore, it seemed the natural place to celebrate what I then considered to be one of the biggest days of my life: graduation.

Graduation was a bigger transition for me in some ways than just completing twelve long years of education. I had recently left a fundamentalist church and was hanging around with a different group of friends. Two of the friends were married to each other and everyone hung out at their place. Hence, I was enveloped into a completely different lifestyle than what I had been accustomed to while in my old church youth group. Because my friends didn't need parental permission for graduation plans (they essentially were the parents), I, therefore, didn't see the need to announce that I would be hanging out at the lake instead of attending prom or any other after-graduation get-together. Blowing off my prom was nothing out of the ordinary for me. School dances had never been on my social calendar throughout my adolescent years. I had attended a church where school dances were not so much forbidden as they were just not accepted or talked about; there was always some other alternative. During my high school years in the '70s, pretty much anything unconventional was viewed as cool, so snubbing the prom was right in line with the accepted view of wearing the same pair of faded Levi's all week long.

I often smile to myself when I hear of all the plans and fuss made over high school graduation these days. In 1978, no one arrived at the prom in a limo; no girl scheduled a manicure and certainly not a pedicure before the dance; and if a girl dared show up with an up-do hairstyle or anything too outside the long, straight, parted-down-the-middle look, she would have been laughed out of the gym or wherever they were holding the thing.

Somewhere I have a picture of myself and two other girls standing on the beach holding up our cake. If we had any other refreshments outside of chips and beer, I certainly don't remember; maybe we had some cheap wine. I do remember a large bonfire and taunts made all night long to the convicts who might be lurking in the trees and bushes surrounding the lake site. Every time someone had to walk off to go to the bathroom, they heard, "Watch out for so-and-so," "Oh, yeah, come and get us, you losers," and on and on.

Our party, somehow overshadowed by the possibility of danger, was also somehow muted effectively by the amount of beer being consumed. Not yet a partaker of alcohol, I watched in amazement as one of our classmates, a boy on whom every girl in our school had had a crush at one time or another, win match after match at seeing who could drain a can of beer the fastest. We timed him over and over at two seconds flat; it was amazing, and he was still standing when it was all over. We managed to endure the night and make our way back home in the morning light. While some of us were sleeping off hangovers or just sleeping in for want of sleep, a gunfight was ensuing in Caddo, Oklahoma, some thirty miles away from where we had partied the night before.

Oklahoma State Troopers had set up roadblocks in southern Oklahoma around the lake and were searching the area. At approximately 10:30 a.m., two highway patrolmen on a lonely country road were met by the convicts in a stolen farmer's pickup truck and were immediately fired upon. One of the officers managed to radio that they had been hit as he lay dying; both officers were killed. An Oklahoma Highway Patrol helicopter pilot, who managed to spot the pair as they sped off, alerted authorities in the area. The escapees headed to the small town of Caddo, Oklahoma, where they set up an ambush site in a residential area. Another pair of state troopers answering the call were met with an onslaught of automatic weapon fire that killed one officer and wounded the other. The wounded officer returned fire, killing the first convict. A neighboring detachment's officer, answering the distress call, managed to bring down the other convict as he tried to escape, thus bringing to an end a month-long killing spree that left eight people dead and three wounded, including the three Oklahoma State Troopers killed in the line of duty.

The escaped convicts had managed to steal vehicles from their victims while covering four states, break through roadblocks and escape while shooting at state patrol officers, had raped, plundered, and killed mercilessly before returning to the region, where one was known to have family, before being brought down violently. In our rebellious ignorance, we had defied the gravity of the situation and had our party on the beach while others paid an awfully high price to ensure we could keep doing so. Shamefully, I don't think we got it at the time, even after reading about it in the newspaper; school was out, and the summer of love and more mistakes lay just ahead. May, it is a time of transition and sometimes goodbye.

May 1, 1993, was another transition point for me. After eleven years of single parenting I decided I was ready for marriage again. Cliff and I were married in the courtyard of a famous old hotel on the Riverwalk in downtown San Antonio, with my son, soon to be in the seventh grade, standing next to Cliff. It had poured rain all week, making me sweat the plans we had made for an outside wedding, but the sun came out the morning of the ceremony, and, with it, the humidity. Then we really did sweat. City buses, rolling by on downtown streets just the other side of the stone wall surrounding the courtyard, caused the preacher to pause every so often just so he could be heard over the engine roar that seemed to repeat itself every ten minutes.

The year my mother died, we celebrated fifteen years of marriage with the two of us going out to dinner. It was nice enough: the conversation flowed well, and it was a chance to get away from the routine struggle of getting kids to eat while at the dinner table, but I wasn't much for celebrating; escape was more what I had in mind. Everything around me felt so trite, so everyday, unimportant, or unimpressive. I felt without purpose, and simple acts, which used to bring some sense of purpose and joy with them, now seemed so *senseless*. Time was of the essence; it was slipping away, and I wanted something to show for the time I had been given. Never mind medical school, past accomplishments, four kids, and my marriage. I wanted something really significant to show for my time spent here on this earth. After all, I had only been given so much. Death sure had a way of making me aware of my limitations.

Desperation and a pain in my chest that threatened to cut off air from flowing in and out of my lungs would particularly flair up at my son's baseball games. I had regularly attended my older son's baseball games with the YMCA while going through medical school in San Antonio, but baseball in North Texas with my younger son was a whole different experience. These people meant business, from the coaches down to the parents and grandparents—oh, yes, they were out there too, parked in lawn chairs, coozies in hand. Fathers still in their work clothes, gripping chili dogs with fries, would be yelling at their kids from behind the backstop, "I don't want to see another ball get by you!" I would find myself backing away from the stands, separating myself from these people whose lives seemed so wrapped up in this world of ten and twelve year olds learning the game of baseball. I was wondering what in the world I was doing living in such a place. So, when I said to my husband, "I need to take another trip," he said, "Go." I called my sister-in-law in San Antonio and asked if she could take a break from her kids' baseball schedule for a couple of days. She asked, "Where are we going?" I said, "New York."

I saw New York for the first time exactly ten months before September 11, 2001. My husband and I decided to attend a medical conference in Manhattan so we could take in the sights as well as visit some cousins on my mom's side of the family I'd never had the chance of meeting. Before leaving for our trip, some well-wishers gave me tips on how to survive the streets of Manhattan: how to strap a purse on so it couldn't be lifted as easily, instructions never to look people in the eye while passing on the street or in the subway so as to avoid soliciting or begging, and to forget about courteous service, particularly during the lunch hour. What I experienced there was quite the opposite. I came away in love with New York—the architecture, the mass transit system, the food, the art, the hustle, but mostly the people.

Much to my husband's dismay I had a blast meeting and talking with people everywhere we went or along the way, whether it was on the subway or just waiting for the subway, questioning cab drivers about their lives and families in Harlem, chatting with our waiters, the hotel clerk, anyone. While he stuck his face in the subway map, I found it much easier and more interesting to stop people and ask for directions; they seemed to get a big kick out of it. Sometimes you didn't even have to ask. They were drawn to your state of confusion over which way was east or west. I did not just imagine the smile on this humongous NYC cop's face who directed us to our first night's show on Forty-second Street in the pouring rain after I'd tugged on his shirtsleeve for assistance.

Maybe that's part of the reason the tragedy of 9/11 in New York struck such a personal chord within me—not to take away from the terror rained down on the Pentagon or the horrible crash of United Airlines Flight 93 just outside of Shanksville, Pennsylvania. Although both were just as tragic, I hadn't been to either of those places. I didn't have a reference point or personal connection like I felt I had with the city of New York. I worried about the lady with a downtown job I had met on the subway one morning. She had a splitting headache she attributed to sinus congestion, and we talked about over-the-counter antihistamines and decongestants. I shared with her some Ibuprofen after discussing my preference of it over Tylenol for stuff like that. In spite of feeling bad, she thanked me before getting off at her stop. I wondered where she was during the morning of 9/11, not to mention some of my own family, whom I had just gotten to know.

Ironically, at the time of the terrorist attacks we already had reservations for another medical conference in New York scheduled for December, 2001. We were still planning to attend before we became part of the post-9/11 baby boom phenomenon; come December I was too sick to travel to New York. We rescheduled our trip for the next year, scratched the medical conference and took our ten-month-old daughter along to see the Big Apple. Looking across to Manhattan from the shuttle platform in New Jersey, we couldn't believe the hole left in the skyline. We turned simultaneously toward each other and in unison said, "It doesn't look the same."

New York was not a disappointment, though. If anything, it refortified my image of the city as a town made up of folk just like me. In the aftermath of such a devastating tragedy, our family had been blessed with a new life, and the people of New York seemed even more aware of it than ever.

As crazy as it seemed to others, taking Aubry along with us was the best decision we ever made. We were treated like royalty everywhere we went. We were removed from lines outside of the restaurants, paraded before people waiting ahead of us and given a table immediately. We were given free dessert; waiters tied balloons on the backs of our chairs; and she turned heads wherever we went. It was as if no one had ever seen a baby before. A group of dressed-up businessmen, having dinner in a private room at Carmine's on the Upper West Side, literally stopped what they were doing and started making goo-goo faces, pointing and laughing with her from behind the glass door that separated them from us while we were waiting for our table. One night, a young man with dreadlocks down to his waist and a beautiful Caribbean accent, selling roses on Times Square, stopped to admire her so boisterously that he drew a crowd of other happy onlookers. She stole the show. They were more interested in watching the baby than viewing the big midtown screens with all their graphic displays. She drew smiles and compliments from people on the subway, in the park, in the museums; and it wasn't just from the older adults; the people were all ages, from all backgrounds, all ethnicities. It was cool. Only once did 9/11 threaten to ruin a good sleep.

While waiting in line to be cleared to tour the Statue of Liberty, Aubry had fallen asleep in her stroller. While searching our bags and other contents, the security personnel informed us that they needed to search the stroller, as well. Could we please remove the baby? Knowing what an ordeal this would be, we begged if there was another way. A supervisor brought over a handheld scanner, and, while gently lifting her up, he ran the device underneath, making sure we hadn't hidden any explosive device underneath the baby. We were cleared, and she slept on, never knowing she was a potential suspect. All was well. In fact, one of the park rangers outside the national monument made a special trip back inside his office to get her a "Junior Park Ranger" badge to remind her of the visit.

While that trip was memorable in so many ways, another trip taken to New York with a girlfriend proved fun in a different sort of way. If we happened to be walking past a store with a sale going on inside, we popped in—unplanned, unrehearsed. We got to try on shoes and buy them if we liked; we stopped at downtown kiosks and bought purses; we darted in and out of shops just to look. Imagine, shopping in New York. What a concept! Outside of a general schedule of what we wanted to do or see that day, there was no rigid time frame, no watches. If we were late, so what? If we wanted to find cheesecake at 2 a.m., so be it. I could get into this: taking a girl to New York was a little more in line with "girls just wanna have fun." So, when my sister-in-law requested no alarms or wake-up calls, no set itinerary, and no cooking in the kitchenette, I said, "I'm good with that. Let's go."

I experienced a familiar rush as our cab made its way through the narrow, busy streets of the Upper West Side in search of our temporary residence. We were so excited; I had reserved us a studio apartment close to the park instead of a hotel room. We had a pull-out bed and a cool mirrored bathroom, a nice kitchenette that we never touched except to put leftovers in the fridge, and our own private balcony just outside the living area that held chairs and a wooden table where we ate our muffins. We felt and acted like a couple of young college roommates, an experience neither of us had shared, although we both had college and professional degrees.

Every morning, after waking up at whatever time, we threw sweatshirts over our pj's and strolled to the corner market for cranberry muffins before crossing the street for our cup of Starbucks. We always toted everything back to our room, where we did hair and makeup to the sounds of the local radio station or the local news broadcast on the television. While her duties as a mom and pediatric ENT nurse demanded that she rise early and remain organized and on schedule, I was amazed at Kahley's flexibility and laid-back manner to how we approached the day, the sites we chose to visit, and off-the-cuff excursions we ended up doing sometimes instead.

For instance, running behind after sleeping in from a big Saturday night, we missed the last boat to see the Statue of Liberty, so we trekked on in the rain down into the financial district. After briefly touring the National Museum of the American Indian, we ate our sack lunch of leftovers from our 2 a.m. dinner on the top steps of the structure while the rain continued to come down. Rather than actually touring the site, we spent most of our time talking to a security guard from Brooklyn who was interested in finding out where we were from, due to "the accent."

With its many different cultures, religions, and ethnicities represented from all over the world, it never ceased to amaze me the interest or disbelief—or whatever you call it—when someone from New York found out we were from Texas. We might as well have said Saturn, unless we ran into fellow Texans. Such was the case on another early morning excursion to our favorite late-night restaurant, Cafe Lalo. There we sat next to four cute girls who were all recent graduates of Texas A&M, two of them living and working in New York.

We went to my favorite restaurants and discovered new ones as well. We shopped briefly, walked a lot while she took tons of pictures, ate fabulous food, and still managed to save room for chocolate espresso cheesecake at 3 o'clock in the morning. We picked a Tony winner to see, even before it was declared a winner (*AUGUST: Osage County*) and found ourselves in constant search of bathrooms with all the sodium-laden food and caffeine we were consuming. While crossing the Brooklyn Bridge on foot one night after eating pizza in Brooklyn, I was in so much pain from having to pee I thought about looking for some bushes to hide in after we got over to the other side. Fortunately, I managed to make it all the way back to our room after riding the subway. Such was not the case with my sister-in-law one early morning.

After listening to jazz sessions in a basement club in Greenwich Village one night, we emerged from the dark to encounter the first rays of the sunrise. After exclaiming to the last of the patrons, "I haven't done this since Mexico," we bid our new friends goodbye and made our way to the subway for our ride to the Upper West Side to get some sleep. We encountered the subway workers with their sack lunches on their way to work. Feeling no pain, I began yelling obscenities at passing cab drivers on a deserted upper west stretch of Broadway for not stopping for us the previous Saturday night when we had tried desperately to flag down a cab in order to make a show. Begging me to stop while laughing so hard, my sister-in-law wet her pants before we could make it back to the room. It was to be the start of a long, interesting day.

A knock on our door from housekeeping around 10 o'clock that morning interrupted our sleep as well as our casually planned last day of stay. Housekeeping was coming to prepare the room for the next guest. I was the one who had the itinerary all wrong; our flight had left without us! We dressed and packed while the vacuum cleaner was running and then, in what felt like a scene out of a movie, we sat on the stoop outside our apartment with luggage at our feet while I made arrangements on my cell phone with the airlines for another flight out that day. We were still under the gun to make the flight on time as we ran to the corner to catch a cab in order to catch a train back over to New Jersey. We bought cheesy souvenirs at the airport, because we didn't have time to shop, and ate cheesy airport food as well, instead of meeting my cousins for a planned dinner that night.

I felt horrible for Kahley. We had planned to see the Statue of Liberty that day; instead, we found ourselves shuffling through with our bags, looking out the windows of the terminal across to Manhattan, wondering if we could catch one last glimpse of *her* while flying over on our way back to Texas. Kahley remained upbeat and saw it as a great excuse to come back the following year, as I sat despondently in the seat behind her. While waiting for our flight to take off, she kept handing me the airline magazine over the seat to look at pages she had flagged, pages of art prints with inspirational messages. In Atlanta, we sat down to strong margaritas, waiting for our connecting flight. I apologized profusely, still in shock over my screw-up. The return to reality was abruptly felt as we drove through the streets of San Antonio after landing, trying to find a place still open to eat dinner, craving the great late-night restaurants we had grown accustomed to. We settled on Denny's; the waitress was really nice and served us with a big smile, somehow easing the confusion in my head.

Kahley had asked me several times about our flight schedule and length of stay, but I kept insisting we were scheduled to leave on Tuesday instead of Monday, never stopping to checking the itinerary in my bag. Thankfully, I had told my family the same, so they didn't expect me to return until the following day. Even though I was covered there, I was still depressed that my oversights had nearly ruined the trip for us. Messing up the flight schedule had only been one mistake in a series of recent brain misfires.

To get to New York, we had flown out of San Antonio. I drove down the day before we were scheduled to leave. I left my home for a seven-hour drive ahead with a half tank of gas, fully intending to gas up down the road. I was having so much fun listening to my new discs I drove on through reports of possible tornados to the west of me all along the Interstate 35 corridor. I finally stopped to purchase an umbrella for the trip, because the week's weather forecast for New York had mentioned rain. It would have been great if I had remembered to glance at the gas gauge while stopped at Walmart, otherwise I wouldn't have run out of gas a little farther down the road, more than an hour away from my destination. Kahley had to interrupt her packing to come rescue me from the side of the road well after 9 p.m. After an hour's drive back to San Antonio and having to finish packing the rest of her stuff, we were looking at about four hours of sleep before having to catch an early flight.

Running late the next morning, we missed the San Antonio airport exit either due to the pouring rain, panic, or a combination of both.

We nearly collided with a temporary concrete embankment while whizzing through the turnaround on our way back to the airport. Would have been nice if I had remembered to grab the umbrella—that one I had stopped to purchase—from under my seat before we sprinted through the rain from the parking lot into the terminal. I could have also spared us the time spent tracking down a Sprint store in the rain if I had remembered to bring my phone charger with me. Then, if the itinerary mess-up wasn't enough, on my way home I cruised into town on fumes and a prayer after realizing, nearly twelve miles from civilization, that my gas tank was on empty—again! If Colorado had shown me that getting away wasn't the answer to my restlessness, New York had revealed to me that it was time to go talk to somebody. I needed an unrelated, objective voice to help me sort through the anger and distance I was feeling toward those closest to me and address this desperate feeling over leaving this earth with nothing left behind to show for my time spent on it. Maybe then my brain would start firing on all pistons again.

While in New York, bombarded by the Who's Who splashed across magazine fronts in all the newsstands on the Upper West Side, larger-than-life ads of the beautiful people in Times Square and models painted on the whole sides of buildings, surprisingly, it was there where a little perspective began to return. It happened where I least expected it. We arrived late for our date with the Metropolitan Museum of Art due to spending too much time getting ready and dallying along the way, darting in and out of shops on Lexington Avenue. Though we didn't have the whole day, we did manage to shut the place down as we made our way slowly through the exhibits. After admission we took a familiar turn that led us into the area of Egyptian art—not my favorite venue. However, Kahley seemed interested in viewing the sepulchers of ancient Egyptian rulers. There, atop a wooden base, a piece of stone dating from sometime around 2500 B.C. stood, encased in glass. It resembled a gray marble headstone like those in cemeteries today, only tiny detailed drawings arranged in neat rows covered the entire surface on both sides. Hieroglyphics, although interesting, had never intrigued me more than a passing glance, until that day. For some time I stared in awe at the intricate piece of work, wondering if one or many individuals had crafted it. I never gained a sense of what it was for or what it represented; I was just struck by the idea that somebody's work had been preserved for others to admire centuries removed from its origination. It could have been a road marker, for all I knew, but the artistry was so beautiful and detailed that I appreciated the time and effort put into the piece that was unsigned and unclaimed.

I had become so overwhelmed with the faces and bodies in the tabloids and news stories, people supposedly envied for their talent and contributions to the arts and entertainment world, that I had fallen for the big-splash hype rather than the idea of leaving something of value behind, recognized or not. It took a gray stone marker to open my eyes to unsigned works of art all around me: masonry work decorating the tops and sides of the buildings, architecture and the magnificence of the bridge we walked across, ornate metal fencing and gates with spiked finials on top. All these works were crafted and constructed by nameless people. They left traces of their livelihood and history behind for others to enjoy, but it wasn't just the art that made me stop and take notice. I thought about the services people offered to others as a daily way of life to support self and family, something exhibited from within an individual apart from the job itself. Maybe that is why the waitress in Denny's left such an impression with me. It was her genuine act of serving that I remembered, not her name, as was the case with the Arabic restaurant owner who was so accommodating in letting us sample and worked so hard to please, as well as the young girl behind the drugstore counter who handed me my newly purchased umbrella with a smile. After all, it was raining in New York as predicted.

Little pieces, fragments, memories, legacy: the very thing I wanted so desperately to leave behind that would validate me as somebody worth remembering, for something done that would be generally agreed upon as good or even great. Legacy was all around me. My mother had instilled in me a love and appreciation for the arts, had given me the opportunities she never had. She had also taught me an appreciation for the simple—the daily regimen lived out by daily people. She pointed out things that some people may have considered trite and identified them as something special, such as noticing that the newspaper comics wrapping the tamales she had purchased were colored with crayons. "Look, Sherry, some child has colored the newspaper probably because they didn't have a coloring book."

May had brought with it a remembrance to look around and take note of the common, as well as the exceptional, and see that often the two were inseparable. Mom had left a legacy of humbleness and had allowed in me, at the same time, the dream of reaching for the stars. I was desperate once again to try. I doubt she knew her leaving would trigger this within me, but with her death came the reclamation of a part of myself I had squelched for years. Long before I could recognize it as such, I was beginning to taste liberation in the midst of grieving: a way of looking at life and living it the way she had always wanted for me.

May, it is often a month of transition and goodbye.

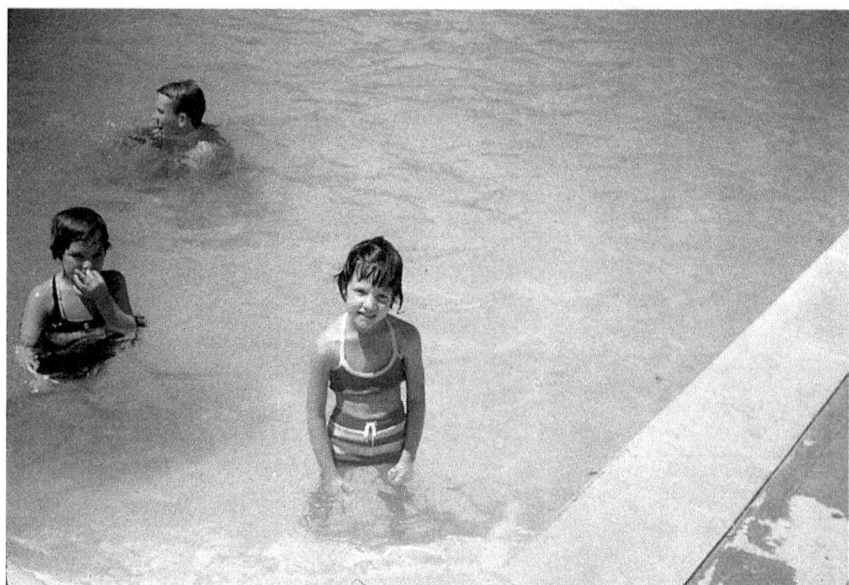

June

*J*une brings the first days of summer, though I just don't recall it feeling like summer so fast. Trying to escape Texas heat so soon brings with it a certain dread for the rest of the summer months. "If it's this hot now, what will it be like in August?" Heat wasn't a concern of mine at a much younger age. I liked the idea of record-setting temperatures. When my dad would say it was "hot enough to fry an egg on the sidewalk," I'd test it myself. The egg would sizzle some, but it never looked like the eggs in my grandmother's cast-iron skillet.

My early memories of June were days filled with play that evolved into different games as the heat index rose. Mornings brought me out of bed eager to get started. I'd find myself sitting on the cold concrete step outside, sorting through my rock collection before the other kids on the block had started stirring. I could just as well fill the early mornings with watching old primetime reruns: *Dr. Kildare, Father Knows Best, The Donna Reid Show*. Once I found someone else up and about, it was play and pretend outside until the heat and our mothers' insistence on lunch drove us all in for a while. I never took naps, so after lunch when the neighborhood took on a hazy stillness, I would fill my time with trips to the neighborhood convenience stores while keeping one eye on the lookout for the snow cone man. He came around every day but at different times. Only once do I remember my inability to run him down, in spite of my tears and pleas for him to stop. When everyone re-emerged in the mid-afternoon, it was time to get wet.

Early June ushered in days of running through water sprinklers across multiple yards, because the only fence-enclosed yard on our block belonged to Mrs. Wilson, our next-door neighbor. Her cyclone fence still allowed full view of the neighbors' yards all the way to the end of the block. My father never liked tall wooden fences in backyards; he said they blocked the view and weren't good for the dogs, who couldn't see out behind the tall wooden planks either. Except for Mrs. Wilson's yard, it was a free run all the way down Nineteenth Street.

Though plastic pools came and went, our mainstay of keeping cool and feeling like we were in the mix of summer was the water sprinkler. I recall the three basic models regularly employed on our street. (The in-ground sprinkler systems of today were unheard of or at least unknown by any of us.) Our household boasted all three sprinkler types. The strip kind consisted of a long, plastic one-and-a-half-inch-wide green strip that lay flat in the grass; the green plastic was pinstriped in white, I guess so we could see the thing, because it resembled a snake laying across the lawn. It had minute holes punched throughout its length that allowed the water to spray up and out in criss-cross directions, creating a mist-like effect. It simulated the mandatory showers we had to run through in order to swim at some of the public pools. Even at a young age I thought that was so anal.

The oldest model we owned consisted of a heavy metal base, once painted scarlet red, which sprouted little metal arms that rotated violently when connected to the water hose, flinging water circumferentially. The trick was to jump over the spinning bands of water. Our newest model, purchased at Sears and Roebuck, was a yellow oscillating version. Its single metal arm rotated back and forth spraying out water through its pinpoint holes in a fan-like pattern: the higher the force of water, the larger the fan. We ran back and forth through the fan, brushing the water aside with our arms. For a different effect we would sit on the thing for as long as we could stand it, water shooting up inside our bathing suits, if we owned them. Water up certain orifices brings to mind a memory that readily evokes the sensation of summers past.

Every house on the block had a water hose attached to the outside spigot, usually located on the front of the house behind the planted shrubs. We all drank from the water hose. It saved time from having to go inside to get a drink, a fact our mothers appreciated, I'm sure. All of this was routine, and we would stand in line, waiting for our chance to get a drink, but every once in a while we were duped by the person manning the faucet. Usually it happened to the first person in line. If we were *fool enough*, we would wrap our lips around the end of the hose waiting for a drink, expecting a gentle stream. What invariably happened instead would be an abrupt force of water erupting from the end of the hose that would find its way up through our cribriform plates—straight up to our brains, it seemed—compliments of the operator in charge of turning on the water. Of course, there was also another way.

In the middle of taking a drink, the stream would magically dissipate, and while we were wondering what happened or who turned off the water, whoever was pinching off the water hose would abruptly release it before we had time to think. Coughing and sputtering from the water that had inadvertently traveled down into our tracheas from the overflow out our noses, we swore we would never fall for that one again, only to have it happen time and time again: the aesthetics of summer.

I was nearly six years old before I got my first bathing suit. It was a yellow one-piece, the color of a French's mustard bottle. It was trimmed in white and had a little black fish located at the bottom of the suit, just above the top of my right leg. I had been comfortable playing in the water in just my underwear until one day I became aware of myself. I was walking down the street to join the water sprinkler brigade, wearing nothing but a towel over my white cotton panties, when I noticed (or thought I noticed) stares coming from the passing cars. I clutched the bath towel around me closely, suddenly aware of my nudity, but I proceeded to play in the water once I got to my friend's house just the same. I must have said something to my mom, though, because the bathing suit appeared soon afterward. It turned out to serve a purpose other than just a fashion statement, I would soon learn.

The Aylors lived directly across from our house on Nineteenth Street. Both houses were on corner lots, with Austin Street on the north side of both properties. Jim and Ruth Aylor were good friends of my parents and had four teenagers who were all around the same age as my brother. In fact, Gwen, the only girl, was in the same grade as my brother. Jimmy was the oldest, my favorite next to Gwen; Eddie, the trouble-maker; Gwen, my babysitter; and Robert, the youngest and babysitter, too. In fact, they all took turns babysitting me at one time or another.

Robert had gotten a new job at the Gordon Country Club as a swimming instructor and had apparently gone around the neighborhood recruiting kids for swimming lessons. I was informed that I would be going. Every day for the next two weeks, three other boys from our street and I would be carpooling with Robert, in his 1963 white Plymouth Valiant (a hand-me-down from the older Aylors, I'm fairly certain).

Robert had a buddy who was a fellow swim instructor at the club. He actually turned out to be my teacher. He also carpooled with a bunch of kids from his block. Little did our mothers know that these two guys had an ongoing bet throughout our two weeks of swimming lessons to see who could pile their kids in the car and get home the fastest after swim time was over. So we kids were basically in a drag race everyday and didn't even realize it.

The road that leads to the country club is pretty much in the same shape today as it was back then. It is a partly paved, unmarked road that turns off Highway 82 west of town. Somewhere along the way, the pavement becomes riddled with potholes then gives way to nothing but a narrow rock road bordered by tall weeds and barbed-wire fencing on either side, no shoulder. Bumping along on a makeshift drag strip felt natural to us: no seatbelts, kids hanging out the open windows with our moms' bath towels flying in the wind. We thought we were just going home really fast until, one day, Rex left his shoes at the pool, and Robert had to turn around and go back and get them. We soon learned that was the only day we had lost a race. Robert just laughed it off. Years and years later, my brother looked him up and bought a Tahoe from him; he owned some big Chevrolet dealership close to Dallas.

My first day of swimming lessons turned out to be my *worst nightmare come true.* No wonder Mom had sprung it on me without consulting me first. The term "crybaby" had to have originated from my behavior those first couple of days. Though Robert wasn't my teacher, by the second day he came over and lifted me out of the water to see what the matter was. During the short course of my life, Robert had already witnessed many of my crying episodes, but I was petrified; this was no fit. I wanted no part of putting my head underwater. This was definitely not as much fun as the water sprinkler.

Under the tutelage of Robert's friend and surrounded by the boys from the neighborhood, after a couple of days I managed to get my head wet without freaking out, and, by the end of the second week, I was swimming underwater. Before the end of our session, I stroked nearly across the whole length of the pool one day but forgot to take a breath. Even so, Robert came over and gave me a bop on the head and told me, "Good job—just need to work on breathing." That small, rectangle-shaped pool with its blue tile border seemed overwhelming to me at the time, but I had conquered my fear of water sometime over the course of those two weeks. Swimming would become a routine part of my summers from then on.

I stayed away from swimming lessons for a couple of years, but after moving to a neighboring town where the public pool was "ginormous" compared to what I had been used to, I picked up from where I had left off and made it all the way up to the junior lifesaving level. Fairview Park Swimming Pool was the social destination for kids in our neighborhood every day during the summer months. The biggest challenge was always how to get there. From our street, the pool was a good mile if we traveled on regular streets; the shortcut was faster, but we had to cross a creek and maneuver through lots of brush. It was such a hassle that we usually went the full mile instead. There always seemed to be five or six kids going at one time and only two bikes (bikes that worked) between all of us. After scraping up a quarter for admission, we would wrap our towels around our necks and take turns riding on the handlebars or on the back of the seat, either being "pumped" by someone else or doing all the hard work of "pumping" when it came our turn, in order to make the 2 o'clock pool opening.

The pool itself had 11,000 feet of water surface area and a great diving end, roped off separately with three boards, including the high dive. In the heat of summer, lines always extended out from each board, but we stood in line, fighting off the monster horseflies that hung out around the big chlorine tanks behind the fence, just so we could do our favorite tricks over and over again. The diving end of the pool was kind of a *turn on* for me. Its deepest depth was twelve feet, and all the bigger kids and teenagers hung out there. There never seemed to be a shortage of really talented divers and tricksters. It was nothing to see one-and-a-halves, double flips, jackknife dives, and a couple of "preacher seats" while waiting our turn. My ace-in-the-hole trick was the handstand; I performed it almost every time I was up for a turn. Once I mastered my fear of the high dive, I thought it my duty to perfect my dive off the thing. Occasionally, I got the landing or "entrance" right, but, for the most part, my face would smack the water so hard that I would come to the surface just knowing my face looked as contorted and deformed as it felt. I think I actually used to ask my friends after climbing out of the water, "Does my face look all right?"

We had "chicken fights," played our favorite songs on the jukebox, ran when we weren't supposed to, had races, played tag, saw who could stay under the water the longest, watched the teenagers dunking each other in a game of flirting, and nearly drowned ourselves a couple of times. We usually stayed until the afternoon closing and headed home with sunburns and ravenous appetites, never having enough money left to buy snow cones from the stand across the street for the long trip home. It wouldn't have seemed like summer without Fairview Swimming Pool, and I thought I'd never outgrow it.

Sometime in 2006, I decided to start swimming at a fitness center for exercise. I had tried this once before when the kids were smaller. I had gotten all fired up after watching the Summer Olympics and decided I wanted to be a swimmer, but I had fizzled out after so many months. I had never really gotten comfortable with swimming laps for an extended time. The fitness and aquatic center was just down the street from my daughter's preschool, so I figured I could get in a swim after dropping off my daughter. Nervous over the daunting task of starting over, knowing how difficult it had been for me in the past, I suited up and entered the enclosed pool area that first day and chose a roped-off lane by the windows.

Two men were swimming laps in the designated swim lanes, and I paused at the edge, prepared to wait until they were finished. One of the men stopped swimming in order to introduce himself. He offered to share a lane with me, because the other half of the pool was designated for the water walkers and water aerobics classes. I didn't know it at the time, but I was meeting my future swim partner. His name was John Norton, and he informed me he had been swimming in this pool since it opened in 1975; he had logged in over 2,500 miles, which he kept recorded in a little spiral pocket notebook. John would be turning ninety on his next birthday.

We got to talking, and I confided my trepidation over getting started and my fear of not being able to carry through with my goal, but also that there was just plain fear present. Maybe it was due to the fatigue and air hunger, or the fact that I had to keep my head under the water the entire time, the isolation of it all. Sometimes I really felt claustrophobic under the water. John told me that for years he had had arthritic spurs in his neck. "They've told me they could remove them but that they would just come back. I didn't see the need in going through that, so I started swimming. To me, this is just like medicine." He had the gentlest smile and laughing blue eyes. When he got out of the water to make his way to the showers, padding along in his Speedo, I could see the effects of arthritis on his petite, bent frame. But when he was dressed and groomed, with that shirt tucked in perfectly, he could easily pass for someone fifteen to twenty years younger. So I started swimming.

I shared a lane with John on Monday, Wednesday, and Friday mornings beginning at 8:30; John got to the club around 7 a.m. on those days so he could ride a bike and lift weights before his swim. I began to increase the number of laps I could complete by adding two more laps every couple of days. The straight crawl was unnerving at first, so I switched it up with different strokes and used my kickboard as well. Even so, that claustrophobic feeling would come over me a couple of laps into my routine, making me feel as if I couldn't breathe. On mornings when I didn't want to get out of bed and go, I would think to myself, "If John Norton can do it, so can I!" I kept at it, trying to work my way up to a mile, which equaled thirty-six laps in that pool. John told me he was back down to swimming only two-thirds of a mile these days; he said his kick was almost gone.

That was the thing about John—even though no one there came close to logging the miles he had recorded, he was so humble and was constantly working on learning and improving. He complimented me on my style and asked how many strokes I took before I came up for a breath. He would comment on how little of a splash I made or how fast I was, even though I was much more impressed with his record. After all, he was one of the main reasons I had stuck with swimming. We always had our chitchat sessions before I started my laps. He would always tell me, "Come on in! I've saved a place for you."

One particular morning we were watching two or three swimmers go through some workout laps to get ready for an upcoming triathlon. To watch them sprint was pretty intimidating. I said something to John about how impressive they looked. John had his back up against the wall of the pool, arms crossed, casually taking in the scene. He said, "Yeah, I've watched a lot of triathlon trainers come and go in my time, and I'm still here."

John was so youthful that I often forgot how old he was until he would tell a story that brought his age into perspective. For instance, he mentioned that his baby girl was sixty-five years old. John's dad had been a pilot in World War I and had been shot down during a combat mission while his mom was carrying him. Until his mom remarried, his maternal grandfather had helped raise him. His "granddaddy" had owned hundreds of acres of cotton-farming land outside of Honey Grove, complete with sharecroppers, land bosses, and a separate house for his kitchen where servants prepared the meals. His granddaddy came away with fifteen acres after the "big crash" and subsequent Great Depression in the 1930s. John himself went on to be a pilot in the Air Force during World War II. Stickers all over his little truck's bumper showed he hadn't forgotten those with whom he had served.

Toward the end of August, 2007, I told John not to worry if he didn't see me for a couple of weeks; my mother was having open-heart surgery the first part of September. John fully understood; he had had a heart operation some years back and had the scar down his chest to prove it. We talked about cardiac rehab and the need for Mom to stick with some kind of exercise program after she had completed the rehabilitation part. I stayed gone from the pool for a long time; in fact, I didn't return until the following February. I guess, by that time, John had forgotten about our conversation, because when I finally did return he didn't ask me about Mom; I never told him she didn't make it.

There is something about keeping my head underwater while the world is spinning over and above me that may help explain why swimming is more psychological than physical, in my book, anyway. Life goes on and the tragedies of the past and anxiety about the future can be overwhelming, can build up inside my head when I am in a place where I can't do anything about it. Such is the way it feels when I enter the pool and begin the lonely task of logging one lap at a time with thoughts of *what if* and *this and that could be happening at this very second all over the world*, reeling inside my head. They cause me to come up out of the water at the end of the lane, gasping for breath, as if somebody or something has been holding me tightly under a blanket. Claustrophobia rears its head when I take worry into the pool. I've often wondered if I will be able to swim if my son ever goes back to Iraq or Afghanistan; the thought of missing a phone call while I'm underwater, or thoughts of what's happening in a time zone fifteen hours away, could be paralyzing. I wondered about such things after Mom had died. *Would I be able to swim?*

The most laps I had done before my exodus was thirty, and I had paid for it; my shoulder had bothered me some, so I backed off. I still couldn't comprehend swimming a mile anyway. It seemed such a daunting task in my mind, and, though I was proud of my efforts, I didn't really enjoy it that much. I would never be as committed as John.

In February, 2008, I came back to the pool, determined to start over, tone up, and do something/anything, to make me feel better about myself. John welcomed me back into his lane as if he'd been saving a spot for me all along. I slapped my goggles in place and promptly swam twenty-eight laps of the crawl without stopping. I blocked out certain memories and cares and, instead, went someplace else in my head. I had gotten very adept at exercising my imagination and found I could go wherever I wanted to go, be who I wanted to be, if the people around me would just give me the space in order to do so. I found that space, under the water.

I fantasized. I pretended. I came up with narratives. I became younger and prettier. I fell in love and inspired songs, poetry, and words. *And I swam.* When panic struck, it was usually toward the beginning of my swim, sometimes as far as six laps out, and then I would begin to pray, *God, take control of my mind,* and every time, the constriction would lift, allowing me to stay in the water. Only once did I come up to hang onto the pool edge and cry.

The words to a song, "Hurting for You," were fresh in my mind. It is a song about loss, loss of a love and the need to go on with life, taking it one day at a time: "Put aside those dreams that keep hurting for you." I felt the pain of my father, waking up every day without Mom, and closing the day without her as well. I could not help him. I felt my own pain: the loss of my dreams, the loss of my youth, things that I couldn't get back, things that were never meant to be, and so I cried at the end of my swimming lane. But, after a time, I put my head back in the water and finished my swim; I had reached a mile, and I wasn't turning back.

Swimming a mile in some ways becomes routine, and in other ways inspires some new insight within that I end up taking with me after my fifty or so minutes spent touching the ends of the pool and counting to thirty-six (lest I forget where I am and have to repeat a lap). It's different every time I enter the water. Sometimes the coffee I've just consumed kicks in, and I go into my strokes excited about my ability to swim; other times, I dread the time spent in order to complete the exercise, and I begin to plow along methodically. Whatever the mood, somewhere along lap six or eight, I reach my stride, and swimming becomes almost mechanical, like being on autopilot. My arms and legs know what to do; my breathing smoothes out as my mind wanders to other places and other times: *stroke, stroke, touch the end of the pool, turn around, stroke, stroke.* If I'm lost deep enough in thought, I don't notice my body, but, if I'm not, somewhere along lap sixteen or greater, I'm aware of my need for fuel. I wonder if the bowl of oatmeal I had for breakfast is going to hold out. Again, my body knows what to do: through a complicated enzymatic process, the glucose that has been stored in my liver and muscle cells as glycogen is broken down and released into my bloodstream to provide substrate for ATP, an energy source for cellular respiration. After an extended period, if my glycogen stores become depleted, fatty acid catabolism occurs to provide another source of ATP. In other words, I forget about being hungry as my body finds the fuel it needs to continue from what it has already stored up for such a time.

I refuse to think of lap eighteen as only halfway there, because I feel as though I've already been swimming for such a long time, so I merely think of getting to lap twenty. Then I can start counting afresh a new set of tens in my mind. I stare at the long strip of navy blue tile on the bottom of the pool. Twelve little individual tiles across make up the strip that runs down the center of the lane. I fix upon the strip and close my eyes when I come up for breath. In this way I focus on the world underneath the water instead of longing for the sun and air above me. My goggles are fogged up by this time, and I can see shafts of light coming through the side windows at different intervals. It pays to keep my eye on the strip; it's the only thing I can see. My mind continues to wander until sometimes I begin fighting the urge to acknowledge the sensation of a full or somewhat-full bladder. *Later,* I tell myself. Pushing through the twenties, I'm sometimes so lost in a narrative that I forget which lap I'm on. Then, at other times, I know exactly which lap it is, and I think I'll never finish: *twenty-five, stroke, stroke, touch the wall, turn around, still on twenty-five, stroke, stroke.* I know I'm almost home when I reach thirty. I switch to three laps of the breaststroke in order to round out the workout on my shoulders, followed by two laps of the backstroke, nervously reaching over my head for the edge of the pool at the end of the lane in order to avoid hitting my head, which I've been known to do. I sprint joyfully during lap thirty-five and slow down to bring it home on lap thirty-six. I'm ready for the showers, which years ago used to be my favorite part, *Thank God, that's over with.* Instead, these days, I feel differently. The joy is in the doing.

Sometimes after the conclusion of a mile and the feeling of having *done it* still fresh, I find myself thinking of the first time I stepped into a pool sporting my yellow bathing suit with the little black fish and how after nearly two weeks I almost swam to the other side. The sense of accomplishment is not unlike the memory of Robert Aylor's bopping me on the head and telling me, "Good job."

The summer after my mother died I was in no mood for chitchat or idle fun, but the kids were out of school and needed to do things besides stay inside with the television and the Wii. My dad wasn't coming over as often to visit, although I would meet him for lunch every two weeks or so. He was staying busy with his volunteering, maintaining the house, and his daily walks, but he was also lonely and looked forward to our visits. He kept inviting the kids to come over and try out the newly renovated city pool, giving them an added incentive for making the hour-long trip. So one hot summer day I found myself returning to my old stomping grounds, some thirty-six years older with three kids in tow. The funny thing was, I kept looking around in earnest to see if I recognized anybody. During all that time I had been away, Fairview Swimming Pool had stayed pretty much the same: same showers, same snack bar area, same sign-in window, diving area, same lifeguard stands. I was curious to see the results a massive reconstruction project made possible by the passing of a city bond. They had basically turned the pool into a mini water park and had significantly raised the prices in order to pay for it all.

The length of the pool was still the same, over Olympic size, but they had divided the length somewhat by placing two gigantic swirling water slides side by side toward the middle of the pool. Adjacent to the slides, in the shallow end, was an area that mimicked a lazy river ride; we could enter the circular area through an opening and the current would pull us around without our having to swim or make an effort, as jet streams of water propelled us along. The jets also arched out of the water sometimes, hitting us in the face. This oblong course circled an inner hot tub area, where the current riders could enter in and take a break as the others floated briskly by. The old baby pool adjacent to the three-foot end had been turned into a miniature baby water park with slides and fountains and giant suspended water buckets that were controlled to dump vast amounts of water intermittently on a person's head. The trick was to guess which one would tip over and in which direction so we could position ourselves accordingly in order to experience the waterfall-like effect.

The only problem was that the baby water park water flowed directly into the large pool; a tiny inlet allowed entrance into the smaller play area. Nevertheless, the two areas were intimately connected. Although diaper technology has come a long way with Little Swimmers, disposable swim pants designed to protect the others who are swimming in the pool with the toddler, they can only do so much. So, for instance, when there is an "accident," the whole pool facility is shut down for a thirty-minute clean-up period, and, in the case of a *catastrophic* accident, wherein the young lifeguards all become grossed out, the entire facility is shut down for a more thorough hygienic cleaning, and disheartened patrons are given return passes on their way to the exit. Such was the case the first day we tried out the new park.

The high dive had been replaced by a small tunnel slide that stood adjacent to one other regular board with all kinds of instructions: only one bounce, no back flips, no gainers, so on and so forth. *So much for showing off.* The snack bar area had been enlarged with awnings and tables; the shower area had been totally remodeled; there were two designated lap lanes and a basketball area in the middle of the pool with an adjacent deck where we could watch slide riders hit the water as they were shot out the end of the chute. The place had been spritzed up, but some elements of the old pool were still left. I couldn't help but miss seeing all the bikes that used to be lined up in front of the entrance in makeshift ladders on the ground with the front tires of the bicycles anchored in the rungs. Oddly enough, I even missed standing in line with a mass of other kids waiting for that wooden half-door to swing open when the big overhead clock read 2 o'clock, and I really missed the quarter admission fee.

The kids took off after having been given instructions to keep up with the youngest one, and I found a place half in and half out of the shade against the fence by the end of the five-foot end, next to the diving area. I found myself sitting close to two "weekend dads"; one had both of his kids with him; the other was a friend along for the afternoon. I didn't know either's custody situation, but overhearing their conversation gave me the impression that they were both divorced and had kids from their former marriages. At any rate, they were all out for a good time, and the two men liked relating stories of days gone by and genuinely seemed to enjoy each other's company as well as that of the kids. They liked talking about their kids and their escapades.

I was determined to stay distanced as I sat and took in the scene in front of me, quietly mourning over *my* days gone by and the passing of the bikini era and smooth brown skin. It wasn't fair. Even on my best days, I never looked *that good,* as I watched young, very young, unassuming preteen and teen girls tear into candy bar and ice cream wrappers, seemingly totally unaware of anybody's watching or envying them. Pool-soaked, bikini-wearing, tattoo-bearing, cell-phone-toting girls, just out for a day with friends at the pool, appearing clueless and uncaring of what life could dish out and how quickly this time would pass. They were just like I had been, though I never looked *that good* while tearing into my bag of barbecue potato chips. The pain in my chest, trying to grapple with the passage of time, was still coming and going. It's surreal sitting in a familiar place and yet being far removed, trying to piece together fragments of time, regain something you can never get back, and all the while searching for a familiar face, hoping age has not disguised too well the friend, the old crush you are looking for.

After a while, I decided to join my kids for a ride on the big water slides at about the same time the two weekend dads had decided to try them. While climbing tiers and tiers of steps to get to the top, I found myself smiling at their stories of the glory days and reminiscences over how mindless they used to be of risk-taking behaviors, particularly the dad with the two kids who kept showing up periodically here and there. On my first trip down, I chose the slide with the tunnel. After having been instructed to lie down and cross my arms over my chest I let go. *Holy shit!* I had forgotten how this felt as my momentum picked up and jet streams of water forced me up onto the sides of the slide. I told myself over and over to keep focused on blowing out through my nose so as to be prepared for the sudden expulsion into the water, as I could not tell where or when that might be. (It was dark in the tunnel, and I had my eyes closed anyway.) It was to no avail: at the end of the slide I was propelled out onto my back, and the water forced itself up through my nose on a course headed straight to my brain, and, suddenly, I was back! I was back in line with a water hose stuck in my mouth and a smooth operator at the other end with the nozzle turned all the way up. I was back into summer.

It no longer mattered about the tan, or lack of one. It didn't matter about the bikini, or the lack of one. I had water up my nose, and I was going back for more. I went back under the water and fished my bathing suit out of certain parts of my anatomy and climbed out of the pool with the two dads trailing close behind. Avoiding the whistle blow by the lifeguard, we did the fast-walk to get back to the slide. You know the one: you can't run at the pool, so you keep your arms down close by your sides, barely swinging them back and forth, and your legs close together, moving your feet as fast as they will take you without breaking into a full-blown sprint in order to beat the rest of the little kids back to the start of the line. We bolted up the steps to the top of the platform ready for another ride down, taking turns between the open yellow slide and the tunneled red slide. At some point later in the afternoon, we headed back to our belongings and towels, threw away all our trash, and herded our kids through the exit to the car. But, for a little while, we were like the uninhibited kids we had remembered ourselves to be. We hadn't forgotten how to have fun, in spite of being all grown up and unrecognizable to our peers who may or may not have been there.

I used to pride myself on doing things with my kids that my mother never did with me, like going to the pool, for instance. Playing tag with my kids in the lazy river while "Smoke on the Water" blared through the outdoor speakers would have never been a shared memory with my mother, but then I would not have allowed it either. It was a different time when I grew up. Except for the small number of mothers over by the baby pool, I never recalled *parents* much at the pool when I was swimming there as a kid. It was like they provided us with a quarter and expected the lifeguards to do their job. But I think it was more than just that; I would have been mortified if my mother had ever shown up at the pool other than just to give us a welcomed ride home. Our mothers weren't for *hanging out* with. They were in the home or at work; they had dinner waiting for us; they signed us up for stuff; they dropped us off and picked us up and were always there at the end of the day, but we did our thing, and they left us to it.

I thought about this as I climbed up the steps to the top of the tall slide. I realized that I had been thinking about it all wrong. I wasn't a better, more interactive mother than my mom; rather, my mom *got it.* She *got me.* My mother had always been there for me, but she afforded me the right to be me and hold her away from me a short distance. I think she not only read the times correctly, but she read me and allowed me some independence and freedom from her. I was never the prettiest girl at the pool. I was just one of the countless numbers of scrawny kids who showed up for a good time day after day throughout the long summer months, but dang if I didn't know how to have fun. My mom recognized this in me: my fierce, independent, "me-first" streak, un-genteel, and usually headed straight toward some disaster, and she loved me anyway. I never told her, but, for that alone, she will be forever endeared to me as the mom I did nothing to deserve but God saw fit to give me anyway.

July

It was July before I noticed the sounds of summer. There was buzzing all around me one hot, humid night in July while on a walk with a friend. No strangers to walking at night (in fact, in the heat of summer I prefer it), my neighbor and I began walking together occasionally, particularly when she needed to talk and I needed to walk away instead of run away. We would walk for miles down darkly lit, narrow streets in a neighborhood that bordered our own, sometimes with nothing but the occasional porch light and street lamps to illuminate our way on moonless nights. I began to be aware of a familiar hum, a constant whir in the background of our conversations. It was the nighttime song or racket, if you prefer, of the crickets, locusts (whether true locusts, which are the migratory grasshoppers, or the loud, single-winged cicadas, I could not say), and possible katydids from the treetops. There are a lot of trees, big trees, where we live; therefore, there is a lot of noise made within their canopies in the summer. Oh, and let's not forget a favorite of the Southwest, particularly among mischief-seeking boys and girls alike: the June bug, belonging to the beetle family. A rather harmless insect with pincer-type claws on the ends of its tiny legs, especially pesky around lights; it can wreak havoc when it inadvertently lands on someone.

My parents were brave enough one year to take three neighborhood girls along with us to the Texas State Fair. We quickly separated from my parents and hit the midway hot and heavy, spending the entire twenty bucks given to me on the rides, save for splitting a cheeseburger with one of my friends, so I didn't have to spend more than I absolutely had to on food. We headed home that night in a blinding rainstorm with my dad a nervous wreck at the wheel during the hour-long drive, as the four of us wrestled and tickled each other all the way home in spite of my father's repeated threats to pull the car over. *Yeah, right, Dad. It's pouring rain outside—like you're gonna get out of the car and make us do the same.* Besides, once the June bug was discovered in the backseat and thrown around at each other, latching onto our thighs in order to catch its balance, it was lost cause of getting us to "settle down."

The bugs in the trees were a gentle reminder, a connection to memories of what used to be my favorite time of the year, summertime. Running barefoot down my grandparents' white-rock driveway only got easier as the summer progressed, and my feet got tougher due to the fact that they never saw shoes until Sunday morning, and, by Sunday dinner, they were off until the next week. The humming in the trees was just something we took for granted while chasing fireflies, or "lightning bugs," as we used to call them. It was the background song of our summer play during nighttime games of hide-and-seek until, one by one, our parents called us home from the front porch door or at the edge of the driveway. Running hard to tag the neighbor's decorative gas lamp in the frontyard as base, I'm sure we interrupted the buzzing insects as we swung around on the pole, *safe* at home. Occasionally, when it was just about time to go in for the night, we could hear a whirring sound coming from the end of the street moving ever closer to us. The object advancing on us had colored lights emanating from it like a UFO. We stood mesmerized until with glee we recognized the mosquito man and were drawn to its DDT mist like moths to the flame. We chased him down the street, lost in the colored fog until he turned the corner, leaving us coughing and laughing at the scent left on our clothes and in our hair.

Whether chasing down the mosquito man or the sound coming from the ice cream truck, summertime was all about being outside and experiencing it with all five senses in heightened mode. Maybe that explained the need for bare feet. Ice cream and watermelon never tasted better, and cut grass never smelled so good (or tasted better, as we sat in it and chewed on the ends of Saint Augustine, discussing our plans for the day). The feel of clover under our feet, vast starry skies we stared up into while lying in the grass, hands behind our heads, spent from a hard day's work of play and pretend, with the sound of the television and conversations spilling out into the yard through screen doors. They were all a part of the symphony of summer. Summertime play made it hard for me to come inside, particularly when certain duties were expected, particularly when the piano had set lonely for too long, according to my parents.

I returned home from school one day to find a weird reflection staring back at me through the darkened front porch screen door. It was the mirror strip along the top of a secondhand upright piano that had been placed against the back wall of our front living room. Without my permission, my mom had gone out and purchased a piano and had signed me up for lessons. The piano was the largest piece of furniture in the house. As kids, we used to climb up on the thing, but the very top narrowed, so you couldn't actually sit on it. It had a narrow, red velvet strip that ran along the back of the keyboard. It wasn't exactly elegant, but it was mine. So I could see to practice, my mom purchased a gold-finished, adjustable-arm lamp that sat upon the high ledge of the light brown piano.

One early fall day, I was dropped off at the home of Mrs. Turner for my first lesson, whereupon entering through the side studio entrance door, I encountered an old black, baby grand piano that Mrs. Turner had played since she was sixteen years old. It was the first time I had ever seen one up close, and I was invited to sit down at it and learn the difference between quarter and half notes playing C and D with my right hand, C and B with my left hand, back and forth. I would enter that studio entrance many times over the next four years, often grudgingly after my short walk from my school down the block, and leave exhilarated and exhausted, only to dread my long walk home.

If Miss Peggy was the epitome of a ballet mistress bent on perfection, the same could be said for Mrs. Turner when it came to the piano. We were expected to take group theory classes as well as our private lessons each week. She penciled instructions all over the page, had us fill out a practice log, and constantly corrected bad posture while at the piano.(I had a bad habit of intertwining my legs so they resembled a pretzel.) But she also placed stickers at the top of each page after we completed a piece, awarded us with little ivory-colored miniature busts of classical composers at the end of the year, and made sure we took advantage of musical culture that came our way.

One Sunday afternoon at the request of Mrs. Turner, my mother dropped me off at Austin College, the liberal arts university in the center of town, to see Handel's *Messiah* performed by the college choir and civic symphony. I was in the sixth grade, and I took a friend along. Sitting on the front row in the balcony, darkness all around us except for the lighted stage, I remember my friend's taking the program from me and studying it closely during the singing of the Hallelujah chorus. She finally turned to me and urgently whispered in my ear, "It doesn't say Hallelujah that many times!" After telling my mother about the incident, she was a little put-out with me for taking my simple-minded friend. "I knew that was not the kind of thing she would have enjoyed or even understood," she said.

Our recitals took place in Mrs. Turner's home and were every bit as big of a deal as our annual participation in Piano Guild (a judged contest whereupon we played a memorized program before a professional musician or a music teacher and received a report card, suitable for framing, that designated our level of achievement). For recitals, our parents sat in chairs either confiscated from the dining room or folding ones that were rented, arranged in rows within the formal living room, facing the piano. Students sat in folded chairs arranged in rows within the studio, on the other side of the piano facing the mob of parents. We were placed next to one another based on our level of performance. Mrs. Turner always sat on a low chair facing the back of the performing pianist with her head bowed. The tension (or excitement, depending on our age and general outlook) mounted as we waited our turn to play the two memorized pieces printed in the program next to our names. I usually sat next to Amy D., a tall, gentle-mannered girl who carried herself a little hunched over due to her discomfort level with her obtained height. She was a grade older and played a bit better than me.

During one recital, Amy got lost in the middle of a piece, completely befuddled to the point that she had to turn around and implore Mrs. Turner for help. I sat and watched in horror as (*Egad!*) Mrs. Turner had to get up and retrieve Amy's music for her so she could continue playing. Amy's face was bright red underneath the blonde curls that fell around her down-turned head. A nervous hush followed Amy's final note, but Mrs. Turner had a way with the parents. She drew relieved laughs from everyone by theatrically proclaiming in that husky Lauren Bacall voice of hers, "Well, you know what they say: at least she didn't fall off the bench." Relief was not an understatement. We students knew the frustration that Mrs. Turner openly exhibited during our lessons, as well as the performance level she expected—or desired—from us.

Mrs. Turner was an avid smoker. Memory does not serve me properly to recall her actually blowing smoke rings around our heads, or ashtrays loaded with extinguished butts on top of the piano, but she spoke in a cigarette-laced voice. We all knew she smoked. During lessons, she had a characteristic ritual of annoyance that corresponded to her mounting frustration with our ineptitude at the piano, obviously due to lack of practice time. (I was known to lie a time or two in my practice log.) She would start out by pursing her lips together as you stumbled through a piece. After asking you to repeat a troubled section, she would let out an exasperated sigh as things were clearly not improving. Stuck in the middle of some blasted piece by Bach, you cringed when she finally turned her head away from you toward the wall with one elbow on the piano, slapping her thigh with the other hand. She never actually said it, but you could almost hear her think, "*God, I wish I had a cigarette!*"

Nevertheless, Mrs. Turner had high hopes for me; she made sure I entered all the regional competitions, praised me for my efforts and accomplishments, and instilled in me an appreciation and recognition for greatness. Some years back, Mom sent me a newspaper clipping of Mrs. Turner's obituary. She had lived many years past her retirement from teaching music. In fact, during my stint at Austin College, she and her husband frequented the private club and restaurant where I waited tables. They ate Mexican food, sipped on margaritas without salt, and never asked for an ashtray. The last time I drove by her house, the familiar side studio entrance door was almost covered by overgrown hedges on either side, the peeling gold and black letters, STUDIO, still visible underneath the curtained window of the door.

I was to be reminded of Mrs. Turner one unexpected Sunday afternoon in July, the year my mother died. During the preceding months, beginning at the end of March, I had picked up my cello and made a stab at playing it again. I had started cello lessons once before, while the kids were involved in string lessons given through the music program at the University of Texas at San Antonio. Just around the corner from us, the kids learned cello and violin during group lessons given by the music majors and even the head of the music department, through a grant the college had received. I thought I might as well take some lessons for myself so I could participate with the kids and keep them encouraged in their playing.

I found a young man named John, who had actually studied at the same college, but had stopped just short of obtaining his degree in music to pursue a career in teaching students of his own. He was an excellent cellist and affirmed me in my quest to learn a difficult instrument. He thought it was very doable. I looked forward to my lessons in his apartment while his wife bathed or played with their adorable, rambunctious son, Fritz, doing her best to keep him from interrupting us. I did my best to prepare, but I struggled with my schedule and practice time. John was very patient, realizing I had a lot on my plate, for John also enjoyed the idea of teaching an adult. So often, instead of playing and working through a piece to completion, we ended up talking politics or discussing matters that may or may not have had any relevance to music or the cello. I felt I never really mastered any aspect of playing, but I must give credit to John for introducing me to an instrument I couldn't leave behind. I packed my cello and moved it, along with my kids' instruments, into our new residence after leaving San Antonio. It stood next to my son's smaller cello in the corner of the study for roughly three years, untouched.

I managed to find private teachers for my kids in the small town where we had moved, and after a while my daughter's violin teacher became very interested in meeting with me to discuss my participation in an ensemble group. I didn't take her invitation seriously until after Mother died. Aching to make my mark in something/anything, I started meeting with Mrs. Williams one morning a week in her home for a lesson. Being a violin teacher, she admitted not knowing a lot about the cello but offered to help me with notes, timing, and rhythm. We struggled along together until she managed to find me a cello teacher somewhat close to home. Toward the end of May, I traveled an hour outside of town for my first cello lesson with David.

To say he and his wife lived a little off the beaten path might be an overstatement, but, considering I had to take a farm-to-market road off the highway in order to reach the white-rock road that led me to the house, hidden behind a fencerow and tall pasture grass, one could see where the description could apply. It was dusk by the time I arrived for my 8 o'clock appointment. Upon stepping out of the car, I was immediately greeted by the sounds of two turkeys in the tall grass just on the other side of the car and eight barking dogs scattered here and there around the property. I gingerly made my way to the house with my cello strapped to my back, avoiding a near heart attack when a huge barking dog lunged at me from behind some tall grass only to be jerked back by the unrelenting chain he was on. Like something out of the British comedy series *Keeping Up Appearances,* this scene would repeat itself every time I arrived for a lesson.

A smiling young man welcomed me. He sported jeans and a blond ponytail. His wife, Claire, wore the same ponytail, only of a different color, and a long blue jean skirt instead of regular jeans. At first glance, they resembled a pair of hippies, but the term "earthy" is probably more appropriate. Claire, a principal violinist, and David, a principal cellist with the same civic symphony, both teach and play in various ensemble groups together when they are not caring for a large menagerie of animals, including their house bunny and the cat that prefers my cello case to nap in during our playing time. Like John, David was immediately encouraging and honored my desire to learn the cello (all over again), and so we sat down to the task at hand of simply re-learning how to hold the bow properly. I struggled along.

Mrs. Williams was ecstatic and insisted I play with her students during their group lesson every other week. She further insisted I play in the recital with her students a little less than two months from beginning my first real cello lesson in over three years. So, there I sat one Sunday afternoon, slap dab in the middle of a bunch of violinists and viola players in a little Baptist church where prayer was offered up before the start of the program. *Thank God!*

Instead of facing my parents, I faced my husband and our two youngest children; my oldest daughter was one of the violinists on stage. I sat in the middle on the back row, next to a young girl who played a lovely viola, and prayed for a good sound during my harmonizing parts. Sitting up there, pretending I knew what I was doing, felt a little bit like a piece Mrs. Williams had given me to read entitled, "Mid-life and the Cello," by Christian Williams, a staff writer for *The Washington Post.* Thinking I might relate to someone else taking up the cello later in life (although I have problems with someone calling himself middle aged at thirty-five), she had hoped to inspire me, but what I found most amusing was a description of an ensemble performance that took place in a church during a rainstorm in the author's fifth year of study.

Just as his bow touched the string to begin the first movement, a thunder clap hit the church with such force that he could hear nothing. Obviously not as experienced as the other musicians around him, he was momentarily stunned and lost his place as the others carried on, unruffled.

> I tried to play, find my place, rejoin my comrades, but in vain. The Niagara above thrummed too loudly. Sweat appeared on my brow as I surveyed the raccoon eyes of the dimly lit audience closely watching. Mortified and lost, I could only raise the bow a few inches above the strings, paste a beatific smile on my puss, and pantomime a happy, confident cellist while not making a sound.

Worked for me.

After the recital, I asked my husband if my squeaks were too noticeable. He replied with something like, "Everybody squeaked. Yours were no more noticeable than any of the others." That was good enough for me. I headed to the reception in the church parlor for punch and homemade desserts with my head held somewhat higher. The exhilaration I felt over having the thing behind me while drinking punch that Sunday afternoon reminded me of eating cookies in Mrs. Turner's kitchen after one of my piano recitals. It had been thirty-six years since I had last played music before an audience.

Some months later, David asked if I might consider taking part in his wife's recital for her violin students; he and I would play a cello duet. Apparently, an "older student" needed some encouragement to participate; she was the mom of a violin student, just like me. On a cold, blustery day just before the holiday season, we assembled in an old country church with wooden floors and a tin roof. Claire's students, including the "beginner mom," performed beautifully. David and I were the only cellists, and all went well with our performance until my brain and hands went in different directions for about two measures during the second piece. Thank God it was a duet. Upon leaving the stage area, I whispered to David, "Well, you know what they say: at least she didn't fall off the bench." He smiled graciously. He didn't get it.

The sounds of my first summer without Mom: bugs in the trees, rock and roll from the '70s, squawks and squeaks from the cello, and 1940s Frank Sinatra hits playing in the kitchen. Sometimes, well, pretty much most of the time, the cello was pretty pathetic. I tried to practice away from everybody, waiting until my husband went out to the garage before attempting long bow exercises. It wasn't the piano, but I couldn't go back even though a beautiful baby grand now stood in my own front room. Cello lessons were another escape for me. On Mondays around 7 p.m., I loaded the big instrument into our old Alfa Romeo convertible, made sure the top was down, and headed out of town with the songs from my husband's iPod Shuffle blaring in my ears. (The radio in the car didn't work.) During the hour-long drive, to and from my lesson, I was somebody else. Come playing time for David, reality hit home, and I was a struggling beginner. But I found comfort in other strings as well.

On hot, sultry nights, I retreated to our upper floor where I had carved out a personal space for creative thought and reflection. In the niche of the middle dormer on the top floor, I placed a desk against the wall, hung a homemade collage above it, and decorated it with various odds and ends. It held everything from decorated bottles to a paperweight and pencil holder, and I hung up a plaque in the same corner:

> LIFE
> is not a journey to the grave with
> the intentions of arriving safely
> in a pretty and well preserved body,
> but rather to skid in broadside,
> totally worn out and proclaiming,
> "WOW, WHAT A RIDE!"

It was there I wrote in my journal and attempted poetry while listening to a CD of English string music from the twentieth century. *Variants on Dives and Lazarus,* a set of variations on old folk tunes, includes some of the most beautiful, moving music. I listened to it for inspiration while tucked away with a glass of red wine. The work is based on a ballad of the parable of Lazarus and the rich man who refused to offer alms to him as he begged outside his door. It reminded me more of a mournful song of the Old South. The music conveyed to me imagery of war-torn Confederate soldiers returning home to all that was lost or burned. I have no idea why. The cellos all but weep in some of those pieces while the rest of the strings rise and fall, eventually ending in some the most beautiful resolutions. The music was mournful; it was sad, but I found comfort and dreamed of being more while listening.

I wonder if that's what Mom had in mind all along. Signing me up for piano lessons and keeping music on in the house at all times. It's not that she exclusively introduced me to the classics. I was far more likely to hear the hits from Henry Mancini or various movie soundtracks such as *Dr. Zhivago* being played on the stereo, but she gave me opportunities that were not available to her. I had been escaping into music for the past eight months in my van, in the kitchen, or in my upstairs hideaway, but, by actually attempting to play music again, maybe I was honoring Mom by drawing the fantasy closer: to be more, to attempt more. Mom had always been aware of the dreamer inside me; she had left me alone to pretend unabashedly. She had always applauded my attempts at creativity whether silly or not, successful or not.

By finding solace in the strings and great music from the past, I was also becoming more attuned to the other sounds around me that I had blocked out for sometime: the bugs in the trees, everyday conversations, the hum of the air conditioner, the laughter of my children. During a hot July with soaring gas prices, the sounds of summer had finally arrived.

One morning during our string practice, Mrs. Williams pulled a John on me. Instead of playing music, she wanted to convey her deeply felt sorrow over the loss of my mother. Mrs. Williams had lost her husband to pulmonary failure the preceding spring. "Sherry, I've lost two husbands in my lifetime, but I believe losing my mother was even harder." She started to cry. Being close to my parents' age, she had to have lost her mom sometime back. At the time, I really didn't want to talk about it. I just sat there and nodded, but I think she was trying to tell me that the psychological impact of losing a mother is pretty universal, and *it runs deep.*

August

*G*as prices that continued to climb in the summer forced our family on a road trip to California in place of purchasing airline tickets for five. We had recently relieved our old red minivan of duty after 205,000-plus miles and had replaced it with a blue one that was begging to be tried out over deserted stretches of highway between Texas and the Pacific coast. We made certain preparations to ensure my sanity: all iPods were charged, TVs were working, and selected DVDs were in their cases and agreed upon by all who would be riding in the back; also, we would only travel on the interstate, so Starbucks could be easily accessed however often I saw necessary. It was a far cry from some memories of *earlier* family vacations indelibly imprinted on my psyche—memories of riding in the backseat by myself, bound for some far away geological national treasure, traveling on two-lane highways the entire way.

Nearly twelve years older than me, my brother had endured such a trip after completing the sixth grade. My parents took him to see the historical monuments in Washington, D.C. They thought he was of the age to appreciate the artifacts of American history. The long ride in the backseat of a 1961 white Falcon without air conditioning almost seemed worth it, hearing tales of his running to the top of the 897 stairs inside the Washington Monument. The illusionary picture of him standing in front of the reflection pool with his outstretched arm holding the monument in the palm of his hand is still cool after all these years, even though he is wearing Sunday-best black pants with a short-sleeved white cotton shirt tucked in.

Some of the longest days of my life I recall were on our family trip to Yellowstone National Park in the *way-up-there* state of Wyoming. It was the summer of 1968. My brother was stationed overseas with the Air Force, so I traveled alone with my parents in our light brown 1967 four-door Chevrolet Malibu. The car is worth noting, because it had a mind of its own. An intermittent mechanical glitch resulted in this irritating jerk that felt like a hiccup. Various mechanics failed to diagnose this problem. When the car's jerking reached violent proportions, my dad would pull over to the side of the road, get out a wrench (which he carried at all times for this one purpose), open the hood of the car, and bang on anything metal he could find. Sometimes this would take several stops, but eventually the jerking would subside for the next 350 miles or so. It always happened on a road trip.

Ah, the days of AM radio exclusively manned by the frontseat occupants (my parents), non-tinted windows, optional seat belts, and two-lane highways that seemed to stretch on forever. I remember the one-sided conversations that went on between my dad and other cars on the road: "Looks like he would pull over after while!" "Is he going to let me by or what?" "Doesn't he know what the shoulder is for?" and on and on. Then there was my mother, trying to read the map, the arguments that ensued over missed turns, the resigned pull-overs to the side of the road to figure out where we were and where we had gone wrong. The trauma of having to exit, turn around, and go back to where we were still haunts me to this day, perhaps explaining my own behavior when I have to backtrack. From my perspective as a kid, I couldn't understand all the lamenting over having to turn around; they carried on as if we'd be lost for days: no hope, no return. And soon the debate turned to where we would stop to eat and, later, where we would spend the night.

More one-sided conversations took place between my father and waitresses who, thank God, never overheard him: "Can't she see me waiting here?" "I wish she would bring the check!" "You'd think she would notice I need a refill." I suffered the trauma of waiting for coffee refills for my mother, who always insisted on ordering coffee on the road though it was never hot enough, either too strong or not strong enough. The imprinted memory of the check arrival, *the blessed check arrival*—such impatience punctured the air, you would have thought we had been waiting for hours. These roadside café experiences were enough to keep me hopping energetically from table to table during my own years of waitressing. I was always trying to remember to deliver the check promptly between running back and forth among my other tables, the kitchen, and the bar for food and drink orders. As a result of my own experiences, I'm a good tipper and am annoyed easily when others in my company grow impatient with the waitstaff. I know full well that *they* have never waited tables and are unaware that tensions and stress in the restaurant business can be likened to working in the emergency room. I know, because I've worked in both. People can be *that* ugly over their food and drink orders.

Then there was the business of finding a motel for the night. It always had to be a motel. My father always said he hated having to go through a hotel lobby dragging all our old luggage in front of everybody. Dad always made sure I had time to swim before dinner, so around 5 o'clock we would begin to scour the neon signs for the cheaper prices, vacancy and pool availability (preferably heated, the further north we traveled). No breezeways; we may have been staying in a room with cinder-block walls, but even Dad had his standards. God forbid if the air conditioner didn't work properly: too much noise, not cold enough, which seemed to plague us more times than I would like to remember. And then there was the Alka-Seltzer frenzy.

For years, my dad suffered from such bouts of indigestion that we all thought he was having "the big one." On road trips, this became a particularly big problem while he navigated the highways and roadside cafes; he seemingly was always either out of his Alka-Seltzer or couldn't locate the ones he had brought along for the trip, stashed somewhere down inside the console tray. We were frequently on a mission to track down the little blue and silver tinfoil packet that "spelled relief." Alka-Seltzer was such a part of my childhood that I actually memorized their commercials word for word and even pretended I starred in a few.

Staying in motels on the way to some destination in the middle of nowhere was as memorable to me as the actual vacation itself. Dad only allowed himself a week of vacation in the summer, so because we usually took two days to get wherever we were going, we usually ended up staying at our destination only two to three days at the most. After the two-day drive home, Dad needed to rest on Sunday before returning to work Monday morning. "Gotta work, kid," he would always say when I complained about the short stay, dreading the long return trip. I was the only kid at home. Why my parents never thought of letting me bring a friend along on trips, I'll never know, but, that being the case, I made many a poolside friend along the way. We would usually end up exchanging addresses and, after the first postcard received, telling each other what we did after summer vacation, what grade we were starting, the names of our dogs, etc., we would end up neglecting any future correspondence and slip from each other's consciousness.

Even though we did not end up exchanging addresses, I still remember the natural comedic style of one boy I met while staying at a motel. It was either in Lubbock, Texas, after returning from our Wyoming trip, or it could have been in Eureka Springs, Arkansas, after returning from seeing some of my parents' friends in Iowa; all the trips run together after a while. Slender and black-headed, the boy was so impulsive and unabashed about making a friendship right out. While swimming together he informed me that the water must be dirty because every time he went underwater he said as many bad words as he could. I can barely see his face, but he's one of many vacation moments, one in which I unexpectedly laughed a lot.

Yellowstone itself did not disappoint. A grizzly bear marched alongside the car in front of us with his paws resting on the half-open window begging for more than just the one handout offered him. It afforded us a great picture while I'm sure at the same time it caused much alarm to the passenger seated next to the window. Old Faithful, the geyser that spews forth steaming hot water on a regular basis some ninety minutes apart from each eruption, was not a disappointment either, particularly the day it decided to spray on the crowd instead of straight up as usual. A vivid image—of grown women tripping backward over the natural logs provided for seating and people scrambling up the hill trying to get away from the spewing steam that smelled of rotten eggs—remains quite intact in my brain. Our stay was short, and the ride was long, but if I thought riding to Yellowstone was a chore, I was in for another treat the following summer when my parents proudly announced we were going to see the Grand Canyon.

In the 1983 movie *National Lampoon's Vacation*, Chevy Chase's character, trying to avoid further scandal over a pocketbook foul-up, hurries his family for a quick picture in front of the Grand Canyon after a long, arduous road trip, before piling them all back in the station wagon to be on their way. The scene rang a familiar bell the first time I saw it. I suffered in the backseat of that jerking Malibu, traveling through miles of road construction in the Painted Desert while looking out the window trying to spot Gila monsters, only to meet the same fate as the Griswold children after finally arriving at the cavernous phenomenon. We got out of the car, stared down into the canyon where the donkeys were making their way along the trail, ambled through the souvenir shop looking for some trinkets, then got back in the car to search for a motel with cheap rates and a pool, my dad popping Alka-Seltzer along the way. If there were not a picture of me sitting on a rock in front of *it*, with my white jeans and gold button-down shirt on, I would hardly believe I had even been to the famous landmark. I do remember looking longingly at the donkeys, with their passengers and trail packs, making their slow descent along the walls and wishing we could go with them and stay overnight in the canyon. We hadn't arranged for that kind of stay. "Gotta work, kid."

When planning for our family trip to California, my husband suggested we make a side trip to see the Grand Canyon. "No, but hell no," was my reply.

So, one Saturday morning in August we set out for California, only about thirty minutes past the scheduled time of departure, as usual. Within the first hour of the trip, not even out of the county yet, we encountered a large black dog on a suicide mission. He came barreling toward us from the left, across the divided highway, as my husband hit the brakes and swerved to the right. The dog continued heading straight toward us. There was nothing left to do but listen for the rumbling underneath the car. At seventy miles an hour, it sounded and felt as if we had hit a large boulder in the middle of the road. The kids looked up from their movie and iPod to see what had just happened. I didn't even turn around to see what was left behind. Just hearing it was bad enough. When we stopped for lunch (the first argument of the trip occurred over eating at a sit-down restaurant versus turning around and eating at one of the fast-food joints located off the exit we had just passed), we discovered that the collision had knocked loose the license plate and dented the front bumper. This complemented the nice scrape down the left side of the van I had acquired a month or so after purchasing it. The impact also caused a tiny hole in the air conditioner condenser to the tune of $600, but it would be sometime before we discovered that.

All in all, the ride to California was not terrible. I guess we had braced ourselves for miles of desert terrain and countless times of being asked, "Are we there yet?" and "How much longer till we get there?" What I found to be more remarkable was the fact that I was able to sit in the front seat, enclosed in a small space over a long period of time with others (others, meaning my family) and be fairly at peace with the situation.

Distancing myself from my family in particular and friends had become pretty commonplace. I was used to being around them as of late, but in small increments only. I had learned to survive the ongoing presence of family by carving up the day into running kids to and from their activities, busying myself around the house at night, and stealing away to the top story with a glass of wine to read or write when bedtime came around. Before school had let out for the summer, I had been nervous about the prospect of not being able to tolerate being around the kids without the distraction of scheduled activities and school hours. I had craved aloneness during the previous winter months. My youngest daughter had been my tether, requiring that I deliver her and pick her up from preschool three mornings a week. She held me accountable for such things as getting her lunch, meeting her insistent demands, and generally just paying attention to her when all I had wanted to do was run away. I wanted to be somebody else, somewhere else.

Distancing myself from those closest to me seemed to be just a part of my makeup, going back to when I was much younger. I distinctly remember the day when I knew it was time to put some space between my mother and myself. The summer before my sixth grade school year, I was getting ready to attend the backyard birthday of a good friend, Wendy. I was not yet twelve years old. Maybe it coincided with my general awareness of how rapidly things were changing in the world around me, but it suddenly felt *uncool* being around my parents; thus, I decided all in the space of one afternoon, to separate a little, both physically and emotionally, from them. Of course, I continued to go places with my family and interact with them as a family unit, but the emotional distancing from my mother would be a pattern I would choose for myself well into my adult years. At times I would seek out her advice, look forward to out-of-town visits, lunches, and outings that the two of us enjoyed—all the normal things families do, but not until I so desperately needed her during my depression would I fully drop my guard and open up to her.

It wasn't as if Mom had not been there for me all along. Mom had always encouraged me in my endeavors, exposed me to the arts and to opportunities that she never had, supported me in times of emotional and financial struggles, and played a vital role in the lives of my children. Even greater, she had stood by and chosen not to interfere when I made life-changing decisions for the good or bad. But our relationship was forged when she became the *rock* in my darkest hour. After that, memories made with her were all the more special, probably because I stopped holding her at arms' length. Such was the case with the birth of my youngest daughter.

Mom chose to sit in the chair next to me throughout the delivery, and I was comfortable with that, whereas before that might not have been the case for the both of us. It was almost as if she recognized the significance of the moment, unaware of future limitations she would face. I had wished for a girl from the start of my unexpected pregnancy. I wanted the chance to name her after my mother. Aubry Alla Elise was named for both grandmothers, the two middle names belonging to them. Alla was my mother's first name. (All three names are applied as the situation warrants it. Names are tacked on one after the other as my frustration mounts, till I finally end up with the whole shebang, "Aubry Alla Elise Scott!") More than just naming my last child after her, life seemed to bring more opportunities for closure and resolution for us right up until the time of her death.

᧦

Our geographical destination was Camp Pendleton, a Marine Corps base on the Pacific coast that encompasses some four hundred square miles between San Diego and Los Angeles on Interstate 5. The entrance gate to where my son and his new little family were assigned was just across the Pacific Highway from San Clemente, California. His new position as a School of Infantry instructor guaranteed him a two-year stint there and new base housing overlooking the Pacific Ocean. The morning after our arrival, he began his first rotation as an instructor with a new class of boot camp graduates; to this day, my son will say he preferred Iraq over Marine Corps boot camp. He spent the next three days and nights in the field with his "boys" while we played in the sand, explored San Clemente, and saw Disneyland for the first time.

Though we sought out quality time to catch up, meeting him for lunch, taking him and his wife out for a special dinner, I was somewhat relieved in a way that he wasn't around so much. I had been afraid Aaron would notice certain changes in me that had bothered him when he visited at Christmas, had persisted and even escalated. I wasn't up to being questioned as to why I needed a glass of wine or two every night before going to sleep. He had always been an expert at pushing my buttons. I blamed the conflicts that would spring up between us, apart from anybody else, on the prolonged periods of separation and our ensuing re-familiarization. It had become a pretty standard ritual with us; this had been going on since he was very young.

I was a single parent of eleven years that spanned the '80s. Child-rearing trends of that time period included: "Quality of time spent with your child is more important than the quantity"—a soother for those of us working mothers—and "It's not enough to tell your child *because I said so.* You should explain your reasons for the limitations you impose upon them. Open give-and-take communication should be your goal." It sounded good enough, but what ensued throughout Aaron's upbringing was a prolonged debate over boundary setting. I was constantly on the defense, being called upon to give reason after reason for my decisions, inwardly rationalizing my guilt while this kid pummeled me with further demands and questions until I finally blew up. It did not help the situation that his two sets of grandparents, on whom I depended greatly for babysitting and support while working and going to school, spoiled him rotten. My dad was the absolute worst; I don't know if he ever told the kid "no" to anything. Aaron loved nothing more than manipulating the situation between me and my parents. He could shift into victim mode in a second to gain sympathy and get his way, or at least cause a big scene in an attempt to get his way.

The relationship between my oldest son and me is best depicted in the American comedy television series, *Malcolm in the Middle*, which ran for seven seasons beginning in 2000. We are a dead ringer for the overbearing mom, played by actress Jane Kaczmarek, and her rebellious oldest son, Francis. Aaron and I have exchanged exactly the same lines of dialogue as the two of them did in many scenes. My husband could never understand how we could have these huge, demonstrative blowups one minute, patch it up, and go on as if nothing had happened the next minute. It's what we became over the years.

When Aaron was thirteen years old, I remarried and promptly set about starting a new family. My outlook had changed dramatically, and I had learned a few things. Three kids later, when they come to me about a decision I've made and attempt to push the matter further, wanting to know why, I snap, "Because I said so, that's why!"

Whether due to Aaron's absence or to the fact we both had resolved to behave, surprisingly there was no conflict and no psychoanalysis over how much I had changed. Instead, I enjoyed learning more about his new job while staying in his home. Just like Francis in the sitcom, he had grown up, married, and had become very disciplined and dedicated to his role as an officer/instructor and family man. But just like on any vacation, there were some glitches, and this time instead of Aaron's being the source of frustration in a debated point, it turned out to be the cops.

The next-to-last day of our stay, I drove the family into San Clemente for some shopping. About to pull out onto the main drag from a side street I sat and contemplated how to navigate, based on a sign in front of me. On the one hand, it read, "No left turn," but, on the other hand, it featured a huge arrow pointing left, indicating that the road was split. I needed to turn left, so I thought about just going for it. (I'm known for ignoring directions I don't see the point in anyway.) Just then, a police car came cruising down the street we were facing. My husband warned, "Don't do it." So, I regretfully turned right, went down the street for a short distance, and pulled into a parking lot to turn around, so I could go back in the direction I needed to be going. I passed the same cop along the way coming in the opposite direction and looked up in my rearview mirror just in time to see him whip around in the middle of the street and come after me. I pulled over to the side of the road, certain I was not speeding, which is usually the case.

He was a no-nonsense kind of guy with a military crew cut. He questioned me about how I ended up going in this direction since he had passed me at the intersection, "Did you make a U-turn?" "No, sir," and I proceeded to explain my confusion over the sign and how I had avoided turning left and went down the street a piece so I could turn around. He stuck his face in my window. "But you thought about turning left, didn't you?" I thought to myself, *Here I am in California where the TV show* Cops *is regularly filmed, and I'm going to get in trouble for* thinking *about making a wrong turn!* "Where are you heading?" he asked after looking over the van and realizing that, despite the Texas plates, everybody inside looked bizarrely normal. "Down to the surf shop on the corner," I replied. After driving off slowly, without a ticket, I remarked to my husband, "He must be bored—probably is an ex-Marine," for we had had our share of dealings with them as well.

Entering the base at the military checkpoint was a new experience every time depending on who was on duty. My son and daughter-in-law repeatedly reminded me not to speed on base: "They will ticket you in a minute." My husband must have encountered a rookie one day as he attempted to enter the base after a day spent on the beach. The state of California had just passed a law concerning *no cell phone usage while driving.* My husband is the least proponent of cell phone use *anytime.* For years, he resisted keeping his on to receive incoming calls, stating he only wanted to use the phone for his own convenience of dialing out, not to be reached by others. He had eventually desisted, and, on this particular day, I had called to inform him I was stopping for Chinese take-out. (We were on our way back to my son's home in separate cars.) The call took no more than five seconds while he was coming off the freeway. He was off the phone by the time he pulled up to the base entrance. The young Marine on duty remarked to him that he had seen him on the cell phone while on the access road and told him to pull over in the designated parking spaces next to the checkpoint station. He then proceeded to hand my husband a ticket for $75 for *seeing him on the cell phone, before even arriving at the base entrance,* which my husband graciously accepted!

I was livid. I was less angry at the young Marine than I was at my husband, for taking the ticket without even putting up an argument.

"I was scared of the guy—he had a gun on him," he explained. There seemed to be some role-reversal phenomenon going on. First, the interrogating cop acted as if he wanted to return to his days as a DI with the Marine Corps, and now some young Marine wanted to play traffic cop on the California freeway. I ranted to my son that evening, "I would have ended up in the brig. There's no way I would have taken that ticket. Does he realize the price of gas and how much it took for us to get out here? He thinks he needs to fund the Marine Corps with my money? I already support them. I drove all the way out here to see a Marine, didn't I? Couldn't he see Texas plates on the van?" My son just listened and shook his head.

Our last night of vacation was spent dining with our entire family on a pier, with the ocean lapping at the wooden supports underneath us. After dinner, away from everyone else, I held my grandson up to watch the train coming around the bend toward us as I had done every morning while we played on the beach. He excitedly pointed at it as it passed between us and the houses located up on the hills, trying to give it a name. I tried to grasp the significance of it as one of life's moments instead of pining for other times and places. This was where I needed to be for a little while until the long road heading back east would take me far away from my grandson, who represented the fruition of my labor to bring up a young man who would go further than I.

After a *full five days* of vacation in California, we headed out, the van packed with all our stuff and all our newly acquired stuff from the beach and Disney. We stopped to fill up with gas while still on the base, taking advantage of a $.05 savings per gallon; they at least owed us that. Interstate 8 led us out of California into the desert of Arizona where we picked up Interstate 10 somewhere at a junction near a little town called Arizola. Interstate 10 brought us over the Texas line at El Paso, leading us to home on the other side of the state, but not before we chocked up some more roadkill along the way.

In parts of New Mexico and far West Texas, Interstate 10 features long stretches where the terrain on either side of the road contains nothing except distant purple, mountainous foothills extending to the horizon. For miles and miles there is not a tree in sight, a blade of grass, or anything green for that matter, and the occasional tumbleweed is only there as the result of a distant dust storm that blows it your way. Out of scenery such as this, a black squirrel came running across the highway heading straight toward us, from nowhere in the middle of nowhere. Like a typical squirrel, it cleared our van's path, changed its mind, turned around, and came right back at us. *Smack.* My husband didn't even swerve the van to avoid it—just laughed out loud and kept driving. Hardened by the road, we were intent on getting home. I don't even think the kids looked up from their movie or iPod. At least it didn't dent the van or knock loose the license plate we had wired back in place.

Before leaving California, staring out at the Pacific Ocean as we drove along the coastline, my thoughts turned toward Aaron and how he had affected my life. As it probably is with all children who intrude into our lives: they cause us to expand. The important life experiences and choices I had made were a direct result of him. He had been the impetus for my setting career goals and achieving an education that eventually led me to medical school. His determination to join the Marine Corps, to which I had strongly objected, had afforded me the opportunity to experience and travel in a great state, one that I fell in love with during my first visit for boot camp graduation. And whether I was prepared or not, my first grandchild had forced me to look forward to a future that seemed a little less daunting whenever he was around. Every event that took place in my son's life had caused a reactive change in mine. So it is with life and death: the coming full circle, the interconnectedness of the two, and how we are constantly being shaped and remolded by both as they occur throughout our lifetimes.

I had survived the summer, a sentiment I never would have believed would come from me, a girl who had once adored summer months, never wanting them to leave. It had been a year since the August wedding that brought our extended family to California, Mom's last trip. Two families from Texas and California were united as we prepared for a union between my son and his bride that we had originally not thought possible. We had all danced in relief and celebration, passing around the baby, not yet a year old, dressed in a miniature tuxedo and red Keds sneakers. Even that hadn't seemed as daunting of a milestone as looking toward the rest of my life from this point. But I had learned to survive. I may have felt as if I couldn't breathe freely at times, may have felt caged and desperate, may have questioned all I ever was, but I had learned enough to keep me where I needed to be and live to see what life would continue to bring my way if I continued to look for it.

September

For me, September has always meant the beginning of a new school year, though schools in Texas have been reconvening in August for as long as I can remember, probably dating as far back to my days in high school. I can't clearly remember my first day of school—kindergarten, that is—but my first day in the first grade at Rosa Pearson Elementary I readily recall because of a certain boy by the name of Burl. Burl was also the name of my grandfather, the only other person I ever knew by that name. Burl sat in the back of the classroom, held on to his plastic horse, and cried the entire day. In Paris, Texas, 1966, kindergarten was elective. Many moms still stayed home during the day; hence, Burl had probably been home with Momma up until day one of the first grade. That memory stands in stark contrast to the scene I witnessed at my children's elementary school when dropping my son off for *his* first day of kindergarten. The kids all waved cheerfully goodbye as several moms stood "boo-hooing" into their Kleenexes just outside the classroom. Even so, it's *my* year in kindergarten that comes to mind when recalling some of school's most significant events.

Robert Fulghum's book, *All I Really Need to Know I Learned in Kindergarten,* is a collection of "uncommon thoughts on common things." It contains various tales from his life experiences. He begins the book with a list of simple, moral rules of etiquette he learned in kindergarten, that if followed would serve us all well as a guide throughout the rest of our adult lives. Included in the list are rules such as "play fair"; "don't take things that aren't yours"; "don't hit people"; and, my personal favorite, "flush." I love the fact that this formative year serves as the basis for relating to stories of his other life events. Bill Cosby once called kindergarten, "The best year ever!" I quite agree.

My year in kindergarten was, in a word, magical. Perhaps I remember it as such because the school no longer exists. I had been away for many years until I was finally able to track down the address of Mrs. Grace Baker while looking through an old city directory in the local library. Mrs. Baker, a widow, lived on Pine Bluff Street in a "huge" Victorian home and ran her one-room school in a small white framed building located behind her house: Mrs. Baker's Little School. As a child, I thought she lived in a mansion. As it turned out, the house was an old two-story with an attic, devoid of any turrets or extremely high walls as I had remembered it. From the dilapidated front of the house and the general run-down feel of the neighborhood, it looked to be occupied by renters. Although the little white building out back was no longer there, the stone steps leading up to the covered porch were still there, giving testament that it had really existed and wasn't something I had just dreamt.

Back in its day, Paris' Pine Bluff Street was lined with beautiful, well-kept, Victorian houses that were home to the some of the town's most influential families. While staring out the window from the backseat, I always knew we were getting close to school when we passed a large yellow-and-white two-story home on the corner that had a sunroom off the front of the house; it was more gorgeous and finer than anything I had ever seen. Walking alongside Mrs. Baker's house on her rock driveway toward our little school in the back, I remember looking *way up* into the second-story windows with their heavy glass panes and dark screens, wondering what was in all those rooms up there. As impressive as Mrs. Baker's house was, it was the simple magic of the school itself that held such rich memories for me. The first and most important rule I remembered was to run "one way"; this was impressed upon us so thoroughly the first day that it was a rare occasion if this rule was ever forgotten or conveniently ignored.

The rule made perfect sense even to our young minds because of the way the house was situated. After passing through the small wooden gate, the yard in front of the school contained plenty of space for running and games, and off the right corner of the school stood two enormous swing sets. But a narrow path, wide enough for single file only, went around the right corner of the house and behind it. The path, bordered by a wooden fence and a thicket of vines, came around sharply at the left back corner of the house. If we were to meet someone running from the other direction it would mean an automatic collision, something kids were prone to anyway while in the middle of a game of chase. I smile at my reluctance to obey such rules now, probably because I don't see the same need for them. They don't make as much sense as Mrs. Baker's list of dos and don'ts.

In a neighborhood off our downtown area, there are several one-way streets that are narrow but can easily accommodate two cars. Different sources give different reasons why these streets are marked one-way. Some say they were put in place many years ago to dissuade drag racing; others say it was to help with the ambulance routes. Whatever the reason, they make absolutely no sense, because they are barely traveled. I smile and wave at the homeowners sitting on the porches as they feverishly flag me down, pointing to the one-way street signs on their corner. *No worry, I'm probably only the third car to pass by here the whole day, and I've got a clear view two hundred yards away. I don't think I'll hit anybody.* And just in case I meet someone, a quick turn down the side street will lead me back to Pine Bluff.

Our little school was a long, rectangular room with an old upright piano on one end and a step-up area at the other end with a small bathroom off to the side. I never ventured into the bathroom and had no intention of ever going in there, because a kid by the name of Kelly was repeatedly taken there for bad behavior. Sometimes Mrs. Baker arranged all the chairs in an oval that encompassed the room, and, at other times, she grouped the tables and chairs throughout the room in sets of four. Several block-paned windows and a set of French doors stood along the back wall, immediately facing the small front door. I recall linoleum floors, a large chalkboard, and the colors mint green and turquoise; I think the piano and its small round stool were painted a light green.

I carpooled to kindergarten every morning with a neighborhood girl who lived two blocks away. Her name was Suzy. Suzy was nearly a year behind me in age but was still eligible to be in the same class, which irritated me in a way. Even more annoying was the fact that she tagged along behind me incessantly due to her shy ways. Every day she followed me into our school and sat next to wherever I sat in our prearranged little wooden chairs with spindle backs. All except one day.

In 1965, Christmas decorations of any sort were rarely displayed in homes and schools until the two designated weeks before Christmas Day. Halloween was Halloween, and Thanksgiving was Thanksgiving. There was no intermingling of the other holidays with Christmas: it stood on its own. Sometime in December, the stores would start putting out their aluminum Christmas trees and decorations, and our neighborhood grocer would start displaying toys above the produce bins. So, we did not think it unusual that, on the day before our Christmas holidays were to begin, our school would finally be decorated for the seasonal party; we just didn't realize how transforming it would be.

Upon arriving that morning, the first thing that grabbed our attention was the *lollipop forest* that was displayed on the wall. It was nothing more than some kind of box covered in tinfoil that had Christmas tree–shaped lollipops sticking out of the surface, but we had learned a song about the "Lollipop Forest," and, when the time came to sing it, Mrs. Baker's assistant, Miss Chess, handed the lollipops to us in the middle of our glorious chorus. The real stunner was the tree. It stood atop one of the wooden tables in the corner. It was flocked in pink and white with twinkly lights all over and a glittery tree skirt at the bottom. Well, that's how I remember it anyway. It was most likely not flocked, but it was beautiful, however it was decorated, so much so that Suzy quickly left my side upon entering the room and took a chair right next to the tree where she continued to stare lovingly up through its branches the entire morning. I admit that I was, surprisingly, a little miffed over being upstaged by a tree.

The most anticipated part of the party was the gift exchange, and it came near the end of the morning. The room had been arranged with all the chairs in a large oval with Mrs. Baker seated in her large wooden chair at the head. Every child had received the name of another child and had been instructed to bring a wrapped gift for him or her. An elderly widow, with her white hair pulled up into a stately bun, Mrs. Baker sat erect and played the party hostess, calling up individual children by name to stand next to her while she opened their presents for them and then showed the class what they had received before allowing them to take their gifts and return to their seats. There was a lot of excitement and talking as we sat side by side, anxiously awaiting for Mrs. Baker to call our names.

I watched Suzy somehow withdraw herself from sitting just under the tree to come and stand beside Mrs. Baker when her name was called. Mrs. Baker proceeded to pull from the box a pair of the prettiest pink nylon panties you ever saw. *Egad! Poor Suzy.* Mrs. Baker held them up over her head, turning them in each direction so the entire class could get a good long look at Suzy's gift. Four or five boisterous boys seated together on the left side of the room got quite a kick out of the display and, understandably, howled with laughter. After she was dismissed, Suzy quietly walked with the box under her arm back to sit beside the Christmas tree.

It seemed to take forever for my name to be called; my last name started with an S. Finally, standing in front of the class for my moment in the spotlight, I watched in horror as Mrs. Baker pulled yet *another* pair of nylon panties from the gift wrap, except, this time, they weren't even pink; they were just plain, nasty white. *God in Heaven*, I felt like snatching the things away from her and jamming them back in the box. *Okay, okay, enough already!* Didn't she have any sense? I was aware of small mercies, though. It had taken so long to get to my name that the group of heckling boys had grown bored with the whole process and were busy playing with their cap guns and other cheap plastic toys instead of watching to see what I had gotten. I quickly returned to my seat fully aware that I had gotten it worse than Suzy. Just barely turned six, I wondered furiously what parent in their right mind would go out and buy a child a pair of underwear for a school gift exchange!

That episode was among many other memorable firsts that happened the same year. In kindergarten I sang my first solo, played a proper percussion instrument (the triangle), wore a tutu, performed in a recital, and started receiving (regular) phone calls from a boy. I got my first black eye that year (just in time for school pictures) and my first pair of boots.

Nancy Sinatra's big hit, "These Boots Are Made for Walking" was all the rage, and I wore out that 45 on my orange-and-white Phonola. One by one, the girls in my class started sporting new pairs of boots (go-go boots, that is) during the winter of '66. But, I have to say, mine were the best. Unlike the shiny patent go-gos with a zipper up the side, my boots were more the style of those worn by a drum majorette. They were white leather with a tassel that hung down the front. I proudly walked in one day wearing them and a cotton gingham dress, the picture of fashion, I'm sure. After all, I aspired to look like Nancy and sing like Julie—Julie Andrews, that is.

Though the movie *Mary Poppins* had been out for over a year, it was still the big movie hit that had all the kids around the block going about singing the songs from the soundtrack. It was a proud moment indeed when I perfected the pronunciation of and words to "Supercalifragilisticexpialidocious." I had seen the movie at the Grand Theatre in downtown Paris, and my parents bought the album. I nearly cried every time I heard Julie sing "Feed the Birds." During the finale of our end-of-kindergarten recital, we stood together on the *huge,* brightly lit stage and sang "Let's Go Fly a Kite" (the movie's finale song) while extending our arms up over our heads, holding on tightly to imaginary kite strings. It was a big night for me as well; I had a solo as head of the *fireflies,* or something like that. Anyway, I wore a tutu, had my hair done that afternoon, and stood center stage under the bright lights. My older brother chose not to come to the performance that night, citing he had other things to do, a decision that did not go unnoticed by me. My big event was just one in a series of celebrations that took place that spring of 1966.

Nearly twelve years my senior, my brother was due to graduate from high school the week following my kindergarten graduation. My brother was born on the same date as my paternal grandfather, June 19. He was the only grandson on that side of the family, my parents' only son. So his graduation and baccalaureate services were some kind of big deal to the whole family. My mom and I went out and bought new dresses and shoes; my grandparents came in from out of town; and Dad made sure he had film and flashbulbs for the camera.

The high school graduation took place at night in the football stadium. I sat in the bleachers on the very end of my family, next to my grandmother, watching and waiting for my brother's name to be called. When it came time for his moment of glory, the one we had all been waiting for, as he rose to cross the stage all lit up by the stadium lights, decked out in his shiny blue graduation cap and gown, I covered my eyes with both hands. "Sherry Larraine!" my grandmother called out while vigorously shaking both my arms, trying to make me watch my brother receive his diploma before it was too late, but I would not yield. He had missed my big night—now it was up to me to return the favor. I did it all right; I missed it, though, secretly, it had been harder to look away than I thought.

The graduating classes of 1966 had their dreams, let's just say, but there are some memories that go beyond nostalgia, that linger on for a reason even though you can't go back and change things. In childhood there seems to be a list somewhere of characteristics that set people apart from the pack—for good or bad. These characteristics may change over time; what was once viewed as good may now be generally agreed upon as bad and vice versa. When I was young, a head of curly hair, a face full of freckles, and names like Phoebe or Meda seemed to fulfill requirements of things sure to cause exclusion from the crowd. It is the only thing that I can think of that would cause me in particular, and others, to act in such a dismissive way toward a certain boy in my kindergarten class.

Donald was a thin boy with a pale complexion and big brown eyes. He had tousled, cotton-top curls all over his head that—even though I'm sure were beautiful—were definitely not valued as an asset back then, not by kids. He always seemed to be hitching up his brown corduroy pants even though his striped long-sleeve knit shirts were always tucked in and belted at the waist. He had lots of energy, was playful and sweet, and, just like Suzy, insisted on sitting by me every day, much to my annoyance.

A revered ritual known as "snack time" happened midway through every morning. There was never a sign-up sheet or a designated parent in charge of bringing the snacks. They just seemed to appear. One or more parents would send a box of something with their kid to school that morning for everyone to share. One girl named Brenda brought Ritz crackers every Monday morning; we could at least count on that. One day, after taking his seat next to me, Donald very proudly showed me the snack he had brought to share with the whole class. He was very excited. He pulled from his pants pocket a box of Spicettes. Spicettes were little gumdrops, sprinkled with sugar or something, that came in assorted colors and flavors. They had a different taste to them, kind of menthol-like, as the name suggests; they weren't a sweet gummy bear treat. I didn't care for them at all, so I couldn't wait for snack time so I could turn Donald down.

Sure enough, when it came time to share his snack, he excitedly turned directly to me (because he was one of the leeches either seated to my left or right) and offered me first pick. Very politely but promptly I said, "No, thank you. I don't like them." I can still see the look on his little face as he pleaded, "Oh, please, just take one?" "No, thanks," as

I shook my head. He reluctantly turned away and went about passing the candy out to the rest of the class.

Included on my long list of do-overs and re-dos in life, this particular incident, for whatever reason, ranks pretty high. Maybe it's because I can't go back and take just one, dismissing the taste while politely thanking him, knowing I was the one with whom he was so eager to share. Maybe it's because I failed to recognize that a moment was passing, the opportunity to befriend a beautiful boy and leave behind a memory of gratitude and grace instead of willfulness that seems so ugly now. Maybe it's because I can still see his pleading, innocent face, and understand better the heartaches of letdown and disappointments, being discounted when you were only trying to be nice and know someone a little better. Maybe it's because I can't trace him and apologize because that time is gone, like so many other precious things and people that pass through our lives, leaving us with only the memory when they can no longer be found.

September of 1965 ushered me toward an education that would challenge me just as much emotionally and socially if not more than intellectually, though obtaining my academic goals probably hinged on what I had learned that first year more than I realized at the time. September of 2007 would usher me on a journey that I was unprepared to take or, rather, forced to take against my will. Now, looking back on the year that followed, I realize my whole life had been preparing me for such a time. The fall had started out muggy and unseasonably warm, but I was in for the winter of my life.

During the latter part of summer, Mom had called to let me know plans to release surgically her carpal tunnel syndrome had been altered, significantly. Mother had been under the care of a cardiologist for some time after coronary artery stent placement in 2000. She had follow-up appointments with her cardiologist every six months. Naturally, before any surgical procedure, especially an elective operation, she would need to be cleared from a cardiology perspective in order to proceed, except this time she wasn't. Instead of carpal tunnel release, she was looking at open-heart surgery, *big* open-heart surgery. We did not know that her doctor had been watching an aortic aneurysm (an out-pouching or weakening in the wall of the artery) for some time. It had ballooned to a size that warranted surgical correction soon, or she ran the risk of imminent death upon its inevitable rupture.

Mom's stamina was deteriorating noticeably: to the point that she had all but given up household duties in favor of naps, reading books in her favorite chair, and games of solitaire at the kitchen table. Ever since her stent placement, Dad, little by little, had taken over household tasks such as grocery shopping, preparing the meals, and major cleaning while Mom continued to do the laundry and make the bed, which was the last chore she finally gave up. Though he didn't realize it at the time, Dad was being prepared for his life ahead; the rest of us had our suspicions. Leading up to the time of surgery, even walking any kind of distance had become difficult for her. Dad began letting her out at the curb during their excursions instead of walking together from where the car was parked. I remember having to do the same while on our last shopping trip together.

In April, I invited Mom to go with me to Dallas to pick up a bridesmaid dress for my daughter and help her shop for a dress to wear to my son's wedding, which was to take place the following month. She accepted but was adamant about not going to a mall where she had to do a lot of walking. After managing to pull an outfit together for her at an individual clothing store, I couldn't wait to take her out to lunch at a little French restaurant I had discovered. I remember dejectedly thinking how different things were compared to when we used to go on outings together when she and Dad would come to visit from out of town. She didn't seem impressed with the café or the meal. The coffee was "too strong," and the conversation that I was looking forward to having with her generally lagged until about dessert time. It just wasn't the same. She wasn't the same.

We did however, after lunch, manage to find a boutique with curbside parking, where we managed to purchase some much-needed clothes for her before returning home that day. We actually ended up having some fun as I ran back and forth from the dressing room to the clothes racks, exchanging various styles and sizes for her to try. I noticed Mom's very protuberant abdomen. It was significantly out of proportion to the rest of her frame, so much so that she had to try on skirts a size larger just to accommodate her expanded waistline. I questioned Mom about her last gynecological exam and checkup; we talked about ovarian cysts and other risk factors in women her age that indicated the need for her to call and make an appointment with her family doctor. At the time I didn't know the other reason for her lack of stamina and overall sense of just not feeling well.

Her latest echocardiogram had revealed such extensive aortic valve insufficiency that aortic valve replacement might possibly be indicated, as well as repair of her aortic aneurysm, if the valve was found to be beyond repair. The aortic valve is basically the point of exit or the "gateway" to the rest of the body for the blood traveling through the heart; the blood is forcefully ejected out this valve to carry oxygen through the vascular network of the entire body. If the valve is floppy or compromised, then this can lead to the heart's being diminished in its capacity to carry oxygenated blood efficiently and effectively to the various organs and tissues throughout the body, resulting in symptoms such as fatigue, diminished stamina, lack of energy, change in color, sleep patterns, appetite—all of which were occurring in Mom.

So, we were now facing major open-heart surgery. Her aneurysm was perched atop the aortic arch, where the aorta exits and arcs over the top of the heart. It is also the site where major blood vessels carrying blood to the head and neck region branch off. One might think of Mom's surgery occurring in the *heart* of the heart, requiring the repair of a threatening aneurysm and the aortic valve. The procedure is considered high risk and carries an even greater risk of complications and mortality if the left side of the heart has been affected negatively by a valve that hasn't worked properly over time. Mother was referred to a renowned Dallas cardiovascular surgeon who was confident regarding her surgical outcome and prognosis. Dad felt assured everything would run smoothly as outlined in the surgical plan (recovery and rehabilitation). Looking back, I think Mom and I had our reservations, for different reasons.

As a physician, I had come to regard working in the ICU as a place where anything could happen. I had worked too long in critical care settings to assume everything would be smooth sailing after surgery. I had witnessed any and every kind of setback during the post-op period, even when the best of care had been given. There were just no guarantees.

While I was in pediatric residency training, a very astute and revered professor of mine described himself once during a lecture as the "cruise director of the ICU." He specialized in critical care for children and explained that it was his job to facilitate the patients safely through their passage while in the unit and hopefully to see them disembark out to the general pediatric floor with their future ahead of them intact. My experiences in the field of medicine had taught me that time spent in the ICU either as a patient or health care provider included a series of ups and downs that demanded patience. Small gains as well as significant losses occurred sometimes, and often minute-by-minute changes could alter the long-term outcome of a patient. Though time seemed to stand still on one hand, on the other hand, people could find themselves in for the ride of their lives.

Though she never voiced it, I could sense in Mom a resolve just to accept whatever was going to happen. Ever since I could remember, this is how she dealt with most things in life, whether big or small. While my dad tended more toward a wringing of the hands, Mom's usual response was, "No use to worry: nothing you can do about it anyway." Since they tended to deal with issues from polar ends of the extreme, Dad began to become increasingly alarmed when she started "getting all her ducks in a row." She pulled out some insurance papers and financial statements from the middle chest drawers one morning to show Dad how she managed their finances and taxes, but he would not hear of it, stating she would be back from the hospital in time to see about all that stuff. He did, however, listen to and carry out some of her requests a week prior to her surgery.

She wanted to put flowers on her family's graves that were located in a countryside cemetery a little less than an hour's drive away from where my parents lived. Dad was appalled that she picked out some cheap plastic dime-store flowers, but he complied with her wishes and helped her set them out. It wasn't about the flowers; Mom was bent on paying tribute and, I believe, finding resolution. She also wanted to visit the graveside of a family friend who had recently died after a brave fight with cancer.

Raymond Woodrow and his wife, Lila, and their three now-grown children, lived down the street from my parents and had attended the same church together for over thirty years. They had recently celebrated sixty years of marriage less than a month apart from Mom and Dad's anniversary. Ironically, his burial site was close by the burial plot my parents had already purchased for themselves within the large local cemetery located in the middle of their small town.

Dad kind of milled around and left Mom to herself. After spending some time at Raymond's graveside, he said she went over and stood next to a small tree with her arm draped over one of the smaller branches, staring out over their town and the horizon, spread out below the knoll upon which she was standing. She stood there for some time before returning to the car to leave. No words were spoken between the two, though Dad wishes now he knew what she had been thinking. I wasn't there, but I have an idea.

My prayer for Mom all along had been for God to steer the boat on her voyage, through whatever darkness lay ahead. I prayed for him to navigate the dangerous waters no matter the outcome, instead of just praying for healing. This image of a boat came to me one night while on a walk. Mom's pending surgery was heavy on my mind, and, when I looked up into the summer sky, I saw this star constellation that reminded me of the stern of a boat. Maybe I held on to this image because I (and possibly she) had a sense of foreboding over what was about to come. Maybe it was due to uncertainty, my jaded past, or the acknowledgement that something bigger than ourselves was in charge of our destiny. Whatever it was, I wished I had discussed it with Mom before the operation. I hated to think Mom had had some fears or reservations that she wanted to discuss with someone, and I hadn't made myself available due to my false optimism. On my part, I resisted broaching the subject for fear of transferring my concerns on her. It's like my dad's wondering what her thoughts were by the tree; I'll always wonder if she wanted to talk to me or would have opened up if I had simply asked, "Are you afraid at all, Mom?" Whatever the case, she was relaxed and at peace when they wheeled her through the operating doors. I wished her well, kissed her on the forehead, and said, "I'll see you on the other side." It was the morning of September 4, 2007.

Mom got into trouble right off the bat. Our family assembled in the cardiovascular critical care waiting room during Mom's surgery. We were called periodically with updates, notified when she was out of surgery, and when she was transferred out of recovery. After coming off bypass, we anticipated for her to remain intubated and on the ventilator for a day or two during her immediate post-op period. I should have known something was up when we received a call from her nurse in the CV-ICU (cardiovascular intensive care unit) to say they were "just getting her settled in," as a reason for the delay in letting the family in to see her. In my experience, "difficulties" in settling a patient in the unit after surgery usually referred to some sort of hemodynamic instability or crisis. Such was the case: Mom had "clamped down" vascularly after surgery, resulting in a drastic plummet in her blood pressure and subsequent cardiac output. This required multiple blood transfusions and a slew of cardiac pressor meds, all hanging like Japanese lanterns from her IV pole, to raise her blood pressure and restore adequate blood perfusion.

She was as white as the sheet that she lay on when I entered the room. It had been a long time since I had seen a Swan catheter (a large central line inserted into the side of the neck), much less interpret the readings that it transmitted upon a monitor. After conversing with the bedside nurse I found out that Mom had destabilized upon transfer. Her cardiac output was at one, a very low reading, indicating how poorly her heart was working to sustain her blood pressure. Sometimes a rough start can set into motion a chain of events that leads to an eventful if not a prolonged stay in the ICU.

That night, Mom experienced a "pocket of bleeding." This required something like four units of platelets due to a surreptitious drop in her platelet count. We learned later that this significant drop was due to heparin-induced platelet antibodies. (She had received heparin as protocol, but her body reacted by making antibodies that attacked her own platelets.). Ultimately, Mom's outcome would hinge on this momentous event. As a result of the extra fluids she required post-op, which included the blood products and IV meds, and on top of an already bad heart, she developed pulmonary distress syndrome from pulmonary edema. In other words, her lungs were "wet" from all the excessive fluid that her heart wasn't strong enough to pump efficiently through her body while she remained in a bedridden state. This all meant longer time spent on the ventilator than the one to two days we had anticipated, edema throughout her body, ongoing IV meds to help her heart beat stronger, and diuretics to help her shed some of the extra volume on board: minute by minute changes.

The first attempt at extubation (coming off the ventilator) was traumatic for Mom. Like surfacing from a prolonged time under the water, all she could say was, "Oh, dear! Oh, dear!" when they removed the tube from her trachea. While still recovering from a newly opened chest, staples down the middle of her sternum still in place, the simple acts of breathing deeply and coughing up phlegm—vital respiratory protocol for keeping her lungs clear from infection—proved excruciatingly painful. Patients in the CV-ICU are given heart-shaped pillows after surgery. They may be autographed, but they are truly designed for patients to clutch and hold close against the chest as they cough or sneeze; we kept Mom's by her side, always.

Due to the extra fluid still in her lungs, she was unable to maintain her oxygen saturation at an acceptable level without the assistance of some positive pressure ventilation given through a face mask. It's considered a step down from the ventilator. She held her own, although extremely uncomfortably, until the third day post-extubation when, no longer able to maintain adequate oxygenation, her saturation monitor dropped, and her heart went out of regular rhythm. After bedside anesthesia was delivered, she was re-intubated, placed back on the ventilator, and her heart was shocked back into rhythm. A large bore needle was inserted into her back and some of the excess fluid was drained from her lungs. It was a difficult setback for us all.

The worst of it was that my dad was at the hospital alone when emergency intervention measures had to be taken. He was asked to sign the necessary papers. Because Mom had been off the ventilator for a few days, my brother and I had gone to our respective homes to get some things in order before returning to the hospital. I was sitting in a coffee shop that afternoon when I got the call. Though I had planned to return that evening anyway, I hurried home, threw some things together and made arrangements for the kids before I raced back to Dallas. I knew that whatever happened would be all said and done by the time I got there.

Mom remained on the ventilator for a total of ten days during her ICU stay. I remember once reading an account of a cardiovascular surgeon who once underwent some kind of operation himself. He wrote that of all that he went through and endured post-operatively, by far, the worst part was being intubated and having his endotracheal tube suctioned.

While ICU patients are immediately post-operative or the sickest, they are kept paralyzed and sedated by IV medications, so as to allow the ventilator to do the work for them. As patients improve, the tricky part comes in weaning them safely off the ventilator, allowing them to wake up for periods and do some of the breathing on their own. "Overriding the vent" involves the tedious process of titrating or lowering the settings on the ventilator and the rate of IV medications that drip into the patients minute by minute. The irony is that, as the patients improve, they usually become more distressed. They are increasingly aware of their surroundings and the horrible sensation of having to breathe through a tube stuck down their throat that is periodically suctioned in order to keep it free from secretions. As their sedation meds are cut back, very often patients may need to have physical restraints placed on them in order to prevent them from pulling out the tube prematurely. It is a fine line to walk. The progression requires patience on the part of the medical staff, families and above all, the patients. Most often, it is the most difficult part for the patients.

To help soothe Mom, I purchased a CD player and some classical music selections that were collected in a format for peace and relaxation. I kept the music on when we were present during visitation hours and asked the staff to keep it playing for her when we weren't there. After a long week, Mom was extubated for the final time and, thankfully, never went back on the ventilator again.

Throughout Mom's hospital stay, my dad and I stayed together at an extended-stay motel just down the street from the medical complex. After Mom's crisis in the unit, I would only venture home periodically, either in the early morning hours around 4 in order to be back by dinner, or leave after the final visitation at 10 p.m. and get back for morning visitation.

We would typically start the day with breakfast in the room, though, as time went by, Dad would be up long before me and have his breakfast already eaten and morning paper and devotional read. After breakfast we would go for our morning walk on the designated walking trail close to the medical center and then walk back to the hospital in time for morning visitation hours. Many a morning when Mom was still in the ICU, I would look up to her corner window while walking up the hospital drive to see if anything indicated things had changed for the worse: the blinds' drawn differently, a flurry of activity seen within. While in the room, we would talk to the nurses and respiratory techs, talk to Mom when she was able, rearrange her pillows constantly, and try to keep her as comfortable as possible.

We would leave the unit at straight up noon and head for lunch downstairs in the foyer. The nicest people ran a family-owned deli-restaurant with a hot lunch line and adjacent Starbucks coffee shop in the main lobby of the medical building primarily designated for cardiac care. We dined there daily. The CV-ICU unit was closed from noon until 4 p.m. every day, so we would find some way to pass the afternoon hours. While Mom was intubated, we never left the hospital during the day, but, after she was extubated and doing better, we began to venture out a little. We might stroll through the nearby mall, go to a bookstore, or travel a little farther away for lunch. We returned to the ICU for visitation from 4 to 6 p.m. and would then break for dinner before returning for the final visitation from 8 to 10 p.m. We always walked to and from the hospital except when we returned from dinner; then we would drive through the parking gate into the designated lot in front of the hospital. I actually looked forward to the ticket agent's taking our ticket and waving us through. It almost felt like we had become friends.

Though we might eat in for lunch, we always ate out at dinner, and Dad insisted on paying the bill every time. We generally went to the same restaurant and shopping area every night, rotating among three or four different restaurants. We had good conversation and became pretty familiar with the waitstaff. Dad always put on a good face, but he was always thinking about Mom back at the hospital. Dad discovered Marble Slab Creamery one night and really enjoyed himself. He had always been a big fan of ice cream. We went there several times and would sit outside on a bench to eat our ice cream until, one night, Dad confessed he felt guilty about going out and enjoying such good food since Mom was unable to. Our days were pretty much rationed: sitting in Mom's room, eating three meals a day, and waiting out time in between.

Toward the last half of Mom's hospital stay we discovered a Jewish deli, Cindy's Delicatessen, run by a Vietnamese family. Although new to us, the deli was renowned to many on the north side of Dallas and had a faithful clientele. Fully kosher, the deli served breakfast all day, had fabulous soups and sandwiches, a no-nonsense waitstaff, and an awesome bakery. We began eating there sometimes during lunch and dinner as well. A lot of the patrons were senior citizens, probably due to the restaurant's close proximity to upscale retirement facilities (not including *The Casket Store*, I swear to God, right next door). While dining with Dad, I would glance around the restaurant, noticing the different elderly couples and singles. I'd wonder what their backgrounds were, where they were from, and what their cultural heritage was.

One night in particular I watched an elderly man eating alone and wondered if he was a widower and, if so, how long had he been alone? Though I can no longer recall his face, I remember my curiosity and how the sight of him sitting all by himself caught my eye. My thoughts did not travel any further, but it was a foreshadowing of the fate of my father sitting across the table from me.

October

O ctober 1 was Mom's birthday. Relatives, friends, and people from the church sent cards and flowers, and I managed to put something together from the gift shop downstairs, but Mom wasn't that interested. She was having a pacemaker put in that morning. After nearly four weeks, Mom had finally managed to graduate from the cardiac ICU after walking the mandatory laps around the unit and proving she no longer required twenty-four-hour intensive nursing care. A feeding tube down her nose replaced the central line that had fed her parentally (through her veins). External pacing of her heart continued, and scheduled routine visits by the respiratory and physical therapists followed her to her new residence on the post-surgical cardiac floor. We were told that sometimes after major invasive cardiac surgery, it is fairly common for the heart to continue to need pacing in order to keep it in normal sinus rhythm. In order for her to go home, however, she would require a pacemaker. The procedure was short and successful, but, after all that she had been through on her way to recovery, it felt like a setback.

Although we were all glad to be out of the CV-ICU, life on the floor meant added responsibility for the patient and family. For instance, getting Mom to eat became our biggest challenge. She had no appetite and was on a restricted pureed diet due to having the endotracheal tube down her throat for so long, but it was imperative she take in enough protein and sufficient calories in order to have the feeding tube that extended from her nose down into her stomach removed. The idea was for her to eat more on her own so she would no longer require supplement calories through the tube; hence, we filled out a calorie-count sheet after every meal. That was the easy part; the hard part was actually getting her to take enough bites of something to be able to record a percentage of her daily intake required to meet her nutritional needs. I had forgotten how stubborn she could be; when she said "Enough," or "I don't want any more," that was that.

Another one of our duties included making sure Mom walked the designated amount required by the physical therapist. While in the unit, only the therapist walked with Mom, but, after she was transferred to the floor, we were expected to supplement the amount of walking; the therapist only came by once or twice a day for scheduled sessions. Again, we had to keep a log of how much she walked daily, recorded as laps around the cardiac ward. The floor was set up as an oval, with the nursing station and offices positioned in the middle. It was standard to see patients, at different stages of recovery after their open-heart surgeries, painfully making their way around the floor with the assistance of walkers or a therapist, some simply gutting it out alone. We exchanged smiles and words of encouragement as we repeatedly passed one another. It was easy to recognize how painstaking the process was by their facial expressions and the snail pace they all seemed to keep. I once praised a very tall, fit man in his forties on how well he was doing while he approached us with the aid of a physical therapist about half his size. Short of breath, he managed to get out, "This . . . is . . . very . . . hard."

Just as painstaking and challenging as the required walking seemed, the discomfort caused by Mom's surgical scar and the pulmonary regimen, which she had to continue in order to keep her lungs clear, proved the most difficult for her. Just repositioning herself in bed caused significant pain, not to mention the deep coughing that the pulmonary therapist regularly forced her to do after inhalation treatments. She wouldn't eat for us; she wouldn't walk as far and as much as she was supposed to, but she was compliant with her pulmonary exercises, much more graceful than my grandmother had been.

When I was just a child, I remember my mom's mother being in the hospital with pneumonia and watching her having to blow into a tube when the respiratory tech would come around with his cart and little machine. She would get so mad during the treatments that she would grab the tube and, with eyes blazing, would blow as hard as she could. Mother never acted in such a fashion. She always smiled at the therapist and blew into the blue tubing, trying to make the little yellow valve bounce up to the designated line.

I knew we had a long road in front of us. Knowing Mom's laid-back manner and her disinterest in exercise of any sort, I began to worry she would not be fully cooperative with outpatient cardiac rehabilitation, which would play an essential role in her continued recovery. Frustration was beginning to mount. I was becoming frustrated with Mom; Dad was becoming frustrated with the hospital.

My dad, who had been so burdened with worry while Mom was in the CV-ICU, now began to rant and rave over things that really did not matter in the whole scheme of things. He became consumed with filling out her menu every day and would head to the hospital early in the morning before I had even risen to make sure her breakfast was correct and to fill out her sheet for lunch and dinner. If there was the slightest mistake or delay, he would become angry and frustrated—as if her total recovery hinged on what was on her plate. It was all he talked about, and he and I began to spar over matters as I tried to explain the workings of a hospital and, specifically, that the difference of being on the floor instead of in the unit was characterized by patients' regaining some independence and being able to participate actively in the recovery phase. I reasoned that there were many other patients in the hospital and that the kitchen was not being neglectful or intentionally messing up her orders. I was looking at the whole process from the stance of a physician; Dad was looking at things through the eyes of a caretaker: a worried, worn-out caretaker.

Because I was so relieved that Mom was no longer on the ventilator and was out of the unit, I couldn't understand why Dad was making mountains out of molehills. How I saw it, having a breakfast tray versus an IV pole (hung with four different drips just to make sure her blood pressure could sustain her cardiac output) signified miraculous improvement. I probably had a glimpse into what was happening, though I was too frustrated at the time to give it much thought. While Mom lay incapacitated in the unit, Dad was totally out of his element and, therefore, felt he had zero control over Mom's care and what was going on. The surroundings and dialogue were foreign to him, not to mention his dismay and consternation over how her post-operative phase had taken a turn for the worse. Every day, upon our arrival, Dad would feel her legs to see if the swelling had gone down; he couldn't get past the fact that she looked like a linebacker lying there. I, on the other hand, didn't give a flip about her edematous appearance; I just wanted her meds tapered off so she could get up and get out of there, and, above all, for her never to have to go on the ventilator again. If she hurt when she coughed, so be it. Just keep those lungs clear. *Let's get the hell out of here.*

As Mom began to improve, Dad began to feel a little more in control of her care and, therefore, his habituated bent toward anxiety began to surface. He could now pace the floors and wring his hands over how little she was eating, obsess over her calorie-count sheet, blast the kitchen downstairs for not getting her tray right, complain that they "just didn't seem to be doing much for her," or blame the hospital when someone did not immediately appear when we rang for assistance. (While on Telemetry, all patients' vitals are monitored continuously in the nursing station. If there had been a real emergent need, someone would have been there, pronto.) At this point, I didn't totally get it, so we exchanged heated words one morning on our way to the hospital. But there would come a time in the not-too-distant future when I would realize how helpless Dad had felt throughout the whole ordeal, and I would make a decision to back off at one crucial junction—a decision I still wrestle with from time to time.

On top of becoming weary of Dad's complaints and the building frustration, I was becoming somewhat angry with Mom. I wanted her to *buck up*, push herself to walk more so her lungs wouldn't get sick, force herself to eat more so we could get the feeding tube out of her nose. I wanted to get her out of the hospital, knowing that, the longer we stayed, she would become increasingly susceptible to a hospital-acquired infection. Sometimes the hospital can be the worst place to be when it comes to being sick.

There is something inherent in the workings of a hospital: the longer people stay, the more difficult a time they have getting out. Once the wheels start turning, the whole hospital experience can actually leave patients in a more vulnerable state than they were before they were admitted: a poorer nutritional state, even with adjunct tube feedings; weakened immunity compliments of a prolonged bedridden state; fatigue and exhaustion due to lack of sleep; and the continual risk of acquiring an infection from a "smart hospital bug" that tends to be more virulent in nature, more savvy in outsmarting the array of antibiotics routinely used on the outside. I thought Mom was not trying hard enough, but maybe she had a truer sense of things internally—not so much a premonition but, rather, a glimpse of the bigger picture.

One night, after Mom was extubated for the last time—still very ill—she lay with her eyes closed and began to voice some complaint over the inner workings of the unit and having to wait for certain things to be done, commenting on the inefficiency of time usage. It was during the last nighttime visitation slot, and I was sitting by her bed, the only other person in the room. She never opened her eyes but started to talk: "I had a dream about my father last night. I thought the doctor was my father. He could make a ruckus and a fuss about things all right, but he could make sure things got done. I miss my father." My whole body perked up as if the Emergency Broadcast System had just delivered an alert. It is standard knowledge in end-of-life-care circles that when a patient begins to hear from or see significant people from the past, those who have died before them, it is a pretty reliable indicator that the patient's end is near. Some experienced hospice nurses give it another twenty-four hours or so before the patient's death. Although Mom recovered and was able to leave the unit several weeks later, that brief conversation stuck with me.

For one thing, Mom never talked much about her childhood or discussed her family in detail, though I knew how much she had adored her father. My brother once told me what a difficult time Mom had had after his death, a little over a year from the date of my birth. Although he was only eleven years old at the time, he remembered her suffering. My father related to me my grandfather's agonizing demise, which occurred in the hospital, suffering from a fatal bout with emphysema. While lying in my mother's arms, he coughed up massive amounts of blood before breathing his last, and there was nothing she could do for him but stay and witness it all.

During the last heart-to-heart conversation we had while still at the hospital, she stated that she wanted to go home; she said, "Daddy could take better care of me there," and she believed that she would do better at home. It was time. I shared with her how close she had come to death and how far she had come since the operation. She knew it; she nodded in agreement and in her tired, small voice she simply said, "That's the power of prayer." We never spoke again of what she had been through, her suffering, or the purpose of it all. Knowing Mom, I sometimes even now believe that she went through it all more for us than herself—a labor of love. When she felt her worst in the unit, she once said to me, "They shouldn't be allowed to do this to old people; they should just take us out back and shoot us."

That was so typical of Mom. She sometimes lacked faith in the medical community and thought many medical treatments were excessive and didn't see the point of people putting themselves through them. Yet she had; without questioning much, she had simply resigned herself to the fact it was something that had to be done, though I doubt she would have done it just for herself. At any rate, Mom seemed very tired, and I wondered if she was slipping into a depression, because she seemed to be withdrawing more into herself.

We had been told that a step-down facility for further rehabilitation might be an option for Mom's continued recovery, but I wonder if Mom's increasing despondency played a role in the cardiovascular team's recommendation for her to be released to go home instead. One day I talked to one of Mom's respiratory technicians about Mom's overall disposition. He said that he had seen depression in lots of patients after open-heart surgery and told me that the doctors really did try to get them out of the hospital sooner than later to avoid risk of infection and to help facilitate the healing process. Therefore, I wasn't totally caught off guard when my sister-in-law called to tell me the hospital was releasing Mom on Saturday morning, just a day away. Of course, a home health agency would continue her care, and she would eventually be enrolled in an outpatient cardiology rehabilitative program, but my brother thought she had no business leaving the hospital so soon, because she really did not seem to be doing all that well, particularly with self-help skills such as eating and walking. I had come home for a couple of days, so I did not get to talk to her doctors about the decision or be present when she was discharged with a stack of prescriptions, home health orders, a list of instructions, and a follow-up appointment with her surgeon.

A weekend discharge meant that my dad would be on his own, caring for Mom until home health showed up Monday to enroll her as a patient. Knowing little of what he was in for, my dad frantically called me Sunday morning asking me to come over and assist him in sorting through her medications and their dosing schedules. I arrived with my family to find Dad in a flurry. He was trying to get Mom to eat his homemade soup. Her medications were lined up on the kitchen table, but he was frustrated over not being able to get all her scripts filled at the same time. Mom was in one of the den chairs, next to the kitchen area, with her feet propped up, head back against the chair, eyes closed. She didn't want to converse. She didn't want to eat or drink much of anything, didn't want to listen to any music (something that was always on in their home, whether from the television or stereo), and resisted Dad's urgings to walk around the hall several times. Of course, upon her discharge, the hospital staff had stressed to both of them that walking a certain amount daily was crucial to her rehabilitation. She seemed to be shutting out everything and everyone.

I helped Dad sort through all the medicines and wrote down scheduled times to administer them. Our family stayed and visited *somewhat* with Mom while Dad ran to the pharmacy to pick up meds that had been delayed in getting filled. Though she smiled warmly, albeit briefly, when my oldest daughter gave her a stuffed bear holding a red satin rose in its paw (she had bought it from the hospital gift shop), I could tell that Mom was in no mood for company. After strongly encouraging her to keep up her nutrition and fluid intake, as well as her walking around the house, I left somewhat frustrated that day. I *knew* my mom was not going to participate in her release orders. She didn't need to be home where no one could monitor and push her to do what she needed to do, and I blamed her in part for not trying. Even in my frustration, I also acknowledged that Mom needed to come home once more. At the time, she was so sick that she just flat didn't care.

The home health agency came the next morning to examine Mom and enroll her as a patient. They set about ordering medical equipment for the home, setting up in-home appointments for respiratory and physical therapy, and assigning her a nurse who would check on her routinely as designated by the physician's orders. Still, my dad called me throughout the day to let me know things were not going according to plan: Mom wouldn't eat, wouldn't walk, and he couldn't keep her comfortable. I volunteered to come over if things got to the point where he needed me. However, he told me to wait until the next day, Tuesday, when my youngest daughter would not be in preschool, and I could just bring her with me.

By Tuesday, things had changed. They had had a rough night together, and, at one point, my dad had my mom use his own respiratory CPAP machine so she could breathe a little easier. I arrived in the morning to find the speech therapist evaluating Mom's ability to take in liquids, since we were trying to advance her diet. Mom was very pleasant and seemed to enjoy the therapist, who was so nice and professional, but Mom sounded raspy and coughed every time she took a drink. Alarmed, the therapist told Dad not to give her anymore plain liquids and called her agency to order a substance to thicken liquids before we gave them to her. She was obviously having some difficulty swallowing. Although the nurse assigned to Mom was not scheduled to visit her until later that afternoon, after receiving the therapist's phone call, reporting the changes that had occurred overnight, the nurse was prompted by the sense of urgency to reschedule her other appointments. She arrived just after the lunch hour.

I listened to Mom's chest with the nurse's stethoscope and could hear some rattles and rales that the nurse verified were not there when she had examined Mom the previous day. It was time to go back to the hospital.

Dad talked to her surgeon's office over the phone, and they recommended she proceed to the emergency room. I wanted to jump in the car and head to the hospital in Dallas, but Dad was insistent on having her seen in the local ER, where her primary physician could be involved. The funny thing was that Mom was totally relaxed and very pleasant; she seemed to be okay with the whole process. She projected no sense of alarm or protest about going back to the hospital.

The ER was a zoo. Mom was immediately triaged into a room, where the staff quickly assessed her and began supportive care; nevertheless, they were extremely busy. Every room was full, and the ER docs were hurriedly moving up and down the halls. The flu season had already hit. They were having difficulty transferring patients out of the ER to their respective rooms, because the hospital was at full capacity, and the ICU beds were all taken as well. While waiting for Mom's chest x-ray results and other lab work to come back, the ER physician explained to Dad that he might have to transfer Mom to the Dallas hospital where she had previously been. I was elated at the news. I knew Mom would basically be considered a "bounce-back." She had probably not been well upon her release (in fact, her blood cultures were positive when she hit the ER doors, suggesting to me that she had had an infection brewing before she left the hospital), and it would be a Godsend to go back to the staff and physicians who knew her immediate medical history the best.

Dad saw it differently. He wanted no part of Dallas; they had been there long enough, and he couldn't see what good it would do for her to be there. "She wasn't getting any better there," he reasoned. He questioned the doctor as to why they couldn't just transfer her to a hospital in a neighboring community. The physician explained that it wasn't that simple, but that he would continue to work on it. I knew that the ER physician had to find an accepting physician to take care of Mom, someone who didn't even know her long-standing medical history. I also knew how difficult hospital-to-hospital transfers could be, but Dad didn't understand such matters. He was frustrated and wanted to keep Mom at home where her own physicians could see to her. Obviously, he didn't understand how complicated Mom's condition really was. Furthermore, her own primary care physician would not be taking care of her even if she were admitted to the local hospital; rather, a team of "hospitalists" working in the ICU would be in charge of her care there.

This is where I fell short. I thought about sneaking out of the room, following the ER physician down the hall, pulling him aside, and telling him behind Dad's back, "Whatever it takes, just get her back to Dallas where she belongs, as soon as possible." But I did not. I decided to let Dad be in control and prayed fate would take a hand in the matter. Maybe all the ICU rooms would remain filled, and we would have no option but to transfer her back.

Mom's ER nurse was a young man who had recently finished nursing school—I knew his pain. He was being baptized by fire that first day on his shift, but he was doing an excellent job of taking care of Mom. (I wish I would have thought to make note of his name.) Because it was a small, cramped space we were being held in, a curtained-off side of the room, Dad waited in the hall just outside the door. My husband was eventually able to come and pick up my youngest daughter, who had been at the hospital with us the entire time. Mom's nurse did his best to keep my daughter occupied while at the same time monitoring Mom and tending to her care. I kept noticing that Mom was having difficulty pronouncing her words, just slightly, and that her bite seemed off, like her teeth were misaligned somehow. I mentioned it to her nurse. He was on it.

He had Mom smile at him, blow out her cheeks, raise her eyebrows, and follow his fingers with her eyes while holding her head still. In other words, he was checking the function of her cranial nerves by putting her through a brief neurological exam meant to look for any acute changes that might be the result of a stroke or some other hematological mishap. For someone just out of school and new on the job, he impressed me. He seemed genuinely interested in Mom's welfare as well. I was leaning over her during the exam, and he pointed to me and asked, "Who's that?" With a smile that lit up her entire face, she softly said, "Sherry."

A moment of such open admiration for me and me alone I recalled witnessing another time not so long removed. Once, while I was changing my youngest daughter's diaper and leaning over and talking to her, she gave me the most rapturous, adoring smile. I remember thinking then, "There's probably nobody else in the world who has ever looked upon me with so much affection, except maybe my own mother, perhaps while changing me." It was the cycle of life right before me, and it did not go unnoticed. At that moment, standing in the ER, a little bell began to ring distantly in my head. That smile conjured up an even more poignant memory, a story my mom had told me while I was in the throes of major depression.

When I was wrestling with painful questions over eternity and hopelessness, my mother very gently and in her own way tried to give me some comfort or perspective by sharing with me the details surrounding my grandmother's death. "If you've ever watched someone die," she began, "I know in the case of my own mother . . . ." My grandmother had been delirious with pain for a couple of days, and I, oblivious to the circumstances, had been sent to spend some

Christmas holiday time at my other grandmother's in order to get me out of the house as they saw the end drawing near.

Mom said that the day my grandmother died was the hardest on her since Grandma had come to stay with us. My mother remained constantly by her side while my eighty-year-old grandmother had cried out deliriously all day, "Momma!" or "Frank!" (her younger brother who had died years before her). The story itself amazed me, because in all my years of knowing my grandmother, she had never talked about her mother, not once. She always told stories about her "papa," a country doctor; Mon Jane, a surrogate grandmother; Frank; or even Frank Jr., his son, who went on to become a prominent cardiovascular surgeon. They were all included in stories she had told time and time again, but there were never any stories about her mother. I don't recall her ever even mentioning her.

Late in the day, after watching her suffer for hours and feeling helpless over how to help her, my mother related, "Then this look of complete joy, rapture came over her face, and she turned and saw me, and she knew me." After that, she slipped into a coma and died a couple of hours later. "All these years, I've held onto that moment, thinking maybe there's a better place somewhere, something better." She spoke with tears in her eyes then and every time afterward whenever she brought it up.

Well *she* had looked at me, and she knew me. Ironically, it would be the last time she would look me in the face and smile at me like that, as her mother had done years before. That little bell was meant to prepare me.

They finally managed to get Mom a bed in the ICU upstairs, and so came the long and tedious process of learning Mom's immediate and past medical history as well as diagnosing and treating what was wrong with her now. Of course we had brought her previous discharge orders and medications with us, but the hospital in Dallas had to fax her complete medical history. The physicians in charge of the unit were a group of hospitalists with an interest in critical care who rotated shifts with one another. They were more than impressed with her delicate surgery and her post-operative complications. "It's amazing what they can do," one said while reading in her chart, "It's almost like they took the heart apart and put it back together."

Understanding the complexity of her case and knowing each time a new physician came on that he or she would have to spend time sorting through Mom's chart and getting to know her, I tried to be as helpful as possible and fill in some of the blanks for them regarding her previous hospital course. Her own cardiologist had been called in to consult on her heart, which checked out just fine. But, even though she had been immediately placed on IV antibiotics for positive blood cultures that indicated a bacterial infection, things pretty much went from bad to worse over the next two days.

For one thing, a barium swallow study confirmed that she had suffered partial vocal cord paralysis, probably due to a small stroke that had occurred Monday night; so, a feeding tube was placed back into her nose and dropped into her stomach to replace oral feedings until she improved with therapy. But Mom did not improve. She began to shut down little by little, and her platelet count continued to plummet even after blood products were given to her. The doctors attributed this to her sepsis (systemic bacterial infection). I was most afraid of Mom's getting into respiratory distress again. The last thing I wanted to see was her back on the ventilator. I was further frustrated by the visitation schedule, which was much more rigid and shortened. Three or four visitation times throughout the day only allowed for an hour at a time, the first one being too early for me to drive over and get to in time. I remembered, while in Dallas, how frequently she had wanted me to help reposition her in bed to get comfortable, and I was unable to be there simply due to the different visitation schedule; she spent far more time alone, without us. After watching her slide downward for two days, I had had enough.

I called her cardiologist, who graciously took my call in the middle of a hectic day of seeing patients in his clinic, and asked for his advice and input about how to go about requesting a transfer. Did I have grounds for the request? He asked me point-blank, "Is continuity of care important to you? Do you think it factors into her outcome?" "Absolutely," I said. "Then you have appropriate grounds to request a transfer, particularly in the light that she is not getting better and would be better served by those who cared for her most recently." I had my ammo. I called my brother and his wife and said we needed to sit down and talk to Dad together after the next scheduled visitation time. Around 5 p.m., we all sat at an outside table adjacent to the hospital café, and I placed the proposition before Dad. He was to the point where all he said was, "Go talk to the doctors." By this time, Mom had actually started bleeding from her left eye due to her precipitous drop in platelets; she looked like she had been punched. What had started out as a severe conjunctivitis had progressed to a hemorrhagic state.

The doctors were gracious when I spoke to them about arranging a transfer. I made it clear that I was not unhappy with the care that she had been receiving. Instead, I believed that continuity of care was in her best interest, because she was a very complicated post-open-heart surgical patient; she should go back where her treatment was initiated. The night before, I had obtained from the unit in Dallas phone numbers to reach her former pulmonologist, including his home number. (It didn't hurt to mention the M.D. behind my name.) He was very nice over the phone and immediately recalled Mom and her prolonged CV-ICU course. He said he would be glad to receive her as a patient but requested that they transfer first thing in the morning; he would be leaving for the weekend and wanted enough time to admit her and get her situated before he left. He assured me that his partner of twenty-plus years, who also already knew Mom's history from working in the unit, would oversee her care while he was gone. Now that we had an accepting physician, the hospital-to-hospital transfer could take place.

I was elated but anxious at the same time. The only stipulation was that she had to be in stable condition in order to be eligible for transfer. I slept very little that night worrying over Mom, praying that she did not get sick or get into any kind of respiratory trouble that would prevent her from being transferred. I had already made up my mind that if it were her time to go, I could live with that if we had gotten her back to Dallas, but I could not live with myself if she had died where she was. From a physician's point of view, I knew she had no business being there in the first place, while, as a daughter, I wanted to do whatever I could to make it right, make sure Mom received the best care possible and be at peace with things out of my control.

I arrived the next morning to the familiar buzz of transfer arrangements amid the busy mid-morning routine of an ICU. The nurse who came in and secured Mom's IV said that the doctor in Dallas had been on the phone several times, anxiously awaiting her scheduled return. "He's on it," she said. There had been a delay involving ambulance availability; finally a unit responded from a small town seventeen miles down the highway, Van Alstyne, a community my dad and his extended family had grown up in and around. To say Mom looked more pitiful than I had ever seen her was not an exaggeration. She lay quite still and had little or nothing to say to us. Her left eye was completely shut and blackened with dried blood. My dad silently cried at the sight of her as we waited for the transport team to arrive.

As the transport team loaded her into the elevator, I told Mom goodbye and that I would see her shortly. I turned to go down the stairs but got distracted in the hospital hallway by running into someone I used to know. By the time I got outside the hospital, I realized it was too late to see her into the ambulance; they were already pulling out of the parking lot. I stood on the curb, watching the back of the red vehicle as it slowly made its way down the street, stopping at the corner and turning left toward the highway. My anxiety had abated, and I felt somewhat exhilarated that things had worked out. I told myself that, if something happened along the way, if she didn't make it, I would be okay, because at least my prayer had been answered: she was on her way.

With the way I drive, even though there had been a significant delay between our departures, I pulled up in front of the hospital emergency entrance in time to see them unloading Mom and rolling her through the sliding glass doors. My dad had some business to attend to; he would be driving down separately. We were back.

It was a sunny Friday morning, and we were readmitted to the cardiovascular intensive care unit in a different room, just around the corner from where we had spent most of the month of September. I was relieved that we were back where I thought we should have been all along, but I was not prepared for the staff's reaction. The last time the nurses in the CV-ICU had seen Mom, she was gingerly making her way around the unit with the aid of a walker and physical therapy tech, proving that she was making enough progress to be transferred to the floor. Now, a little less than three weeks from her unit discharge, she was back: looking sick, with IV antibiotics on board, a feeding tube down her nose due to partial vocal cord paralysis, shut down emotionally, and with a blackened eye to boot. "What happened to her eye?" one of the nurses pointedly asked me while another nurse was getting Mom situated in her bed. I had started to say something about her platelet count being low when her surgeon purposely strode in and announced that she had heparin-induced platelet antibodies and that her platelet count was dangerously low at 30 (normal range is 150,000–300,000). He was ordering platelets immediately. That was the first time I had ever heard those words: *heparin-induced platelet antibodies,* though I had seen a sign, NO HEPARIN PRODUCTS, taped to her CV-ICU door.

I do not know whether Mom's peripheral IV had been flushed with heparin during her stay at the local hospital (though a rapid drop in platelets can occur if heparin is given to a patient with circulating antibodies). However, the medical staff had most assuredly overlooked the issue of her heparin sensitivity, because they had attributed her falling platelet count to bacterial sepsis instead of her circulating antibodies to heparin. Heparin sensitivity should have been in her chart. One thing was certain, before being readmitted through the emergency room, Mom had suffered a slight stroke caused by the continuous coagulation, or clumping, of her platelets within her intravascular system. The irony of this immune-mediated adverse drug effect is that, while the platelet count continues to plummet, the ongoing danger is a result of those platelets' clumping together, risking thrombosis (formation of a clot) within the veins and arteries.

I gave the nursing and medical staff a detailed medical history, describing the events following Mom's hospital release up through her readmission, including her change of status, ER evaluation, and events surrounding her medical transfer. Internally, I found myself feeling somewhat defensive. I did not want the staff to think she had not been taken care of properly while at home, or that we, her family, had been negligent in getting help for her when things began to go south. I knew what it was like to be on the other end. As a medical caregiver I remembered the frustration over having a patient bounce back as a readmit. After spending time and effort pulling patients through medical crises, it was disheartening to see them readmitted in conditions as bad or even worse than when we had started. If we weren't careful, it was easy, if not automatic, to assume that noncompliance on the part of the patients or the families was the reason for their quick return.

My father had done the best he could: medications and schedules, cooking meals and encouraging Mom to eat and walk, arranging home health care and constant surveillance. The truth was, she should have never been released to go home on a Saturday after such an extensive hospital course; on the day of discharge, she was barely taking in enough calories to justify removal of her naso-gastric feeding tube. Mom's flattened effect was most likely due to a bacterial infection brewing rather than hospital fever, because her blood cultures were positive upon readmission. Still, I was glad we were back and knew she would get the best of care, whether the staff believed my story or not.

My dad and I settled into our old routine. He booked a week's stay at the same extended-stay motel near the hospital. We followed the same visitation schedule as before: we left the hospital to eat dinner that night and returned for the last visit of the night in the unit, before I drove home to make arrangements for the weekend. Everything was the same, except Mom was different. She kept her eyes closed, remained withdrawn, and only conversed with me when she needed me to ask the nurse for some medication to help "ease" her.

My son had a soccer game the next day, so I arranged for him to stay with his coach and her family, because my husband was out of town for the weekend, and my two girls and I would be traveling back to Dallas to spend the weekend at the hospital with my father. The next morning we opened the car door to load our bags and discovered that someone had stolen dual TVs and a borrowed cell phone sometime during the previous night. I had been too tired and/or careless to remember to lock up after unloading.

The girls and I arrived at the hospital shortly before noon Saturday, and we all ate lunch on patio tables outside the hospital café. The staff from the family-owned deli recognized us immediately, because we had had many meals there during Mom's previous hospital stay. The day was uneventful. The girls were not allowed to visit Mom while in the unit, so they explored the different gift shops and watched TV in the waiting room. Mom was too weak to sit up that afternoon, though she tried. The nurses were under strict orders by her cardiothoracic surgeon to get her up in a chair several times a day to help prevent her from getting any sicker from respiratory complications; the goal was to keep her lungs clear. However, her nurse just didn't "have the heart" to make her get in the chair when she saw what a struggle it was for her. Mom remained quiet and withdrawn during the day, her eye still blackened and closed.

That evening between visitations, Dad and I took the girls to eat at the little kosher deli. Though I knew Dad was discouraged, it did him some good to get out with the girls and be distracted by them and their pleas for the petit fours they found displayed in the glass cases full of dessert items. We returned to the hospital for the last scheduled visitation from 8 to 10 p.m., leaving the girls to watch TV in the waiting room down the hall. Again, Mom lay with her eyes closed, uninterested in conversing with us except to ask me to tell the nurse she needed something to help ease her. Before visitation hours were up, my dad decided to call it a day and head back to his room. He saw that Mom really did not seem up to having us there or even feel the need to acknowledge that anybody was there with her. I stayed until 10 o'clock.

Just as I had done so many times before, I sat in a straight-back chair next to her bedside, taking in all the details of my former professional life. I stared at the cardiac monitor that was mounted on the wall up over her head, the hanging IV bags of fluids and antibiotics, the computer screen that contained her medical chart and medication schedules, the locked cabinets and her specialized bed with all its buttons. The chair put me a little lower than the level of the bed frame, so I found myself staring down at the foot pedal on the side of the bed.

The pedal is metal and long with the two ends distinctively marked with arrows pointing in opposite directions for emergent positioning, based on what the medical staff wants to do with the patient. Step on one end of the pedal, and the bed immediately puts the patient in Trendelenburg position, where the patient's legs are raised above the level of the head to facilitate adequate cerebral blood perfusion during a severe hypotensive crisis, or it is also used in several procedures, such as central line placement in the great venous structures in the neck. Step on the other end, colored bright red and marked with the capital letters CPR, the bed immediately puts the patient flat in order to allow easy access for administering cardio-pulmonary resuscitation, or as it is known by the staff: running a code.

I thought to myself as I had done numerous times before, *I would hate to have to run a code on this floor, particularly in this cardiac surgical unit where everybody has already been split from stem to stern, and they still have staples and sutures in place. What a mess to deal with.* I couldn't imagine. Unlike episodes on television where cardiac resuscitations appear glamorous, and everyone performs their jobs with the perfect skills and timing needed every time, that is simply not always the case. Codes are anything but glamorous and not even viewed as heroic by most professional medical staff. I dreaded codes on patients who were well known to me, patients who had a long-standing history or who "had been with us for a while," patients whose families we had come to know very well.

When I was working, there was a familiar pit in my stomach when the call "code blue" came over the hospital speakers or when, rotating through one of the intensive care units, a nurse would rush up to tell me that someone was in trouble. Ideally, as you begin to work on a patient, a "disconnect" happens, otherwise emotions may cloud your medical judgment and impair your skills when, for example, an endotracheal tube must be placed promptly down a patient's throat in order to establish an airway. It had happened to me before.

I stayed until visitation hours were over and left the hospital that night, forgetting the ruminations that I had had while sitting next to her bed.

Back at the motel room, we were camped out: three of us were sleeping in a double bed, and my oldest daughter was asleep on the floor in a sleeping bag. At 4 a.m., awakened for whatever reason, I got up to take my youngest daughter to the bathroom. It was no use; she was too sleepy and agitated over being hauled out of bed to cooperate, so we climbed back into bed and immediately fell back to sleep. At 5 a.m., I was abruptly awakened by a ringing I mistakenly took for the alarm clock. My dad was tumbling around on the floor next to his side of the bed looking for something he had dropped. As my mind cleared, I realized it was the phone. For all the times we had left our phone numbers on the board in Mom's room for staff to call us in case of an emergency, this was the one time that it had happened, and neither one of us had heard our cell phones ring. I was still in too much of a fog to realize what was going on when I heard Dad say something and hang up. I asked him what the call was about, "Something about your mother," he anxiously replied. We both jumped out of bed, struggling to put on our clothes. I told Dad to go on ahead of me—I had to get the girls up—and that I would be right behind him. I had been so consumed with the fear of Mom's having to go back on the ventilator that I had tuned out anything else that could have possibly gone wrong. If I had been in my right mind, I would have realized the reason for such an early morning call, instructing us to come to the hospital without giving a full explanation as to why.

I entered the huge glassed-in hospital foyer with my two sleepyheads in tow and deposited them on couches in the same waiting room where our family had waited on the day of Mom's surgery. As I walked into the unit, I immediately saw Mom's nurse standing at the corner of the nurse's station with the most haggard look on his face. He looked as if he hadn't slept in days, sporting a 5 o'clock shadow on his face when it was only a little after 5 in the morning. Behind him, Mom's door stood slightly ajar. I could see my dad sitting in the same chair I had sat in hours earlier, silently weeping by her side. I knew.

"She didn't make it, did she?" I asked.

Death is a routine occurrence within a hospital, in some areas more than others. This is especially true for the intensive care units, medical or surgical, and more common on the adult side versus the pediatric or nursery units, though, of course, death does occur there too. Even so, it takes a toll on the staff, particularly when there has been prolonged contact with the patient and family. This may often prove more difficult for the nurses than the physicians. Generally speaking, physicians may view the death of a patient as a failure, a reflection upon themselves, though through no fault of their own. The loss may feel more personal to nurses, because they provided the continual bedside care and, often, were the liaison between the physician and the family, helping to ensure a clearer understanding regarding the care of the patient. The greater the investment of time and effort, the greater the loss is felt by all involved with the patient including physicians, nurses, respiratory therapists, physical therapists, aides, and other ancillary staff.

He began to describe the events that had taken place around 4 o'clock that morning. He was at her bedside, beginning to do some routine hygienic bedside care, and was making light conversation with her when she suddenly looked up at him with a startled look. And that was that. I'm certain that, at that point, all the bells and whistles went off, and staff had come running from all over. In fact, later in the morning, when I turned to leave from the room for the last time, I noticed the trash can by the door with its hinged lid slightly ajar from the overflow of disposed paraphernalia, tubes and packaging from *other stuff* used in a code.

As I entered the room and rushed to her side, two things immediately came to mind. The first thought I voiced out loud with a broken sob, "Mom, I'm so sorry." Sorry for all she'd been through and how it had ended. Sorry no one was there with her, not any of us, anyway. Sorry for the suffering she hadn't bargained for. As I stroked her curled fingers bent with arthritis (just like her mother's and sister's hands), I was sorry for all the times I had pushed them aside when she had tried to brush the hair from my eyes or made some attempt at intimacy with me during those *distancing years*. Sorry for all the bad she had endured because of me.

The second thought came painfully close to the first: *I wish I had loved you more.* Even though our relationship up to that point was as strong as it had ever been, I knew she had deserved better from me over the years. Now that she was gone, a nagging regret hung over my head—over something I could never get back. The chance to show, to share, to tell a loved one just what she had meant, and how I had come to realize all that she had done for me, just how much I really loved her, although I had not always shown it or even known it at the time.

We stayed with my mother two and half hours after she had passed away, waiting until my brother and his family arrived to say their goodbyes. I took both my daughters into her room as well. The staff left us to ourselves, and we did not feel hurried in the least, especially since Mom and Dad already had their advanced directives and their funeral arrangements in place. Many times at the time of death or soon afterward, body fluids escape from the patient and though not seen outwardly, the putrification process (decomposition of the body) begins to take place on a microscopic level. Standing by her bedside, the smell of death began to permeate my nostrils. It seemed that nature itself was indicating to me the time had come to say our final goodbyes and leave. She looked restful, at peace, beautiful albeit very white, and I knew it was time to go. Along with the rest of the family, my father left the intensive care unit for the last time, leaving a spouse of sixty years behind. I stuck around to talk to the attending physician.

There is more than one perk for having the initials M.D. behind your name. One of the blessings I took away from that morning was the conversation I had with the physician who had been in charge of mother's care that weekend. Though not wholly detached from the situation, I knew the questions I wanted to ask. I wanted to know the intimate details surrounding my mother's death. For me, it was more than medical inquisitiveness, it was closure. I also wanted to make it clear that my mother's medical and physical condition upon re-entering the hospital was not a reflection on the care she had received from my family, particularly my father.

We sat in the middle of the nurses' station while staff bustled around us, making arrangements for transporting Mom. The pulmonologist/critical care specialist had attended the same medical school as I had. Though he had completed his medical training years ahead of me, we both knew some of the same professors of that institution. As we began to talk, he readily furnished me the nugget of truth I was seeking. It had been quick; she had gone in a second. In his professional medical opinion, the reason for such a total circulatory collapse was either one of two possibilities: (1) a blood clot had moved, or (2) her graft had ruptured (the site of repair to her aneurysm) secondary to her systemic infection. The latter scenario would have been ironic—that the very thing she had gone into surgery to have repaired, the very thing that would have caused imminent death in time if left unattended, theoretically could have caused her quick demise anyway, after going through an intricate surgery and an extended hospital course. He felt the first case scenario was more likely, though.

"Heparin-induced platelet antibodies." There it was again, the reason she had bled out the first night after surgery and why she had not responded readily to platelet transfusions. Her body continued to attack the platelets with the antibody attached to them even after the heparin had been discontinued, and, though her platelets were being consumed (hence the reason for the low platelet count), within the blood vessels themselves the platelets were still coagulating together, setting up the formation of a clot. It only takes one clot to dislodge itself from the wall of a blood vessel, travel quickly through the circulatory system and lodge in a prestigious site (for example, a coronary or cerebral artery that is vital for function), to cause stroke, heart attack, or even sudden death. The fact that Mom had partial vocal cord paralysis and slight changes in her mental status the day she was forced to go back to the emergency room indicated that she had had a small stroke the night before. The coagulation process had apparently been ongoing, down to that very morning, her last one.

❧

For as long as I can remember, Sunday mornings have always had *a feeling* all their own. Maybe it is because I was raised in a family where Sundays were set aside for church and a mid-day meal together, a day in which the usual or routine was not expected. For whatever the reason, Sunday mornings feel different to me, always have, even when church was not a part of my day. I found this particular Sunday morning no different. Looking through the hospital foyer's glass ceiling, I saw the sun, brilliant against a sky so blue; it felt like Sunday, though it wasn't like any other I had ever experienced.

Our family gathered at one of the tables just outside the hospital café. It was a surreal experience for all of us, as we sat trying to take in what had happened that morning. I felt especially bad for my brother, a man of few words, especially when it comes to voicing his emotions. He said quietly, "I've never seen anybody like that. I've never seen anybody lying dead like that before, like Momma." It had been a traumatic experience for us all in one way or another. Upon my entering the coffee shop, the owner immediately saw something in my face and came over to ask me what was wrong. It seemed we had grown to know each other pretty well in the short time of interacting with each other over coffee and lunch orders. I felt comfortable in relaying to him the news that my mother had just died, though I faltered as I began to voice the reality of it all.

Our group eventually broke up after having made arrangements to caravan back to my parents' house, where we would receive extended family and friends. Our departure felt not unlike a losing team's departing the field for the lonely ride back home. We had lost; nothing we could have done or do now would change the outcome; it was a simple matter of eventually getting over it and moving on. My nephew drove my father back home while my brother and his wife and I drove separately. As I pulled out of the parking lot, I turned to see the sun brightly reflecting off the windows of the third floor. The room where Mom had stayed for so long was now occupied by someone else, and the room in which she had died was around the corner, its blinds pulled down and blanketed by the sun. With that parting image in my rearview mirror, I drove away from the hospital toward the freeway entrance. It was to be the beginning of a long day.

Epilogue

ews travels fast. By the time we arrived at my parents'
home, neighbors on both sides and across the street from
them had already heard. In fact, my parents' good friend
who lived on one side of them had her yard man out
mowing Dad's front lawn when we pulled in the drive. I will never
forget their condolences and the honest look of sorrow and apology
in their eyes.

There are little moments that I like to think of as buoys in the
sea of life. Bobbing up and down surrounded by the whitecaps and
current, they demark safety zones: places our minds can retreat to
for reassurance, things that will always be there to grasp. I've come
to think of such moments as points of validation, if nothing else, a
sense that God has just nodded in my direction. That day, between
the comings and goings of everybody, there was a time that Dad and I
were left alone when such a moment happened.

My dad is not a procrastinator, so after discussing some things of
Mom's, he went straight to her jewelry box to locate her original set
of wedding rings. Her jewelry box was located in her middle dresser
drawer where, alongside her pajamas and lingerie, we were liable to
find anything. Unlike other mothers who keep scrapbooks and files
of their children's mementos and memorable *firsts,* my mother tucked
these things in and among her underwear and slips. She stuffed into
her drawer cards we had given her, pictures we had drawn, snippets
of our hair, and even an old clay pot my brother had once made that
eventually disintegrated into dust within the handkerchief that held
it. In fact, in the top dresser drawer, which contained a slide-out tray
for makeup and hair accessories, I found rings and hair barrettes of

mine, even a necklace with Tinkerbelle sitting within a gold hoop. My aunt had brought it back from Disneyland for me when I was very young. Although Mom kept her personal belongings folded and neatly arranged, there was no real order, rhyme, or reason to why she kept some of the other things.

Dad opened the drawer to get the jewelry box and something *popped out* at me. Dad took no notice. He was too bent on looking for her rings, but I immediately saw it and grabbed it. It was a black-and-white striped headband, the circular type made of cotton nylon that slips easily over your head. It used to be pretty common to see this variety hanging in packages or in pairs on the hair accessory aisle in the grocery store or at five-and-dime variety stores. Before I had even started elementary school, someone had given Mom a whole sack of these headbands. I think it was our former neighbor, Gwen Aylor, with the probable intent of giving my mother some way of controlling my unruly hair.

I had worn the thing as a kid. In fact, out of the whole bunch, it was the only one I had liked or even attempted to wear for any length of time, speaking in terms of thirty minutes or so. There is a picture somewhere of me wearing it with my semi-rolled hair sticking out in all directions from underneath it. One thing that was certainly true of me at that age was that I gave little priority to my appearance, especially my hair. I have school pictures to prove it.

And yet, there it was! After all the years, a little something left behind that spoke volumes to me and of me. It said all that was needed, just what she would have said. It was me: this silly, black-and-white, ridiculously stupid-looking headband that represented a tangible memory of who I was to her. The waywardness, the imperfections, the unorganized and untimely, the unkempt, headstrong, opinionated, determined-to-be-me and do-it-my-way right up to the bloody end, all wadded up in my hand. I had opened that drawer lots of times looking for something, and I had never seen it there, not before that day.

I was remembered fondly. In a tiny moment I learned better than I ever could from anything else that it wasn't as important that I hadn't loved as I should have. It was more important to know, really know, that I had been loved and loved unconditionally. It was a tangible symbol of a love that didn't need to control me or even understand me—a love shown to me by a mother who watched me soar, fall, and climb back up for more, without ever denying me the experience to learn from it for myself. All the regrets I had been feeling since that morning suddenly seemed dimmed by the awareness that, though I didn't do enough or say enough while she was alive, I could have never out-given or out-loved her. It was just who she was.

∽

What I took away with me the year my mother died was more than a striped headband. In the days that followed, when I needed it the most, her voice was very resolute in reminding me of how she had been with me and what she had meant to me. When I told God to give me some space, when I withdrew from my family and defiantly wished to remain separated, even as I remained fearful of the consequences of my actions and inner flights of fantasy, I would hear her say, "It's okay." Mom took away the judgment of God, or how I had come to view God's thoughts toward me over the years. Only after her death did I truly realize just how much permission she had given me all along to be me, to test the waters, to learn for myself. In time everything would turn out as it was meant to. Her unshakeable confidence in me liberated me.

It was during my time of rage, when I defiantly dared God to put another car in my lane, when I told Him, "Screw this! What else would you have expected? You made me like this!" that I slowly began to realize that not only was he not going to zap me or abandon me, more importantly, he was not going to withdraw from me. God just came in through a different door. In the year my mother died, I discovered my mother's God, and, in my grieving, I found freedom.

Much of the literature on loss and grieving speaks in terms of a two-year time frame, advising against such things like making rash decisions and/or life-altering plans during this time. Recent palliative/hospice publications emphasize the individual's experience more than time. One end-of-life care booklet published by the Texas Cancer Council says it beautifully: "It is important to remember that there is no magic timetable as to how long the intense pain or grief will last. Grieving is a learning process that takes time and is unique to each individual."

For me, two years did make a difference: I experienced a slow returning to "perspective" and a realignment of goals. Rediscovery.

Even so, I could have never been prepared for how that first year played out. I unraveled just enough to remember who I was, what I had left behind, and then, I moved forward. The funny thing was, Mom's voice, her thoughts toward me, and the patience she had shown me all became clearer, more real, and infinitely precious after she had gone. I finally got it.

❧

One life, so unselfishly lived; one love, so freely given: my mother.

Thank you for allowing me to dream.

About the Author

Sherry Scott, M.D., is a pediatrician who has practiced palliative/ hospice care for children. She completed medical school and residency training at the University of Texas Health Science Center at San Antonio. Her memoir, *The Year My Mother Died*, is her first literary work. She lives in Paris, Texas.

Printed in the USA
CPSIA information can be obtained
at www.ICGtesting.com
LVHW041618201223
767019LV00006B/126

9 781456 737795